SECRECY OR FREEDOM?

Declaring War
on
Political Dissimulation

D1601531

Alan B. Jones

ABJ Press

ISBN 0-9640848-2-1

Copyright 2001 by Alan B. Jones

Library of Congress Control No. 00-092804

ABJ Press
P.O. Box 2362
Paradise, CA 95967

CONTENTS

INTRODUCTION

There is a large and growing number of Americans in our country today who perceive that our society is rapidly sliding down a slippery slope toward world socialism, and that no levers seem to be available to bring that slide to a halt, much less to reverse it. We are fed soothing platitudes by our national news media concerning world politics, while our entertainment media keeps us distracted with sports, sex, and violence. Our schools indoctrinate our kids with socialism, ensuring the future predominance of "liberal" legislatures. Our politicians keep their eyes on their single main goal, which is to get reelected. Our families hardly have the time or energy to think about what is really wrong, and what might be done about it, because two paychecks are now needed just to keep bread on the table and a roof overhead.

The purpose of this book is to outline the crucial history revealing who the culprits really are who have brought us so low, and what their main weapons have been in the war that they are waging against us and against all aspiring middle classes around the world. This knowledge will in turn reveal to us their Achilles heel – a weakness which has always existed, but which can now, for the first time in modern history, be successfully exploited. An action plan is outlined to regain control of our country for the benefit of We the People, and to the benefit of all peoples throughout the world.

It can be done! If you are one who still wishes to save for your children and grandchildren the freedoms that were won by our founders and preserved for over 200 years by the blood, sweat, and tears of our ancestors, I invite you to take part in this great struggle for which our ultimate victory can, for the first time, be dimly seen on the horizon.

The historical outline which I shall develop will utilize reviews of a carefully selected set of books, some old, some new, but all carrying their own bibliographic references sufficient to support their credibility. I have sequenced the chapters roughly in the order in which the covered knowledge has become known to the several truth-seeking authors. Each of these works is currently available, and I have included at the beginning of each chapter the address of the publisher or other source from whom the work may be purchased.

Alan B. Jones
November, 2000

Chapter 1

"Memoirs Illustrating

THE HISTORY OF JACOBINISM"

(By Abbé Augustin Barruel. Orig. pub. 1797. Pub. 1995 by American Council on Economics and Society, 34152 Doreka Dr., Fraser, MI 48026. Available also from Omni Publications, PO Box 900566, Palmdale, CA 93590, 805-274-2240.)

This work is the 800-page *magnum opus* of a French Jesuit priest who studied the causes of the French Revolution as it was developing, and who escaped to England in 1792 with the anti-clerical revolutionists in hot pursuit. His escape has provided us with the most detailed description presently available to us of the actors and organizations most culpable in bringing about that social cataclysm. We will, in the chapters which follow, show that Barruel was in fact describing the evil works of the same movement which, in the year 2000, continues to seek the enslavement of the entire population of this planet.

We will use Barruel's work as the starting point in assembling a chain of historical evidence extending both forward and backward in time, to construct our present picture of the nature of the conspiracy facing us, and from whence it came. Equally important, we shall seek to highlight the mechanisms utilized by the conspirators which have enabled them to attain their present successes. So let us start with the three-pronged movement described by Barruel which he says paved the way to the French Revolution.

Barruel starts (p. 3) with his overall characterization of the scope of the conspiracy along with its chief enabling characteristic: secrecy. He states his theme: "We shall show that, even to the most horrid deeds perpetrated during the French Revolution, everything was foreseen and resolved on, was premeditated and combined: – that they were the offspring of deep-thought villainy, since they had been pre-pared and were produced by men who alone held the clue of these plots and conspiracies, lurking in the secret meetings where they had been conceived.... The grand cause of the revolution, its leading features, its atrocious crimes, will [be seen as] one continued chain of deep-laid and premeditated villainy."

Furthermore, its long-term scope was not to be limited just to France. He continues, "I will show that... the French Revolution is but a sportive essay of [the conspir-acy's] strength, while the whole universe is its aim. If else-where the same crimes are necessary, they will be commit-ted; if equal ferocity be requisite they will be equally fero-cious; *and it will unavoidably extend wheresoever its errors shall be received.*"

The three conspiratorial elements which coalesced to produce the French conflagration of 1789 were, says Bar-ruel, a conspiracy against Christ, a conspiracy against kings, and a conspiracy against all civil society, even all property whatsoever. Participants in these elements he labeled ad-epts of impiety, rebellion, and anarchy respectively. Corre-sponding organizational entities were, respectively, a rather loosely organized secret group of self-styled "Philosophers," a more tightly organized group of Freemason occult lodges, and a highly-structured, extremely secret group called the Illuminees, or Illuminati. The first three parts of Barruel's book deal in turn with these three elements, and the fourth part deals with how they historically grew together to bring about the French catastrophe. Our review will follow the same pattern, beginning with the anti-Christian movement.

The leader of the anti-Christian element of the conspiracy was one François Marie Arouet, born in 1694 the son of a minor French official. Early in life, he gave himself the more pretentious name by which he became famous: Voltaire. During his formative years he acquired, says Barruel, "a thirst for dominion over the literary world," along with a hatred of Christianity. He was educated by the Jesuits at the College of Louis le Grand, at which one of his professors, the Jesuit le Jay, rebuked him and predicted as follows (p. 9): "Unfortunate young man, at some future day you will come to be the standard bearer of Infidelity."

Following college, he sought the company only "of men whose profligate morals could strengthen his infidelity." He shortly thereafter emigrated to England where he found a literary community more generally supportive of his life style. His disciple, confidant, and historian Condorcet later listed (p. 243) Collins and Bolingbroke as members of that community, and asserted (p. 11): "*There it was* (in England) *that Voltaire swore to dedicate his life to the accomplishment of that project* [the overthrow of religion]; *and he has kept his word.*" Voltaire returned to Paris around 1730, with a firmly fixed lifetime goal: to overthrow the Christian religion.

Encountering opposition to his numerous impious or obscene writings, he observed that he would have to hide his true objectives, and that he couldn't do it all himself. To help hide his objectives, he named his group of Christianity-hating admirers and disciples the Philosophers, a name which Voltaire apparently encountered during his sojourn in England, where, says Barruel (p. 10), libertines under Collins and Hobbes had likewise named themselves Philosophers. To enlist the help he needed, Voltaire appointed his second-in-command, D'Alembert, from among his growing group. Barruel describes D'Alembert as "...cold, reserved, prudent and crafty, ...carefully guarding against [any] reply that may expose him; his steps, mysterious and indirect, conceal his design."   In comparison, Barruel describes Voltaire as fiery, passionate, and impetuous. The two personality patterns neatly complemented each other, to the great benefit of the conspiracy.

The third member of the leadership of the anti-Christian conspiracy was none other than Frederick II of Prussia, better known as Frederick the Great. Frederick was born in 1712, and was thus 18 years younger than Voltaire. He was attracted by Voltaire's writings, and a correspondence developed between the two by about 1736, four years before Frederick's ascension to the throne. The correspondence was to last throughout their lives. The origin of Frederick's anti-Christian mind-set remained obscure to Barruel, who noted only that the young Frederick "unfortunately was surrounded by [religion's] calumniators."

Voltaire, naturally, enthusiastically embraced him, knowing the great value such a powerful figure could have in helping him attain his goal of obliterating the Christian religion. Voltaire lived in Frederick's court for about 3 years starting in 1750, but left following a disagreement which they rapidly put behind them. Barruel notes, "Though not in friendship, they were soon united in mutual hatred to Christianity; and though they never met again, their plans were more easily formed, and intelligently conducted, in their future correspondence."

Barruel devotes a whole chapter to convincing his reader via the written words of the conspirators that their hatred of Christianity was virulent. The common phrase appearing over and over in their private correspondence, almost as a slogan, was *écrasez l'infame!*, translated as *Crush the Wretch!*, referring to Christ and the whole Christian church. Voltaire is quoted, "I am weary of hearing people repeat that twelve men have been sufficient to establish Christianity, and I will prove that one may suffice to overthrow it." And elsewhere, "Could not five or six men of talents, and who rightly understand each other, succeed after the example of twelve scoundrels who have already succeeded?" Barruel's research on this point is very convincing.

Of even more importance to us in the present day is to take close note of two crucial means utilized by Voltaire's "Philosophers" in working toward their goal. First, and most important, they realized that maintaining secrecy in their efforts was absolutely mandatory. Thus, in their writings to each other, they frequently used code names, to discourage identification should the letters fall into the wrong hands. "In their correspondence, Frederick is often called *Luc*, and D'Alembert *Protagoras*, though he often styles himself *Bertrand*." A secret language was developed: "For example, *the vine of truth is well cultivated* is tantamount to saying, we make rapid progress against religion."

Though the conspirators were open with each other, they were continually exhorted to maintain secrecy with respect to the public. "The Mysteries... are not to be divulged; ...the *monster* (religion) must fall, pierced by a hundred invisible hands; yes, let it fall beneath a thousand repeated blows." Again, "Confound *the wretch* to the utmost of your power; speak your mind boldly; but when you strike, *conceal your hand....* The Nile is said to spread around its fertilizing waters, though it conceals its head; *do you the same*, and you will secretly enjoy your triumph."

Barruel continues, "No precept is oftener repeated by Voltaire than this: *Strike, but conceal the hand."* He further records with what great skill D'Alembert had mastered the art of secrecy. Concerning their third leader, Barruel comments, "Frederick not only approved of this

10

secrecy, but we shall see him playing off all the artifices of a dark policy to ensure the success of the conspiracy."

Barruel spends the next 150 pages or so of his great book to describe the primary mechanisms which the conspirators utilized to turn the minds of the intelligentsia away from religion, with its inherent personal morality, and toward the notion than man's reason should be the only guide to his morality. This latter was then gradually perverted by imperceptible steps to the common moral dictum held by tyrants everywhere: the ends justify the means. Barruel writes (p. 179): "What motives to virtue did these chiefs [i.e., Voltaire, etc.] suggest to their adepts when they declared that a God neither regards their virtues nor their vices, that the fear of this God is an absolute folly, or when, wishing to stifle all remorse of conscience, they tell them 'That the man void of fear is above the laws – *That a bad action, when useful, can be committed without remorse –* That remorse is no other than the fear of men and of their laws.'"

Barruel readily perceived the profound immorality of the conspirators, but never explicitly sought any further motivation than their obvious hatred of Christianity. We will deal further with this issue in later chapters.

So how did the conspirators go about it? The second of the two crucial means referred to above was, in a word, to gain control of the mass media of the day and to utilize it for their propaganda. We will merely itemize the various thrusts of this program.

First, they realized that the use of force was many years premature, and that such force would have to be preceded by the weakening of public opinion which supported the church. D'Alembert, in a 1762 letter (p. 32), criticized Voltaire for being too hasty, saying, "If mankind grow enlightened, it is because we have used the caution to enlighten them by degrees." He then proposed their famous

Encyclopedia project, which was enthusiastically taken up by Voltaire and the others. In this project they brought together the talents of a great many French writers and experts in all manner of human arts and sciences, e.g., Religion, History, Physics, Geography, Commerce, Poetry, Grammar, Oratory, Architecture, and more. The grand scope of the project won it widespread public acceptance, especially by the more literate French intelligentsia. However, its dark and secret object, says Barruel, was "to convert the Encyclopedia into a vast emporium of all the sophisms, errors, and calumnies which had ever been invented against religion, ...and these were to be so artfully concealed that the reader should insensibly imbibe the poison without the least suspicion."

The Encyclopedia ultimately appeared in many editions, of all sizes and prices, always with sophistical praises as to its literary magnificence. They were lodged in libraries everywhere, and all men of "learning" had to have their own. The numerous editions were increasingly open in their criticism of religion, as the conspirators took the opportunity of each new edition to introduce additional misinformation under the pretense of "corrections." The last such additions were ultimately made just prior to the outbreak of the physical revolution in 1789, long after the death of Voltaire in 1778, by "petty infidels" of that later time, as Barruel characterized them.

Next, using a strategy proposed by D'Alembert, Voltaire set about to take over the prestigious French Academy, membership in which was the common goal of French writers seeking public honor and acclaim. Using deceit and deception to hide their hatred of Christianity, Voltaire and D'Alembert finally each obtained admission to the Academy, and then set about to bring in those others of their group of "Philosophers" who were secretly but reliably anti-Christian, while denying membership to pro-Christian writers. The Academy was thus converted, in a matter of relatively few years, from one in which "Any public sign of infidelity was a bar against admission" to one which had been "converted into a club of infidels." D'Alembert's plot thus "conferred the laurels of literature solely on the impious writer," while the defenders of religion were "to be covered with reproach and infamy."

Having attained the highest mantle of respectability, the conspirators then proceeded to deluge Europe with a flood of impious literature, aimed at gradually bringing the whole people to a condition of universal apostasy. Barruel starts the chapter discussing this matter as follows: "That, ...particularly during the last 20 years of Voltaire's life, all Europe has been overrun with most impious writings, under the forms either of pamphlets, systems, romances, or feigned histories, is one of those self-evident truths which needs no proof." He then sets about to show by example how Voltaire, D'Alembert, and Frederick conspired and aided each other to produce the desired flood. Their letters to each other, to which Barruel became privy, discussed how pressure could be brought against booksellers to cooperate with them, including pressure exerted even by Frederick the Great himself. Voltaire writes to him, "But, Sire, cannot you, without exposing yourself, have some of the Berlin booksellers encouraged to reprint them [Voltaire's current batch of anti-clerical works], and to distribute them throughout Europe at a price low enough to ensure their sale?" This proposal did not displease the book-huckstering King of Prussia, who responded, "You may make use of our printers as you please; and as they are connected with those of Holland, France and Germany, I have no doubt that they have means of conveying books whithersoever they may think proper." Thus the conspirators endeavored to gain their ends, as in today's world, via manipulation of the intelligentsia, the politicians, and the mass media of their day.

The conspirators' strategy was to clothe all their efforts in restrained, thoughtful, *moderate,* language, as is the case today. However, the means which they always held in reserve were much more violent. Thus Voltaire, in 1743, "was plotting with the King of Prussia to plunder the Ecclesiastical Princes and the Religious Orders of their possessions.... In 1770 he writes to Frederick, 'It is noble to scoff at these Harlequin Bull-givers [the clergy]; I like to cover them with ridicule, but I had rather *plunder* them.'" D'Alembert concurred, though he counseled a cautious approach; Frederick likewise ultimately concurred, writing: "[The Revolution] will never be perfected but by a superior force: from government must the sentence issue that shall crush the wretch. Enlightened Ministers may forward it, but *the will of the sovereign must accede.*" He was presuming, of course, that he or someone like him would be the acceding sovereign.

Voltaire's initial targets, notes Barruel (p. 147), were "among those who governed, or were made to govern, and among men of letters." Separate chapters are devoted to the conspiracy's very successful efforts to enlist Europe's "Crowned Adepts" (i.e., various of its reigning monarchs), its lower levels of royalty, its nobles, government ministers and other bureaucrats, and its men of letters into their antireligious movement. Monarchs included Emperor Joseph II of Germany, Empress Catherine The Great of Russia, King Frederick of Prussia, Queen Ulrica of Sweden, her son King Gustavus III of Sweden, King Poniatowski of Poland, and King Christiern VII of Denmark. These monarchs, and the nobility below them that they influenced, were highly useful in providing financial support, legal protection, and new adepts to the movement. The "men of letters" were given a platform for their works, and sinecures for their maintenance, in return for their outpourings of anti-Christian literature.

A little later, the common people of France were included in the targets of the Conspiracy. When a vacancy was detected in a country school, great efforts were made to assure the promotion of a secret "Philosopher" into that position. Anti-Christian literature appeared in great quantity, and at negligible cost, from country peddlers loaded with various goods for sale. An investigator questioning several such peddlers reported that the books cost them nothing, that they received bales of them without knowing where they came from, they being asked simply to sell them at whatever low price they could get. Barruel adds that this account "perfectly coincides with what I have heard many rectors of small towns and villages complain of. They looked upon these hawking booksellers as the pests of their parishes, and as the agents of the pretended philosophers in the circulation of their impiety."

Barruel then records a remorseful confession made in September of 1789, shortly after the commission of the first atrocities of the French Revolution, by one Mr. Le Roy, an academician and member of the royal household, concerning the existence of a secret committee, or Academy, of which he had been the secretary. This "Secret Academy" was started by D'Alembert, between 1763 and 1766 by Barruel's calculation. Le Roy is quoted (p. 152):

"This society was a sort of club that we Philosophers had formed among us, and only admitted into it persons on whom we could perfectly rely. Our sittings were regularly held at the Baron D'Holbach's. [Barruel thereafter refers to the group as "Holbach's Club."] Lest our object should be surmised, we called ourselves Economists. We created Voltaire, though absent, our honorary and perpetual president. Our principle members were D'Alembert, Turgot, Condorcet, Diderot.... Most of those works which have appeared for this long time against religion, morals, and government were ours, or those of authors devoted to us.... Before they went to press, they were delivered [to] our office. There we revised and corrected them.... In a word, we made our writers say exactly what we pleased.... When we had approved of those works, we began by printing them on fine or ordinary paper, in sufficient number to pay our expenses, and then an immense number on the commonest paper. These latter we sent to hawkers and booksellers free of cost, or nearly so, who were to circulate them among the people at the lowest rate. These were the means used to pervert the people and bring them to the state you now see them in."

Barruel notes that Le Roy also explained that the characters "ECR: L'INF" with which Voltaire concluded many of his letters stood for "écrasez l'infame" (crush the wretch), and that "all those to whom Voltaire wrote under that horrid formula were members or initiated into the mysteries of this secret committee." Barruel then quotes from a Voltaire letter of April 1761: "Let the Philosophers unite in *a brotherhood like the Freemasons,* let them assemble and support each other; let them be faithful to the association.... This *Secret Academy* will be far superior to that of Athens, and to all those of Paris. But everyone thinks only for himself, and forgets that his most sacred duty is to *crush the wretch.*"

Barruel does not, to this point, claim to understand the motives of the plotters. He does, however, grasp the impact of their program on its victims. The high-sounding name of Philosopher could henceforth be used to excuse the misdeeds of "the faithless wife; the profligate youth; the man practicing every art, whether just or unjust, to attain his ends; even the loose women whose characters were openly disparaged." The Philosophers "had erased from their code all those virtues which religion maintains to be descended

16

from heaven." The morals of the victim people were *targeted* for corruption, and the means for accomplishing that result was the destruction of the religion which enthroned their code of morality. But why corrupt the people? We will return to that question a little later.

Barruel does make very clear, however, a point which is critically important to us today, and to which we alluded at the beginning of this chapter. That point is that the Anti-Christian effort could never have been successful without the great care taken to maintain its secrecy. Suppose that, during the early years of the conspiracy, the secret orders to "*strike, but hide your hand* had been known, [or] that the people had been acquainted with all the tortuous means secretly used to seduce them," would not the conspiracy have been stopped in its tracks? Suppose the people had known that "teachers, who had been appointed to instruct the rising generation, were only the impious emissaries of D'Alembert, sent to corrupt its morals; that all those hawkers of books sold at so low a rate were the agents of the Secret Academy, employed to circulate its poisons from towns to villages, and thence to the poorest cottages" – could then the Conspiracy possibly have succeeded? The question obviously answers itself. Even two centuries ago, secrecy and *media control* were necessary keys to conspiratorial success, as they remain up to the present day.

The second of the three conspiratorial elements which coalesced to produce the French revolutionary tragedy was the conspiracy against the monarchy. Barruel traces the path of Voltaire in first opposing and then finally supporting this movement, though its much more potent supporters were found in a sect that Barruel calls the "Occult Masons." Voltaire, having expended a great deal of effort in bringing King Frederick II not only into the fold, but into the leadership of the Philosophers, was obviously intent on not antagonizing him by letting the Philosopher adepts publicly express any anti-monarchical feelings. At what point Voltaire himself acquired such feelings is not clear, but his correspondence clearly shows him admonishing his followers, as late as 1765 (p. 190), to respect the King, be faithful servants of the King, pray for the King, etc. Considerably earlier than this, however, he shows his truer colors in a 1757 confidential letter to D'Alembert in which he says of King Frederick, "Those men who put themselves in the way of a musket or a sabre.. are most abominable fools. Don't betray my secret either to Kings or Priests." By 1764, 25 years before the French Revolution, he writes (p. 197), "Everything is preparing the way to a great revolution, which will undoubtedly take place; and I shall not be fortunate enough to see it.... The uproar will be glorious. Happy those who are now young, for they will behold most extraordinary things." D'Alembert, Condorcet, and other names among the Philosophers are shown to have harbored similar feelings.

In about 1770, Voltaire is seen (p. 274) agitating for the overthrow of the government of Geneva, which was not even a Monarchy, but a Republic. In 1774, he was finally initiated, as an octogenarian, into the Occult Masonic system, which he found heavily peopled with many of his own Philosopher adepts, who had long preceded him in accepting and acting upon the anti-regal Masonic keywords of Liberty and Equality (p. 368). Voltaire died in 1778, making his prediction come true of not living to see the Great Revolution.

The philosophic justification (or rationalization) for merging the efforts of the Anti-Christian and Anti-Monarchical activists was provided by the major works of Montesquieu and Rousseau, on which Barruel spends several chapters. He summarizes as follows (p. 242): "Montesquieu taught [the people] to govern themselves, and make their laws in conjunction with their Kings; and Jean Jacques [Rousseau] persuades them to expel all Kings, and to govern and make their laws themselves. The Sophisters no longer hesitate, and the overthrow of every *throne* is resolved on, as they had before resolved on the destruction of every altar. From that period the two conspiracies are combined and form but one in the school of the Sophisters."

Barruel then quotes extensively from Condorcet, the "Philosopher's Historian," who exults in the labors of the Philosopher writers in leading the people in the coming overthrow of all Altars and all Thrones, and who names the leaders (p. 243): "In England, Collins and Bolingbroke; in France, Bayle, Fontenelle, Voltaire, Montesquieu, and the schools formed by these men...." Barruel summarizes the significance of Condorcet's panegyric as follows (p. 244):

"Let the historian seize on this avowal, or rather this eulogy, of plots. He will find concentrated and flowing from Condorcet's pen everything that the most daring and the deepest initiated conspirator could have let fall, to characterize the most authenticated and most universal conspiracy, planned by those men called Philosophers, not only attacking the persons of particular Kings but of every King, and not Kings only, but the very essence of Royalty and all Monarchy. The commencement of this conspiracy was when *Collins, Bolingbroke, Bayle, and other masters of Voltaire,* together with that Sophister himself, had propagated their impious doctrines against the God of Christianity." (my emphasis - ABJ)

Condorcet's words are followed by the corroborative testimony of Mr. Le Roy, quoted previously, who spells out the same set of facts, but from a heart filled with shame and remorse. Both men give testimony of the art and guile with which the Philosophers set about to destroy all religions and all monarchies. Barruel concludes (p. 253), "When such opposite passions, such different interests and sentiments, agree in their dispositions on the same conspiracy, on the same means, and on the same conspirators, truth can require no further proofs; it is evidence, it is demonstration itself."

Barruel notes how identical the conspiratorial mechanisms used against the Monarchy were to those used against the Church (p. 254). Following upon "that inundation of Anti-Christian writings which we have seen flowing like a torrent through every class of society, [there came] a second inundation of Anti-monarchical writings, by which the Sophisters were in hopes of perverting the sentiment of confidence and respect which the people had for their Sovereign into hatred and contempt, [which] was only a continuation of those means which they had employed against their God. These writings are issued from the same manufactory, composed by the same adepts, recommended and reviewed by the same chiefs, spread with the same profusion, hawked about from the town to the village by the same agents of Holbach's Club, and sent free of cost to the country school-masters, that all classes of people from the highest to the most indigent might imbibe the venom of their Sophistry."

The anti-monarchical writings of the Secret Academy did not go unnoticed by French officialdom. In August 1770, the Attorney-General of the Parliament of Paris issued an accurately composed denunciation of the group (p. 265): "An impious and daring sect has raised its head in the midst of us, and it has decorated its false wisdom with the name of Philosophy.... With one hand they have sought to shake the Throne, and with the other to overturn the Altar.... And Government should tremble at tolerating in its bosom such an inflammatory sect of unbelievers, whose sole object appears to be *to stir up the people to rebellion, under pretence of enlightening them.*"

The hour, however, was late, and the conspirators felt secure in coming out of the closet with their aim of overthrowing the Monarchy. Frederick himself finally realized that he too had been duped, and had been let in on only half of the overall program. He then turned on the Philosopher writers, but only with respect to their writings against the Throne, continuing, in effect, to defend and support their efforts against the Altar. Barruel remarks that Voltaire and D'Alembert did not at this point try to convince Frederick that they meant no harm to Monarchies. Rather, their correspondence showed them prudently staying silent, so as not to further provoke Frederick into more detailed proofs and accusations.

In 1785, just 4 years before the onset of the Revolution, Barruel notes that "Condorcet and the other editors" made a large portion of the voluminous correspondence between Voltaire and D'Alembert public, though with some letters obviously suppressed. Condorcet and the other adepts, he says, "must have had even then a strange confidence in their success" to publish the letters for the benefit of history. One is led to compare this action with that nearly 200 years later of Professor Carroll Quigley in exposing the work of the New World Order conspirators in his book Tragedy and Hope. Quigley felt that the NWO could no longer be dislodged from its path, and that history deserved to know who the real movers and shakers of the world were. The conspiratorial leaders of that later time did not agree with him, however, and tried to suppress his book.

We turn now to Barruel's look into the world of Occult Masonry. He starts with a two-pronged disclaimer (p. 299), first excepting the great bulk of all lower-level Masons around the world who know nothing of secret Masonic goals of which they would disapprove, and second the English Masonic lodges in particular, which were peopled by "those upright men, who, excellent Citizens, and of all stations, are proud of being Masons, and who may be distinguished from the others by ties which only appear to unite them more closely in the bonds of charity and fraternal affection." Barruel continues such disclaimers from time to time, which we will duly note and then comment upon as the issue becomes ripe.

Barruel then turns to the great secret which Freemasonry had heretofore held dear to its heart, but which they publicly revealed on August 12, 1792, when Louis XVI was formally taken prisoner by the revolutionists. They publicly read a decree proclaiming: "We have at length succeeded, and France is no other than an immense lodge. The whole French people are Free-masons, and the whole universe will soon follow their example." Barruel, present at this event, notes: "I saw Masons, till then the most reserved, who freely and openly declared, 'Yes, at length the grand object of Free-masonry is accomplished, Equality and Liberty; *all men are equal and brothers; all men are free.* That was the whole substance of our doctrine, the object of our wishes, the whole of our Grand Secret.'"

In reality, says Barruel, that revealed secret is what is known in secret organizations as a lesser mystery, common to all degrees within the sect. Though the words of the secret remain the same in the higher degrees, their interpretation, innocuous in the lower degrees, becomes monstrous in the higher degrees.

The three lower degrees of Masonry are labeled *Apprentice, Fellowcraft,* and *Master.* Barruel was himself importuned to be initiated. He refused, particularly objecting to having to take an oath of obedience to an unknown Grand Master for unknown objectives, which he suspected would conflict with his remaining obedient to the Church. He was nevertheless invited to a dinner by Masonic friends, following which he found himself in a lodge meeting from which he could not withdraw, and was led through a fore-shortened version of the initiation rites for the two lower innocuous degrees. For the third degree, however, he was asked to respond to the following: "Brother, are you disposed to execute all the orders of the Grand-Master, though you were to receive contrary orders from a King, an Emperor, or any other Sovereign whatever?" He answered "No," but was ultimately "initiated" anyway, so determined (or under orders) was the officiating Master to ensnare him. The initiation ritual was then completed, and Barruel was later permitted to attend meetings of a regular lodge, where similar initiation rites were held for others. He quotes the words of the officiating Master upon the conclusion of the initiation: "My dear brother, the secret of Masonry consists in these words, Equality and Liberty; *all men are equal and free; all men are brethren,*" the same as proclaimed in the decree of August 12, 1792.

Barruel is finally led to note that, of those who had received him in initiation, "except for the Venerable [the initiation Master], who turned out to be a violent Jacobin, they all showed themselves loyal subjects at the Revolution." Thus only in the higher degrees were the revolutionaries to be found, and the bulk of those in the lower degrees remained innocent, though duped. He remarks further on the English: "Few English craftsmen are acquainted with more than the first three degrees already mentioned, and the reader may rest assured, that with the exception of the imprudent question on obedience to the Grand Master of the Order, there is nothing which can render the secret dangerous, were it not for the Jacobin interpretation. The English good sense has banished such an explanation. ...Though the English have everything in common with the craft of other nations, ...yet as they generally stop at the degree [of Master], they never are initiated into the Grand Mysteries; or we should perhaps be more correct if we said they had rejected them. They have found means of purifying Masonry." Hmm... Perhaps.

Barruel then proceeds to a description of the next six higher degrees, and the secrets revealed to the adepts of each. These "Occult Degrees" are the *Elect,* three successive *Scotch degrees,* the *Knights of Rosæ Crucis* (i.e., Rosicrucians), and *Kadosch.* We will paraphrase Barruel's descriptions, omitting the allegorical folderol used to rationalize the revealed secrets to the adepts.

Elect: In the initiation rites, the adept is first led to commit a play-acted murder of a person seeking to discover and expose the secrets of Masonry, and secondly to play-act the role of Pontiff, dressed in priestly robes, and offering bread and wine. These acts prepare him for later violence against the enemies of Masonry, and encourage him to believe that all men are equally free to interpret religion, as opposed to the distinction made in the Christian Church between Priests and Laity.

Scotch Degrees: The adept emerges from these three successive degrees as *Scotch Master,* and in the character of *High Priest of Jehovah,* free and equal to all other Scotch Masters to practice the true religion of Deism which has been secretly passed down to the present Freemasonry via the "Masonic Sages," namely Adam, Noah, his great-grandson Nimrod, Solomon, Hugo de Paganis (the founder of the Knights Templars of the Crusades era), and the Templars' last Grand Master Jacques de Molay. This "true religion" is based on human reason rather than revelation, and declares its priesthood to be freed of the mysteries of the Gospel. The Knights Templars carried their precious knowledge to Scotland, where, under the name Knights of St. Andrew, their first lodge was established. Its successors are today's Masters of Freemasonry.

Rosicrucian: Adepts to this degree discover that their true religion proclaiming the unity of God was destroyed by Christ himself, who was an ordinary mortal, was the great enemy of Jehovah, and is therefore deserving of our hatred rather than our allegiance.

Kadosch: Here the adept again takes the role of play-acting assassin. The victim is Philip le Bel, King of France, who outlawed and destroyed the Order of the Templars. The person being avenged is Jacques de Molay, the Knights' Grand Master, whom the King executed. The adepts further learn that assassination is the proper end of Princes and Priests everywhere, as they have too long abused the goodness and simplicity of the people. The universal extermination of all Thrones and Altars is revealed as the grand object of Masonry.

Barruel notes the great gap in the Masonic responsibilities seen by the adept between the latter two degrees. Becoming a Rosicrucian only involves what appears to be a personal attitude toward one's own personal religion, whereas becoming a Kadosch involves the willingness to sanction, even participate in, regicide, obviously a capital crime. Operating the filters of the preceding degrees will have produced the desired result for the higher-level conspirators, however, of developing a small pool of activists willing to commit such crimes upon the order of unknown leaders. Barruel again takes the opportunity of noting that the huge preponderance of Masons, quietly residing in the lower degrees, have absolutely no knowledge of or predisposition to being connected with any such crimes, and remain instead faithful to both Altars and Kings.

Having now defined the pinnacle of the Masonic goals, Barruel again seeks to defend English Masonry. He notes (p. 321) that "they allow only of the three first degrees." ... "Nothing appears in their mysteries tending toward the hatred of Christianity, or that of Kings." ... "A Mason should be a peaceable subject, and cheerfully conform to the laws of the country in which he resides." However, he also notes: "We perfectly well know that many English are initiated in the occult mysteries of the Rosicrucians and Scotch degrees; but it is not their occult science which constitutes them English Masons; for the first three degrees are all that are acknowledged in England." Not acknowledged, though many are initiated? Barruel does not follow this loose end any further, at least at this point.

Barruel makes short shrift (i.e., just one chapter) of the three doctrinal classes into which Masons divide themselves: the Hermetic, the Cabalistic (which includes the Martinists), and the Eclectic. The Hermetic is the class which we have described above, which includes the Scotch degrees, and which embraces Deism. The Cabalistic is a class having a complex belief system involving dual deities of Good and Evil, each accompanied by an army of either good or bad spirits (angels or devils). The Martinists were a modern example (to Barruel) of Cabalists, who were notable for harking their Masonry back to its ancient roots, as we shall shortly discuss. The Eclectic is a class which permits of any religious view which denies all authority other than one's own reason, and which rejects all revealed religion. It is notable by the brand of anti-religious thought introduced by the Philosophers of Barruel's time. The three classes are in agreement on only their core beliefs: their hatred of Christianity, Kings, and all revealed religion.

Barruel now sets out to examine the history of the Knights Templars, seeking the historical roots of Masonry. The accepted history is straightforward. The period of the Crusades ran from about 1096 to 1270. The Knights Templars Order was founded in 1119 by Hugo de Paganis, and later blessed by Pope Eugene III (reigned 1145-1153). Its ostensible purpose was to safeguard Christian pilgrims journeying to Palestine. At first virtuous, the Knights grew in both fame and reputation. Their Order spread into Europe, and thereafter began to acquire immense wealth.

High morality soon gave way, says Barruel, to "plans of ambition, pleasure, debauchery, and unjust and tyrannical usurpation." For example, the Order was accused of treasonably communicating the whole of Frederick II's plans to the Infidels during the Sixth Crusade in about 1228. Philip le Bel, King of France (1285-1314), was made aware of certain crimes of the Knights, and ordered the arrest of all Templars in his Kingdom. Pope Clement V (reigned 1304-1314) first opposed the King in this matter, but after his own personal investigation, without threats of torture, he became satisfied that the charges were true, and permitted the King to proceed with the trials. Many of the charged Knights were found guilty. Many were executed, including the Order's Grand Master, Jacques de Molay (in 1311), and the Order of the Templars was abolished. These same actions were repeated in England, Scotland, Ireland, and Italy.

And what were the tenets of the Templar Order, which apparently made it so attractive to the Hermetic Masons? Barruel summarizes from the depositions of the accused: "The Knights Templar on their reception [initiation] denied Christ, trampled on the cross, and spit upon it; ...they promised to prostitute themselves to each other for the most unnatural crimes; every child begotten by a Templar was cast into the fire; they bound themselves by oath to obey without exception every order coming from the Grand Master; to look upon every thing as lawful when the good of the Order was in question; and above all, never to violate the horrible secrets of their mysteries under pain of the most terrible chastisements."

Barruel records that only a minority of the Order indulged in these practices, many others knew nothing of them, and probably many more who did know did not approve, but were coerced into silence. He estimates that at least two-thirds of the Order must have known what was going on. He also notes that between thirty and forth thousand Knights survived both Philip le Bel and Clement V, suffering only canonical penance or short imprisonment. From such as these men, says Barruel, have the Masons truly descended. To the corrupt anti-Christian conspiracy of the Templars has been added hatred toward the King and the Pontiff who were responsible for the execution of their Grand Master, and by extension hatred toward all Kings and Pontiffs.

So, did the eighteenth century Masons descend in an unbroken organizational line from the fourteenth century remnants of the Knights Templar? Or did the Hermetic Masons of Barruel's time, observing a congruity of outlook, simply adopt the anti-Christian beliefs, the secrecy oaths, and the immorality of the Templar Order, plus even the names and events concerning the Order's dissolution in their allegorical initiation rites? If these were the only alternatives, it would seem to make little difference as to which is closer to the truth. But another issue intrudes.

Where and how did the Templars acquire such beliefs, oaths, and immorality, in light of their having been created to assist Christian pilgrims in the Near East? Barruel suggests an answer (p. 345): "[The Templar] crimes, however infamous and incredible, only serve to [illuminate the existence of] the abominable Sect which introduced [those crimes] among their adepts, and from whom the Templars evidently learned their frightful mysteries. That hatred of Christ, that execrable immorality, even to the atrocious infanticide, are all to be found in the tenets... of that incoherent medley of *Begards*, *Cathares*, and that [group] of sectaries which flocked from the East to the Western States about the beginning of the eleventh century [i.e., about a century before the Crusades]." Barruel is suggesting a look further backwards, which he next undertakes.

28

He first notes that he was saved a great deal of research labor by the Philosophers' "historian" Condorcet, who was apparently equally curious about Masonry's antecedents. That worthy produced only the outline of his grand historical work before the Reign of Terror caught up with him. The outline, however, was enough to lead Barruel to the sources that he was after.

Condorcet gave the following general outline: In southern France, prior to and during the period of the Knights Templars, there were other anti-Christian movements which gave men full freedom to interpret religious tenets however they saw fit. These movements were violently put down by the armies of Christian Princes in one location, only to find them cropping up in another. The invention of printing helped them grow, said Condorcet (p. 356), until their power was sufficient "to deliver a great part of Europe from the yoke of the Court of Rome.... We will examine whether, at a time when Philosophic Proselytism would have been attended with danger, *secret associations were not formed, destined to spread and perpetuate privately and without danger, among a few adepts, a small number of simple truths as certain preservatives against predominant prejudices.* We will examine whether that celebrated order (the Templars), against which the Popes and Kings so barbarously conspired, are to be numbered among these associations."

These "men of the South" were especially strong throughout Spain, Italy, France, and Germany, says Barruel, during the reign of the Holy Roman Emperor Frederick II (1235-1250). He lists the names of a dozen or so of these sects, labeling them "the most direful enemies of morality, government, and the altar that had as yet appeared in Europe. I have studied their tenets in their divers ramifications...." Having done so, he found religious principles paralleling the three classes of Masonry discussed above, as well as the same principles of secrecy and immorality. (The code of Manes, however, went one step further in the direction of Communism. It demanded (p. 358) that "the whole belonged to all, and that no person had the right of appropriating to himself a field, a house, etc.") He concludes that Condorcet found, and he, Barruel, confirms, that a direct line of succession existed between these several sects and the Templars, and thence to the Jacobins of the Occult Masonic Lodges.

Barruel then makes his final, but giant, backward step in time. He focuses on possibly the largest of the eleventh century sects: the Albigeous (or Albigenses, after Albiga, a town in southern France). That sect claimed that no submission was due to any "Spiritual or Temporal power," and, says Barruel (p. 357), they went about *"beating down the churches and the religious houses, killing without mercy the widow and the fatherless, the aged parent and the infant child, ...and, as the sworn enemies of Christianity, ravaged and destroyed every thing both in Church and State."* The antecedents of the Albigeous, however, were not unknown. "What all history asserts," says Barruel, "[is] that the Albigeous and all the ramifications of those sects of the South... were really no other than Manicheans...." (Our encyclopedia says the Albigenses 'constituted the western branch of the Cathari, who had adopted certain Manichean doctrines.')

Manicheanism, however, is a movement named, some 16 centuries before the French Revolution (i.e., circa 200 AD), from a slave named Curbicus, who took the name Manes after being freed upon the death of his mistress. He formed a secret sect aimed at avenging himself on society because of his being born into the status of slave. Manes thus did preach "Liberty, because he had been born in slavery, and Equality, because [of his having been] born in the most degraded class of the human species." Condorcet

30

himself, said Barruel (p. 357), "pointed out the offspring of Curbicus [appearing] in the sectaries of the South, [and] in the order of the Templars."

Barruel relates further proofs of the connection between the sect of Manes and eighteenth century Occult Masonry, including such things as secrecy, the organization of degrees, the acceptance of immoral principles, the goals of "Equality and Liberty," the secret signs and grips, etc. In addition to opposing Kings and Altars, Manes aimed also at the abolition of *all* laws, i.e., producing anarchy. (Our encyclopedia also notes that the Manicheans rejected both the Old Testament and whatever parts of the New Testament displeased them.) We will discuss just one additional connection: the incorporation of the circumstances surrounding the death of Manes into the initiation rituals of Occult Masonry. Barruel relates the pertinent history (footnote 7, p. 335):

"*Terebinthus*, a disciple of *Scythian*, a conjurer, finding that the Persian Priests opposed his designs, retired to a *widow's house* in Palestine to whom he left all his money and books. She bought a slave named Curbicus, whom she afterwards adopted and caused to be instructed in the sciences of Persia. After her death, he quitted the name of *Curbicus*, to blot out the memory of his first conditions, and took that of Manes, which in the Persian language signifies *discourse*.

"Manes [now wealthy] had the insolence to promise the King of Persia that he would cure his son by his prayers [à la Rasputin in the 20th century], and the credulous Prince, believing him, sent away his physicians. The son died, and Manes was thrown into prison; but, escaping from thence, he fled into Mesopotamia; after various adventures however, falling into the hands of the King of Persia, he was flayed [skinned] alive, and his carcass cast upon the dunghill to be devoured by wild beasts. His skin was stuffed, and hung up on one of the city gates. His followers honored him as a martyr, and, in memory of his being flayed with reeds, *they slept upon them.*"

The allegorical rites of the high-degree Masons reflect these events. The meaning of a portion of the initiation ceremony is given the Masonic label *Mac Benac*, which was defined by Masons to Barruel as meaning literally *the flesh parts from the bone.* This clearly hearkens back to the manner of Manes' execution. Again, says Barruel, "The Rosicrucians begin their ceremonies by seating themselves sorrowfully and in silence on the ground, then raising themselves up and walking each with a long reed in his hand," reflecting back to the role that reeds played in Manes' death. The early rites of the Manicheans contained the same allegory, in a ceremony which they called *Bema.* There is nothing in the known history of the Templars which could give rise to such a rite, however, confirming that the Masonic roots did go back beyond the Templars to the Manicheans. The Templars simply substituted a new martyr, Jacques de Molay for Manes, and a new figure for hatred, Philip le Bel for the King of Persia. The hatred of Kings and Christianity remains intact, however, from the Manicheans to the Albigeous to the Templars to the Occult Masons.

Barruel terminates his look backward into history by once again complimenting the good sense of the English in rejecting the higher Masonic degrees, along with the "dangerous principles" emerging from the explanation of their mysteries. "Let us admire and applaud [the English]," he says (p. 363), "for having transformed this conspiring Sect of other states into an association evidently useful to their own." He does not elaborate this ambiguous statement, nor does he yet suggest a rational motive behind the secret movements of his time to destroy European society.

Before going into the merger between the French Philosophers and Masons, Barruel notes (p. 366) that the Masons of his day were claiming that the Scotch Grand Lodge was the source from which Masonry spread, "through England into France, Germany, and other states." Though this might be true with respect to the then-current forms and institutions of the various lodges, he offers documentary evidence showing that the deeper mysteries surely did not originate in Scotland, or even with the Knights Templar.

He describes (p. 386) a manuscript, preserved in an Oxford library, which is a copy of questions posed by Henry VI, and answered by a questioned Mason, written in the King's own hand in about 1460. Concerning the origin of Masonry, the adept "makes no mention of the Templars, [but] on the contrary says that all the important secrets of which [Masonry] is in possession were brought into Europe by Venetian merchants coming from the East." The ancient manuscript also reveals, says Barruel, that "Even in England, Freemasonry already [included] all those systems of *Cabal*, of *Astrology*, and of *Divination* [predicting the future], sciences all founded on the twofold principle of Manes."

In short, English Masonry, and likely the systems of Masonry throughout all of Europe, arose from the Manicheanism transmitted from the East by Venetian traders; only later was the history of the Templars incorporated into the Masonic rituals. Barruel suggests that this substitution may have been motivated by a desire to suppress the lowly social origin of Masonry's founder, and to supply a replacement origin in the person of Jacques de Molay, about whom a more positive spin could be generated. An alternative motivation occurs to us, namely, to hide the involvement of "Venetian traders," which could suggest a more commercial or political aspect to the Masonic movement. More about that later.

The European principalities were not unaware of the Masonic threat, and proscriptions against them were issued in Holland (1735), France (1737), Pope Clement XII (1738), and Switzerland (1748). The lodges survived, however, by avoiding the limelight and maintaining strict secrecy, except as to the identity of various adepts among the nobility whom they were able to dupe into membership. These noble adepts were able to quiet the fears of the reigning monarchs, including Louis XV, and the Masonic system survived the proscriptions.

The Sophisters and the Masons quickly identified each other as allies in a common cause. The Masons saw the Sophisters and their Holbach's Club as a new means of multiplying their lodges; the Sophisters saw the proliferation of lodges as the answer to their problem of raising street-level manpower for the revolution. Barruel notes (p. 368) that, many years before the conflagration started, "it was difficult to meet with a Sophister who was not a Freemason." Even Voltaire was finally initiated, in 1774, upon which he found that the great bulk of his own adepts had themselves previously been initiated. Upon this defacto merger, the adepts of French Masonry bought into the religious orientation of the Philosophers, and shortly, says Barruel, "The Martinists alone, with some few Cabalistic Lodges, remained true to their slave Curbicus; all others adopted the impiety of Voltaire." Thus, as suggested above, did the clouding of the true origins of Masonry occur in France.

Barruel describes the strategy of the conspirators for raising street-level mobs, in the elegant language of 200 years ago (p. 369): "To secure the triumph of Holbach's Club, the Sophisters had only to assure themselves of the support of the pikes [i.e., foot-soldiers carrying pikes]; and by means of the interior intercourse of the Masonic Lodges they hoped to effectuate it." By "interior intercourse" he is referring to the system of correspondence by which orders were directed from the Grand Master of the Grand Orient, that is, from the nominal head of French Masonry, to the heads of each of the subordinate lodges throughout France. Such transmissions were enveloped in a system of secrecy, with unquestioned obedience expected, and with the threat of dire consequences for failing to act or for revealing any Masonic secrets. The system was ideally suited for creating instant riots or mayhem wherever and whenever desired. Recruitment of adepts who would become such street troops was regarded as a simple matter, since for such persons indoctrination into the Occult Mysteries was entirely unnecessary, "the warhoop of Equality and Liberty [being] more than sufficient to excite their enthusiasm and direct their blows." Barruel provides documentation of such efforts being directed by the Grand Orient as early as 1776.

In 1787, a new secret organization calling itself Friends of the Blacks was formed in Paris. The name, denoting opposition to slavery in America, was merely a cover for the Sophisters and revolutionary Masons who created the new group. It's purpose was revealed to Barruel by a French noble, the Marquis de Beaupoil, who stayed in the organization only long enough to find out what it was about. Its purpose was to bring together Masons and Sophisters and any others having complaints against the Church or the State, and letting them discuss strategy. Its deeper purpose, however, was to provide a cover for the meetings of a "Regulating Committee," whose ostensible purpose was to guide those strategy discussions. The Committee contained the hard core of the revolutionists, however, including Condorcet, Mirabeau, Syeyes, Lafayette, and others less well-known, and was secretly engaged in its *raison d'être*: directing the field recruitment operations leading up to the Revolution. When the Revolution actually started, the organization named Friends of the Blacks was thrown aside, but the Regulating Committee remained, operating even more secretly, to direct the ongoing revolutionary activities in the field.

In Barruel's words (p. 381), "Of all the means adopted by the Regulating Committee, that which contributed the most to form the immense multitude of armed men which they wanted, was their correspondence with the Masonic Lodges dispersed at that time all over France in great numbers. In Paris alone there were one hundred and fifty.... Deliberations taken at the Regulating Committee were transmitted to the *central committee of the Grand Orient*; thence they were sent to the *Venerables* or Masters of the different Lodges in the Provinces." The first such missives to the hinterlands contained orders to punctually perform orders given, to make no inquiry as to why or from whom the orders came, and to remember the consequences of violating one's initiation oaths of secrecy.

The recruitment efforts were highly successful. Barruel estimates (p. 382) the number of French Freemasons at six hundred thousand, with about five hundred thousand of those "...zealous for the Revolution, all ready to rise at the first signal and to impart the shock to all other classes of the people. The Sophisters [in estimating a much larger figure] had already boasted that it was not such an easy thing to triumph over three millions of men."

Note that, while the Grand Orient was regarded as the seat of government of French Masonry, its Grand Master, says Barruel, was in fact obeying the orders of the Regulating Committee, which he elsewhere identifies (p. 369) as a group of "the most profound adepts." The Marquis de Beaupoil named those he knew on the Regulating Committee, including Condorcet. But who else

36

might have been running the show from behind the scenes? Might someone else have been guiding the Regulating Committee? One additional strand of the tangled web is identified by Barruel (pp. 372-375), as follows:

Condorcet and Syeyes founded a new lodge in Paris, "presided over by the Duke de la Rochefoucault, and more particularly frequented by the profound Masons." A German physician, researcher, and writer named Mr. Girtanner lived in the midst of the French Sophisters and Masons, gained their confidence, and later wrote his Memoirs on the French Revolution, plus other correspondence to which Barruel had access. The new lodge, says Girtanner, called The Club of the Propagandists, had a much larger goal than did the lodges which were planning and organizing just the uprising in France. Rather, its primary focus was to spread revolutionary incitement against government and religion throughout the whole of Europe and of the whole world. The Club was in existence, he says, at least by the year 1786.

(What we will find later in this review is that one of the intended roles of the Propagandists was to prepare the way for the armies of Napoleon during his conquest of most of Europe following the overthrow of the French monarchy. Condorcet was by that time dead. Again we ask, Who or what intelligent entity had the foresight to see that such a role would be needed, and had also the power to put it in place?)

Upon reception of an adept into the degree of Kadosch, he was judged ready to be considered for initiation into the Propagandists. He was told that the first requisite for such initiation was to promise to maintain the most profound secrecy. He was then told that the number of Propagandist adepts was immense, and that they were spread all over the world. Club membership consisted, said Girtanner, of about 5000 dues-paying subscribers, and perhaps 50,000 non-paying members. Club assets, he said, amounted in 1790 "to twenty millions of livres [pounds of silver] in specie," with ten million more expected before the end of 1791. We wonder where it was stored. But much more we wonder what manner of intelligence must have existed behind the scenes to create and direct an organization of such wealth and extent.

The Code of the Propagandists, says Girtanner, rests on the following basis: "Want and opinion are the two agents which make men act. Cause the want, govern opinions, and you will overturn all the existing systems.... [Their Code further] instructs the brethren not to try their plan until they are certain of having *created want*. It also says that it would be better to defer the scheme for fifty years than fail in it through too much precipitation." These immoral tactics were obviously used before and during the French catastrophe, and may still be seen, not so dimly, governing events in today's world. The long-term vision of this international "club," extending beyond the lifetime of any one member, can clearly be seen in the words of their Code which Girtanner and Barruel have managed to preserve.

Although aimed at larger targets, the Propagandists were also highly successful in their proselytizing efforts on behalf of the French Lodges. As Barruel put it (p. 375), "It was to the Propaganda that [French Masons] were indebted for the immense number of their adepts; or rather, in rendering impiety so common, the spirit of Philosophism had gained so much ground that it was scarcely necessary to be initiated into the Occult Mysteries to be a complete conspirator."

With Barruel, we now turn to the third leg of the Triad giving rise to the French Revolution: The Illuminati.

The name Illuminati was not original with its founder, Adam Weishaupt, observes Barruel (p.393): "It was the name which Manes and his disciples first affected.... The first Rosicrucians also, who appeared in Germany, called themselves Illuminees. And later, in our time, the Martinists... have pretended to Illuminism." Further, Weishaupt did not create his sect from his exposure to Masonry, since the founding date of the Illuminati, May 1, 1776, was a year before Weishaupt himself became a Mason, and began to find out what its mysteries were (though he worked at least until Dec. 20, 1781 on perfecting his organization). So what was his source of knowledge?

Weishaupt was born in Bavaria in about 1748, says Barruel (p. 400). "Of mean birth, his youth was passed in obscurity.... It is not known, and it would be difficult to discover, whether Weishaupt ever had a master, or whether he is himself the great original of those monstrous doctrines on which he founded his school." There exists, however, a tradition among his adepts, according to which, in about 1771, a European merchant who had lived in Egypt arrived in Europe proposing to initiate people into the "ancient mysteries of Memphis [the ancient Egyptian capital]. Barruel says he learned, "from more exact information," that the merchant had stopped in Malta, from which he was ejected for teaching the people "the disorganizing tenets of the ancient Illuminees, of the *adopted slave* [Manes]...." The merchant then proceeded into France where, the tradition has it, "he met with Weishaupt and initiated him in his mysteries."

Whether or not this tradition was factually true, Barruel concludes that Weishaupt must somehow have acquired an affinity for the ancient Illuminees, for he adopted both their name and their principles of Liberty and Equality, and recommended the study of Manicheanism to his adepts. He adopted also a pure Atheism, rejecting not only Christianity, but also Deism and even the twofold Deity of the ancient Manicheans, though he adopted those of the latter's doctrines which "threatened every government, and led to universal anarchy." Most significantly, he also adopted their view on property, which was that property, being the *cause* of inequality, should itself never be *owned* by any man. We previously noted Barruel's description of Manes' code regarding property, which stated (p. 358): "Lest there should be either poor or rich, [Manes] inculcated that the whole belonged to all, and that no person had the right of appropriating to himself a field, a house, etc." Thus the Communism of Marx is seen to have preceded Marx by around 1600 years.

Weishaupt adopted one other important attribute of his sect from an outside source, namely, the Society of Jesus, better known as the Jesuits (founded in Paris in 1534 by St. Ignatius Loyola). The Jesuits were running, among many others, the University of Ingolstadt, where Weishaupt, having attained the grand age of 28, had gotten himself named the chair of Laws (p. 404). What he borrowed from the Jesuits was their quasi-military organizational system, which so successfully "directed so many zealous men dispersed throughout the world toward the same object and under one head." He conceived that he might use the same forms, though aimed at opposite purposes from the Jesuits. Weishaupt thought to himself, "What these men have done for the Altar and the Throne, why would I not do in opposition to Altar and Throne? With legions of adepts subject to my laws, and by the lure of mysteries, why may not I destroy *under the cover of darkness* what they edified in broad day? What Christ even did *for* God and for Caesar, why shall not I do *against* God and Caesar, by means of adepts now become *my* apostles?" This was in fact the plan – one might justifiably say the Devilish plan – which Weishaupt adopted, as was documented to Barruel by Weishaupt's letters to various of his adepts.

We are led, however, to raise another questioning eyebrow. Both Voltaire and Weishaupt received their educations in Jesuit institutions. What a striking coincidence that both should have emerged leaders of violent anti-Christian movements! Shouldn't one have been able to expect the opposite of persons educated by religious scholars dedicated to the expansion and well-being of the Christian Church?

Weishaupt spent five years after founding the Illuminati in working out the details of its organizational procedures, much to the distress of his impatient helper-adepts. Upon conceiving a new element of the plan, his mind immediately went to the obstacles which might be raised to thwart it, and then to think through responses that could be made to such obstacles. He would take the time to try out the new element, with real people, to "experimentally" evaluate its worth before deciding whether to keep, modify, or reject the element. Two of the organizational principles which emerged from these deliberations are described below.

First, he observed, "I cannot employ men as they are; I must form them; each class of my order must be a preparatory school for the next; and all this must necessarily be the work of time." Barruel notes that to speed up the process, Weishaupt deliberately set out to seduce *young men* into the Order, they being more ignorant of the world, more responsive to their passions, and therefore easier prey for seduction.

Second, the maintenance of absolute secrecy was paramount. Weishaupt writes, "You know the situation in which I stand. I must direct the whole [conspiracy] by means of five or six persons. It is absolutely necessary that I should during my life remain unknown to the greater part of the adepts themselves." The same would apply at all levels, with no adepts generally knowing more than a very few adepts above them.

He continues, "The grand art of rendering any revolution certain [is to] insensibly turn the public opinion to the adoption of those changes which are the given object of the intended revolution. When that object cannot be promulgated without exposing [its author] to public vengeance, he must know how to propagate his opinion in SECRET SOCIETIES. When the object is an universal Revolution, all members of these societies, aiming at the same point, and aiding each other, must find means of *governing invisibly, and without any appearance of violent measures.... In silence, but with the greatest activity possible, direct the scattered inhabitants of the earth toward the same point.*" His empire of Illuminism, he says, is to be grounded on this force of secret societies. Once the Empire has been established "by means of the union and multitude of the adepts, *let force succeed to the invisible power.*" In a word, once secrecy is no longer necessary, pull out the guns and physically crush those whom you have not been able to convince (p. 413).

During his five years of organizational contemplation, he never changed the ultimate goal of his labors, which he states (p. 411): "Yes, princes and nations shall disappear from off the face of the earth; yes, a time shall come when man shall acknowledge no other law but the great book of nature: This revolution shall be the work of the SECRET SOCIETIES, and that is one of our grand mysteries."

Barruel spends the next hundred pages or so describing in detail the organization of the degrees which Weishaupt created for his sect. We shall present them, but severely digested, and concentrating on the principles underlying and holding the structure together.

To start, to provide for the growth and propagation of the sect, every Illuminatus who seeks internal advancement will at some point be required to play the role of recruiter ("Insinuator") of new adepts. Targets for recruitment are carefully selected, sometimes without their knowledge, and an appropriate Insinuator assigned the recruitment task. Potential recruits are wealthy, or politically strong, or societally influential, or possessing some other attribute or material good useful to the society. The Code contains pages of instructions on what kinds of people make desirable recruits, including educators, booksellers, discontented youth, etc. The Insinuator is motivated by being rewarded with long term control over the recruits he brings in, as well as those whom his recruits in turn attract. As the code expresses it, "Every Illuminee may form to himself a petty empire, *and from his littleness, emerge to greatness and power.*"

The Insinuator is required to keep a detailed diary concerning his probing into the habits, relationships, strong and weak points, etc., of his target recruits, and to transmit those written findings to his superior. Before any recruit is ultimately admitted, he too will have to write and transmit a highly detailed autobiographical account of his life, including his preferences, desires, weaknesses, relationships, etc. Thus, detailed knowledge is ultimately available to higher-order Illuminees on *all* lower-order members, a key element to enabling successful internal control and discipline. Various subterfuges and snares are then applied by the Insinuator, all aimed at inspiring the candidate with the wish to enter the Order. Upon the candidate's acquiescence, he is admitted to the degree of Novice if he is previously inexperienced, or to an appropriately higher degree if the candidate is a man of importance and previously disposed to the more secret goals of the Order.

The first three Illuminati degrees, of Novice, Minerval, and Minor Illuminee, parallel the first three in Masonry, of Apprentice, Fellowcraft, and Master. The newcomer's term as Novice is his time of trial, which may last from one to three years. He is asked to absorb a heavy load. He is imbued with the need for secrecy, and signs a declaration never to reveal anything he learns about the Order, even its existence, to any person, excepting only his Insinuator, who will lead him through his trials. The identity of no other Illuminatus is made known to him unless and until he completes his novitiate. He is made familiar with the use of assumed names and ciphers and codes to be used for internal communication. He is assured in his signed declaration that "Nothing is ever transacted in this society hurtful to religion, morals, or the state," though this statement will ultimately undergo a complete reversal. He is made to read and report on books assigned to him, to study and regularly write reports on others with whom he comes in contact, and to suggest which others might make good members. The Insinuator is simultaneously following the Novice's progress, and writing his own reports to *his* superior.

Toward the end of the trial period, the Novice is confronted with the demand for total obedience, which his Insinuator is charged with extorting from him. He is asked to write his answers to a long list of questions, which include the following (p. 434):

"VI. Should you ever discover in the Order anything wicked, or unjust to be done, what part would you take?

"XI. Do you, moreover, grant the power of life and death to our Order or Society? On what grounds would you refuse... it such a right?

"XX. Do you subject yourself to a blind obedience without any restriction whatever?"

When the Novice convincingly answers these and the other lesser questions satisfactorily, the Insinuator sends the responses and his recommendation to his superiors, and upon their approval, the Novice is presented with his final vows, which include the following:

"I promise ardently to seize every opportunity of serving humanity....

"I vow an eternal silence, an inviolable obedience and fidelity to all my superiors and to the statutes of the Order. With respect to what may be the object of the Order, I fully and absolutely renounce... my own judgment.

"I promise to serve [the Order] with my life, my honor, and my estates. Should I ever [perform an] act contrary to the laws or to the welfare of the Serene Order, I then subject myself to whatever punishment it may please to inflict upon me."

Upon this oath being signed, he is formally admitted to the degree of Minerval, and is told that he can expect to know only those of the same degree who are under the same Superior. The new Minerval is thus tightly bound to the Order long before he has the remotest clue as to its grand object, which is precisely what Weishaupt carefully planned.

Minervals are organized into sort of "Literary Academies," each consisting of a dozen or so Minervals headed by a Superior about two degrees above them. The single major purpose of this degree is to separate the sheep from the goats, that is, those who will continue on to the higher mysteries within the Order, as opposed to those who, showing insufficient promise, will be left behind. The means of discrimination involves the study and group discussion of literature selected by the Superior. Following such discussions, the Minervals are each required to write reports covering the books and the discourses, and announcing and criticizing not only one's own prejudices that may have been uncovered, but also the shortcomings and prejudices of other Minervals in the group. That is, they are taught to spy on each other and report their findings to their Superiors, a practice which was designed by Weishaupt and carried on throughout the Order, in order to protect the Order by finding and getting rid of potentially unreliable members.

Other means of sheep/goat discrimination have to do with satisfactory discourses on the Order's demand that they submit to torture, or even suicide, rather than reveal any information about the Order; that they accept as moral that books for their study were being stolen from wherever they may have been found; and that, more generally, they accept the Order's precept that "the end sanctifies the means," up to and including calumny, theft, or homicide (p. 444). Those who pass these tests are passed on to the degree of Minor Illuminee, while those who still retain "religionist inclinations" are granted instead the first three *Masonic* degrees (i.e., Apprentice, Fellowcraft, and Master), in which, as Barruel puts it, they may molder away the rest of their lives studying Masonic hieroglyphics, albeit under the eyes of Illuminati superiors.

As Minor Illuminees, two elements are added to their education: a deeper involvement with the *principles* of Illuminism, and training in the process of educating those in subordinate degrees. The former involve the use of sittings similar to those used by Minervals, but in which the adepts are presented with hints about how the wrongs of the world might be righted, especially via the energetic efforts of nobly-directed Secret Societies. The adepts are then led to believe that they themselves are gradually thinking up and working out the principles toward which the Illuminati should be working. As Barruel notes (p. 446), "The Minor Illuminees are imperceptibly [led] to become, as it were, the inventors and authors of Weishaupt's principles; that, believing them to be the offspring of their own genius, they may more zealously defend and propagate them." No definitive statement is yet presented to them, however, as to what specifically are the wrongs to be righted, and who specifically are the perpetrators of those wrongs.

Progress made in the matter of principles prepares the adepts to better perform their second task, which is to learn and to practice how to educate the adepts in the lower degrees. Thus, a few Minervals are selected for the Minor Illuminees to practice on, under the direction of higher degree superiors. This task is preparatory work for one of the primary responsibilities of the adepts upon advancement into the next degree, that of Major Illuminee. But before that advancement is offered, the Minor Illuminee is required to respond to searching inquiries about every aspect of his life, until his Superiors may finally agree that they have a viable candidate for promotion.

When and if that time comes, the candidate is then required to compose a highly detailed and candid account of his whole life, excluding nothing good or bad, positive or negative. When it is ready, a reception ceremony is held at which he hands his sealed autobiography to his Introducer. It is opened and read to the assembled company, and immediately followed with a reading of an essentially identical compilation of facts and characteristics which the Order had itself previously accumulated about the candidate. For the first time, the adept is forcibly made aware that the Order has learned the most private aspects of his life in incredible detail, and that it has thereby acquired effective control over his future well-being. As Weishaupt expressed it (p. 454), "Now I hold him; I defy him to hurt us; if he should wish to betray us, we have also his secrets." And the candidate now knows it.

The candidate is thus forced to choose between the dangers of withdrawal and the emoluments of advancement. The latter are of course urged on him, provided that his answers to a new set of interrogatories are satisfactory. The most important is his promise to report to his superiors on any advantage which might become his to bestow (e.g., a contract, or job, or gift), and to follow his superior's direction to give it to a fellow Illuminee. Thus, while defectors face punishments up to and including death, those remaining loyal could expect to be rewarded by being helped along in life by the whole body of those remaining in the Order. Weishaupt's hand is again clearly visible.

Upon the candidate's positive response, a dissertation is delivered on the goal and the plan of the Order (p. 458). Who stands in our way? "We are counteracted by the Princes and the Priesthood." Was violence to be used? Heavens no! Our plan? "We must insensibly bind the hands of the protectors of disorder, and govern them without appearing to domineer. In a word, we must establish a universal empire over the whole world, without destroying the *civil ties. Under this new empire, all other governments must be able to pursue their usual process, and to exercise every power, excepting that of hindering the Order from attaining its ends and rendering virtue triumphant over vice.... We must encompass the Power of the earth with a legion of indefatigable men, all directing their labors, according to the plan of the Order, towards the happiness of human nature* – but all of that is to be done in silence; our brethren are mutually to support each other, to succor the good laboring under oppression, *and to seek to acquire those places which give power, for the good of the cause.*" Doesn't that describe pretty well the "shadow government" that seems to be running today's world?

The candidate is thereupon admitted to the degree of Major Illuminee, and handed the portions of the code describing the techniques for learning about the lives and the secrets of Minervals, over whom he will preside as one of the major responsibilities of his new rank. Upon his study of this code, he learns for the first time how it was that the Order managed to learn so much about his own self.

The Major Illuminees' skills as "Scrutators" [examiners] are honed by their leadership position over the Minerval Academies. When a candidate has shown sufficient skill in extracting and laying bare a man's deepest secrets, he will be advanced, after taking suitable additional oaths, to the next degree, called The Scotch Knight of Illuminism, or Directing Illuminee.

Weishaupt created this "Scotch" degree for the single purpose (p. 462) of providing "a point of union between the Masonic Lodges and Illuminism." Specifically, the Major Illuminee (also called Scotch Novice) and Scotch Knight degrees of Illuminism could be announced to the Masons as equivalent to the "Scotch" degrees of Masonry, ending with Scotch Master. Perceiving the near-congruity in philosophy between the higher degrees of Masonry and Illuminism, he saw that he could very rapidly expand his own Order by capturing the Masonic Lodges, including their upper-level intelligentsia and their lower-level hordes. To accomplish this purpose, he set about to create "Masonic" lodges of his own, but composed of and secretly run by his own Scotch Knights, and into which existing Masons could be drawn. At the same time, he sought to insert his Scotch Knights into existing Masonic Lodges, where, as a secret society within a secret society, the Order could be expected to quickly gain control. By these mechanisms, "Illuminized Masonry" would be created, and would flourish.

Installation of a new Scotch Knight takes place in a "Secret Chapter" of the Knights, replete with the trappings of Scotch Masonry. Following the candidate's "knighting," a Superior delivers a discourse to the new Knight (p. 463), outlining a made-up history alleging to show how man, living in a state of primitive dignity, went through a great Revolution which deprived him of his ancient splendor. The secret principles governing that primitive state were, however, preserved by schools of ancient sages, including the schools of Illuminism and Freemasonry. Jesus of Nazareth was himself among those sages, though Christianity has since been falsified and perverted. Freemasonry, though well-intentioned, has also drawn away from those true primitive roots, and its lodges have "gradually subsided into seminaries of ignorance and error. The Illuminees alone are in possession of the real secrets of Masonry, many of [which] are even still to be the objects of their researches; and the new Knight is to devote all his attention to their discovery. He is particularly recommended to study the doctrines of the ancient Gnostics and Manicheans, which may lead to many important discoveries on this real Masonry." They should expect this research to be obstructed by "ambition and other vices which make humanity *groan under the oppression of Princes and of the Priesthood.*"

This allusion to the "oppression of Princes" is carefully explained away to Prince adepts, but this degree is as far as any such adept is to go, since the next higher degrees are going to be directly attacking the system of monarchy. The degree is also the stopping point for many others, including those deemed never likely to buy into Weishaupt's principles of anarchy and atheism. Such persons might, however, still be useful as agents of destruction, and could be expected to follow directions when the time comes. Those Knights who are *not* to be sidelined are installed in the "Secret Chapters" noted above, where they may work on their study of Manichean philosophy (i.e., down with altars, thrones, and property), in intellectual preparation for the next higher degrees.

The active Knights have several remaining duties written into their Code of Instructions (p. 465). One is to watch over the interests of the Order, particularly its financial interests, within the district of a Knight's purview. That means to find ways of attracting money into the Order's coffers. Another duty is to oversee and report on the activities of the Major Illuminees in their running of the Minerval Academies. A third is to acquire absolute sway in the Masonic Lodges, i.e., establish new ones, and reform or destroy existing ones. An exception is made for lodges "constituted under English diplomas" [my paraphrase], for which no visiting in either direction is to be permitted, for undisclosed "strong reasons." A fourth is to install auditors from the Secret Chapters into lodges "which do not pertain to our system. In general, the money which these lodges spend in a useless manner should be converted to the advancement of our grand object."

Weishaupt didn't think much of this degree, except for its ability to expand Illuminism by capturing Masonry, but Barruel thought even less of the thieving Scottish Knights. "[These] Knights Brigands," he says, "were but pitiful and miserable indeed."

After spending some time as a Scotch Knight, during which his enthusiasm and competence in directing others is carefully monitored and measured, he may be selected as a candidate for the next higher degree – that of Epopt, or Priest of Illuminism. The candidate is required to write out his answers to a set of ten questions, aimed at measuring his degree of acceptance of the history presented to him upon his acceptance as a Scotch Knight, and where such acceptance might lead. For example, What means should be employed (legal, revolution, or whatever works) for returning to our primitive happy state? Doesn't personal interest presently predominate over general public interest? Shouldn't we remedy that before trying to regain our Golden Age? Shouldn't we keep up our efforts via Secret Societies?

Given these questions and his recent study of Manicheanism, the candidate obviously knows what is expected of him, and upon his enthusiastic correct responses, the Superiors assent to his advancement to the degree of Epopt. (Curious spelling. Try it backwards.) Following the obligatory initiation ceremonials, the presiding Superior delivers of himself a long discourse, from the Code of the Mysteries composed by Weishaupt and his closest lieutenants, instructing the new Epopt on what he must now understand, and what duties lie ahead. We will try merely to identify the principle themes (pp. 472-494).

The Candidate is first flattered that he is entering into the leadership ranks of their secret Order, whose intent is to solve all the alleged evils of the world via a worldwide army of intelligent, accomplished men, acting together within secret societies rather than the civil constitutions of states.

There follows a lengthy elucidation of the "history of man" previously presented more briefly to the Scotch Knight candidates. Briefly, as families of primitive man multiplied, the means of subsistence began to fail, the nomad life ceased, men built homes and became farmers, bringing *property* into existence, and then mutual defense to protect a person's property rights, leading to strong leaders, armies, tyrannies against men, and the loss of both Liberty and Equality. In the end, this long discourse shows all Princes (i.e., civil authority) and Priests (i.e., church authority) and human greed (i.e., property ownership) to be the ultimate sources of man's griefs, curable only by the wise actions of secret associations. By those ultimate actions, Princes and Nations shall non-violently disappear from the face of the earth, and each father shall once again be Priest and absolute Sovereign of his family. Reason shall be the only law, the sole Code of Man.

But the gloves progressively come off. Later in the discourse he speaks of the recovery of man's liberty, "not by rebellion or violence (*for the time is not yet come*), but by the force of reason." Still later, the Superior reads, "Serve, assist, and mutually support each other; augment our numbers.... When you shall have acquired strength by your union, *hesitate no longer, but begin to render yourself powerful and formidable to the wicked* [i.e., the non-Illuminati].... *You will soon acquire sufficient force to bind the hands of your opponents, to subjugate them, and to stifle wickedness in the embryo.*"

Barruel here quotes Weishaupt exhorting his followers to weaken the multitude's ties to its civil institutions by diminishing the wants of the people. [E.g., walk, don't drive; set the thermostat to 62, not 72.] The mercantile community, one of his most hated societal structures, can help out, says Weishaupt. "He who wishes to subject nations to his yoke, need but to create wants which he alone can satisfy. Erect the *mercantile tribe* into an hierarchical body; that is to say, confer on it some rank or some authority in the government, and you will have created the most formidable, the most *despotic* of all powers. You will see it giving laws to the universe, and on it alone will rest the independence of one part of the world and the slavery of the other. For that man dictates the law who has it in his power to create or foresee, to stifle, weaken, or satisfy want. And who are better able to do this than merchants?" Such men, notes Barruel, who support the Conspiracy "with a view to partake of the government, are precisely those whose profession [Weishaupt] chiefly detests in every form of government." Weishaupt's sympathies are clearly somewhere else than with local merchants. Business Council, nota bene. (See also "mercantile despotism" in the Index.)

To keep those Epopt candidates from too abruptly learning that the Illuminati intended to jettison Christianity, Weishaupt (and his cohorts Knigge and Zwack) created what Knigge called a "pious fraud." In a letter to Zwack, Knigge wrote (p. 488), "We therefore assert here that Christ did not establish a new religion, but that his intention was simply to reinstate natural religion in its rights.... [His] intention was to teach us the means of governing ourselves, and to reestablish, without the violent means of revolutions, the reign of Equality and Liberty among men.... We add, that this religion, so simple in itself, was afterwards defaced.... In the last mysteries, we have to unfold to our adepts *this pious fraud*, and then by writings demonstrate *the origin of all* religious impositions," at which, presumably, "true atheism" can be extolled. Weishaupt himself is elsewhere quoted (p. 474) concerning his religious adepts who were accepting the fraud: "Poor mortals! What could I not make you believe? Candidly I own to you, that I never thought of becoming the founder of a religion."

The sophistry relating to the uprightness of the ancient history of Illuminism is essentially complete with the elucidation of the mysteries of the Epopt degree. However, much more in the way of *political* strategy is to be revealed immediately ahead in the degree of Regent, or Prince Illuminee. Those who distinguish themselves as Epopts, who show skill in dissembling when persuading others (i.e., are accomplished hypocrites), and who show that they are entirely devoted to the interests of the Order, may be selected as candidates for that next degree. The Preamble of the rules governing the degree of Regent introduces the new political emphasis, and contains the words (p. 495), "[Candidates] must indeed have clearly manifested their *hatred for the general constitution* or the actual state of mankind, [and] have shown how ardently they wish for a change in the government of the world...."

Thus, in Weishaupt's Instructions for conferring the degree of Regent, he lists questions to be asked of the candidate, including:

"I. Would you think a society objectionable... whose invisible means should prevent all governments from abusing their power? Would it be impossible, through the influence of such a society, to form a new state in each state, *status in statu*?"

"II. [Suppose] it to be objected that such a society would abuse its power? ...Is this power as secure from abuses in the hands of Princes, as it would be in those of our adepts whom we train up with so much care? If then any government could be harmless, would it not be ours, which would be entirely founded on morality, foresight, wisdom, liberty, and virtue?"

"VI. Supposing despotism to ensue, would it be dangerous in the hands of men who, from the very first step we made in the Order, teach us nothing but science, liberty, and virtue?"

Barruel's paraphrase of question I is, "Would it be impossible to subject the rulers of every state to this Illu-minizing Society, and to convert them into mere tools of the Order even in the government of their own dominions?" We would today simply ask, Don't you think that our Soci-ety could successfully form shadow governments in every state around the world? We noted an allusion to such shadow governments back in the instructions addressed to those undergoing Major Illuminee initiation. Here, much more explicitly, the strategy for gaining control of a country is spelled out.

In question II, Weishaupt acknowledges that Power Corrupts, but that wouldn't likely happen in the Order's virtuous hands. In question VI, acknowledging that when the Order's government *does* become despotic, it won't be dangerous, since it is steeped in "science, liberty, and virtue." The adept here is being given a demonstration of Newspeak, a term which came into the public vocabulary with the publication in 1949 of the novel *1984*. *("Ours will be a virtuous despotism.")* The candidate is certainly aware of the "morality" which says any means is justified (theft, murder, etc.) which promotes Illuminati ends, including the use of misleading, coded language. He is also aware that if he is to advance, he must mandatorily respond with the proper, lying answers.

The thrust of this latest filter is to eliminate anyone who cannot lie with skill and ease, and who cannot accept criminal means for subverting established governments, fully justifying the labeling of the Illuminati as a *criminal conspiracy*. Weishaupt, in his correspondence to Zwack, represents the instructions given to the adepts during initiation to Regent (p. 497) as "infinitely more important than those of the preceding degree."

When selected for admission to Regent, the candidate is required to make a will containing a clause assuring that any papers involving the Order will, upon his death, be automatically removed from "prophane" hands and destroyed. Upon completing this arrangement, the initiation is held, during which all the papers which had heretofore been prepared by or about him are returned to him, and he is told that he is now free and independent, and trusted not to abandon the Order. (He probably won't forget, however, his vows of silence under penalty of death, or his susceptibility to blackmail.)

Weishaupt, after five years of defining the structure of the degrees in his Order, ended up with just two more degrees, covering what he called his Grand Mysteries. The first of these was called Mage, or Philosopher, and covered his final words on religion. As noted earlier, all that remained in this area was to show that the religions of the world were all man-made impostures, and that Weishaupt's "true atheism" could then easily fill the vacuum. Barruel quotes as his primary source a man who went through all the degrees of Illuminism, the better to unmask it (p. 395). That man, writing anonymously, but nicknamed Biederman by his German supporters, penned the following words describing the degree of Mage (p. 510): "[This degree] contains the fundamental principles of Spinosism. Here everything is *material*; God and the world are but one and the same thing; all religions are *inconsistent*, chimerical, and the inventions of ambitious men."

Barruel indignantly reviews the twists and turns of the religious guidance which the various degrees of Illuminism have given its adepts, only to renounce all their previous assertions of never being hurtful to religion or morality, a sugar-coating which made their anti-monarchical pills go down more easily, and finally to unveil their grand secret that Christianity and all other world religions are false, and that Atheism is the only residual truth. He writes, "The first object of these grand mysteries of Illuminism, prepared with so much art and cunning, is no other than to plunge the adepts into a monstrous Atheism, to persuade all nations that religion is but an invention of ambitious impostors; and that to deliver nations from this despotism of imposture, and recover the famous rights of man, Equality and Liberty, they must begin by annihilating every religion, every worship, every altar, and cease to believe in a God."

The last and highest degree is that of Man King, into which Biederman was also initiated. Barruel quotes him as follows: "The second degree of the grand mysteries," he says, "called the *Man King*, teaches that every inhabitant of the country or town, every father of a family, is sovereign, as men formerly were in the times of the patriarchal life, to which mankind is once more to be carried back; that, in consequence, all authority and all magistracy must be destroyed."

Barruel puts some flesh on the Illuminati's final action item, *"All authority and all magistracy must be destroyed."* Not just kings, but all governments, all laws, and all civil societies, whether monarchies, aristocracies, republics, or democracies, are to be destroyed. Each man's own will is to be the only law. How can men, assembled in towns, protect their homes and property from marauders? Answer: they should desert and burn those towns and houses, since ancient men, enjoying Liberty and Equality, didn't need them, or any other property, and so didn't need any civilly guaranteed "rights" to protect them. Men will become citizens of the world, because, without law, the concept of "jurisdiction" will disappear, and national boundaries will cease to exist. A return to the nomad life will reinstate the Liberty and Equality enjoyed by the earth's early Patriarchs.

Barruel recalls the many hints given throughout the Order's successive degrees that universal civil destruction was in fact the action that was ultimately to be demanded, though it was originally specifically denied that the Order intended anything hurtful to the state. He also points out that the Order's revealed goal was hardly original with Weishaupt, since he had been philosophically preceded by both Rousseau and, centuries earlier, by the slave Manes. Rousseau is quoted, "The man who, having enclosed a piece of ground, first took it upon himself to say *this is mine*, and found beings *simple enough to believe him*, was the true founder of civil society.... What horrors would [some prescient] man have spared mankind... had [he] called out to his equals, 'beware of hearkening to this impostor; you are ruined if ever you forget that *the fruits belong to all, though the land belongs to none.*'" We noted above in discussing Weishaupt's early education his acceptance of the similar Manichean views on rulers, law, and private property.

Barruel expostulates that these goals are, on their face, absurd. "What can these men want with their monstrous Equality, with their plots against our civil laws, our title to even the very name of property? Must we then, to please them, abandon our habitations; must we renounce all arts and sciences, and end with burning our cities, towns, and villages, to follow them in herds like the savage and nomad clans? Are half the inhabitants of the globe to be slaughtered, the better to scatter the roaming herds?" Disbelieving that the conspirators are presenting an honestly-held program, he asks himself, "What can these men want? Have they not fortunes to preserve... or children in their families? Can they be conspiring against themselves? Or, are they ignorant that their conspiracies will fall back upon themselves?"

The best that Barruel can come up with is that they are caught up in an irrational enthusiasm, and should be viewed as barbarians, like the Huns or Ostrogoths of old. Indeed, Barruel quotes from Weishaupt's lecture to future Epopts (p. 519), extolling the virtues of the Goths and Vandals who descended upon and laid waste to Europe in its early days. Those invasions operated, Weishaupt said, "to infuse new life into the enervated species of the south [Rome, Gaul, Spain, and northern Africa], and with new laws and morals to restore vigor to human nature...."

It appears to us, however, that so glorifying medieval despoilers did not represent the true mind-set of the Order's top leaders, but was only a means to incite the lower-level adepts to the acts of savage violence that would later be required. As to Weishaupt's real motivation for helping to plan and organize the destruction of Europe, we are more inclined to ask, with two hundred more years of history available to us, "Cui bono?" Who benefits? Suppose existing civil governments are destroyed, perhaps one by one, via the action of shadow governments? Who will then be capable of taking control of such governments? Let's keep following the history which we are attempting to uncover.

Weishaupt's papers show that certain of his Man King adepts, those selected under the title of Areopagites to serve on the governing council of the Order, are to be told the final Mystery, namely that Illuminism was founded not by ancient sages, nor by the founders of Christianity or Masonry, but rather by modern philosophers. "In a word, it is of our own invention. The *true father of Illuminism is no other than Spartacus* [his Illuminati name] *Weishaupt.*"

We have several reasons to doubt the whole truth of this revelation. First, we can see no profit accruing to Weishaupt himself by his unilaterally deciding to create an organization to someday accomplish the destruction of Europe. Second, large parts of the Order's philosophic goals were created by others who preceded Weishaupt by many years, even centuries. Third, it appears unlikely that one person, and he a young man of modest means, could so astutely build such a successful secret society from scratch, without both financial support and considerable advice from conspiratorial predecessors to guide him concerning what does and does not work. Fourth, conspiratorial efforts consistent with those of the Illuminati continued smoothly up to and beyond the time of Weishaupt's death, suggesting an ongoing higher intelligence. And fifth, in the initiation rites for Regent, adepts are told that the names of the Order's founders would "forever remain in oblivion," and that all documents which could identify them have been burned. This may in fact actually be true, but if so, why does Weishaupt now claim himself to be Illuminism's "true father?" A possible answer might be that he was ordered to do so, as a more effective way of convincing others that looking for founders or directors above Weishaupt would be a waste of time.

Barruel then turns to a discussion of the internal organization of the Order, and the duties incumbent on those holding organizational responsibilities. In so doing, two new ploys not previously mentioned are outlined, which remain of interest to us to this very day. The first involves the assignment of those holding Epopt degrees to one of seven sciences in which each Epopt is to specialize. The seven sciences are Physics, Medicine, Mathematics, Natural History, Politics, The Arts, and The Occult Sciences. Each adept is to master his assigned Science sufficiently to turn the knowledge so acquired to the use of the Order in attaining its ends. As Barruel puts it (p. 534), "The united efforts of the Epopts are concentrated in their pursuit of science *only to debase it*, by directing all its powers toward the overthrow of Religion and Governments." Some examples in today's world of the still ongoing perversion of science are 1) the progressive socialization of medicine (Medicare, FDA, AMA, HMO's, etc.); 2) education perversions (Look-Say, New Math, dumbing down); 3) societal degradation via the arts (crime, sex, and violence in TV, movies, and music); 4) natural science perversions (global warming, ozone holes, carbon taxes, spotted owls, etc.)

The second new ploy is contained in a directive to Epopts (p. 537) to "incessantly form new plans, and try every means, in your respective provinces, to seize upon the public education, the ecclesiastical government, the chairs of literature, and the pulpit." Voltaire's Philosophers had advanced to the writing in their Holbach's Club of propagandistic literature for the schools, but Weishaupt, while including his own substantially identical goal of dominating literature, goes much farther by directing the infiltration and take-over of both public education and theological seminaries. This latter ploy, it is obvious, could only be of value in the long run, taking at least several generations to have an appreciable effect. The long-term outlook of the Illuminati is again apparent. Present-day reactions to these efforts involve vouchers to get away from government schools, and the surge of independent, fundamentalist religion.

More about the scope and the long-term outlook of the Order's efforts are revealed in Weishaupt's directives to his Regents; for example (p. 547):

"XXII.   A cloak is however always necessary, for in secrecy our strength principally lies.

"XXIII.   The inferior lodges of Freemasonry are the most convenient cloaks for our grand object, because the world is already familiarized with the idea that nothing of importance, or worthy of their attention, can spring from Masonry...

"XXIV.   It is of the utmost importance for us to study the constitutions of other secret societies and to *govern* them....

"XXVI.   Never lose sight of the military schools, of the academies, printing presses, libraries, cathedral chapters, or any public establishments that can influence education or government, ...and form plans for making us masters of all these establishments.

"XXVII.   The grand object of our Regents must be [to] add to the perfection and to the power of our Order, that it may become *for future ages* the most perfect model of government that can enter the mind of man."

Barruel takes several chapters to outline the internal command structure of the Illuminati, which we will briefly summarize. Below are the names of the hierarchy of managers ("Prefects"), and the scope of authority of each.

Prefect	Scope
Superior	Lodge
Dean	District
Provincial	Province
National Director	Country
Supreme Council	World
(of Areopagites)	
General of Illuminism	

Prefects will all have advanced at least to the degree of Regent (p. 542), while the Areopagites will have attained Man King. Individual lodges might be of several kinds, depending upon the degree of the members, or upon whether grounded in just Masonry, or in pure Illuminism. When lodges exceed about 10 members (p. 555), they are split up, to help maintain secrecy, and a Dean is appointed to oversee the Superiors and lodges in his district. Similarly, the Provincial oversees the Deans and lodges in his province, and the National Director oversees the Provincials and lodges in his country. Each National Director reports to one of twelve Areopagites, and they in turn, as the Supreme Council, oversee all the National Directors and lodges throughout the world. The General of Illuminism oversees and presides over the Areopagites on the Supreme Council.

Every member of a lodge knows the other members of his own lodge, including his Prefect, but has no knowledge of the identity of any of his Prefect's superiors, or who is a member of any other lodge. He attends regular lodge meetings where orders are given on tasks to be undertaken, and where his upwards communications are tendered. The system of vertical communication is the Order's primary mechanism for maintaining the coherent discipline which enables world-wide or country-wide actions to be taken simultaneously with the appearance of spontaneity. Not only is every lodge member required to write regular reports on everything that he sees happening which has any bearing on his life as an Illuminati, he is also encouraged to write criticisms of his own Prefect, to be opened and acted upon only by the Prefect's superior; i.e., he is encouraged to *spy* on his Prefect, and the Prefect, knowing it, is strongly bound to adhere to the Order's straight and narrow. Further, each Provincial is *required* (p. 560) to establish his own secret spies in each of the lodges in his province, enabling him to spy on Prefects and other persons *below* him. All of this spying activity, plus the regular periodic reports written by everyone, are reported up the chain of command, ultimately to the General, enabling him to better reward exemplary performance and punish traitors and incompetents. The General, of course, can delegate as much of the monstrous volume of paper work to his subordinates as he wishes, so that he can concentrate on his Big Picture.

Weishaupt insisted on the strict obedience of his Supreme Council in carrying out his decisions and orders. Upon encountering some opposition from his highest lieutenants, he fought for their allegiance by quoting Machiavelli to them (p. 571): "It seldom or never happens that any government is either well-founded at first, or thoroughly reformed afterwards, *except the plan be laid and conducted by ONE MAN ONLY*, who has the sole power of giving orders and making all laws that are necessary for its establishment. A prudent and virtuous Founder... ought to endeavor by all means to get the supreme *authority wholly into his hands*; nor will a reasonable man ever condemn him for taking any measures (even the most extraordinary, if they are necessary) for that purpose. The *means* indeed *may seem culpable*, but the end will justify him if it be a good one...." Weishaupt did, in the end, convince his Areopagites that their General, holding the helm of the Order, should be its absolute master. He later took pride in the power he held in his hands, communicating to certain of his adepts about how well he could precipitate the simultaneous actions of thousands by initiating orders given to only a few of his immediate subordinates at the apex of the Order, very much like a five-star General giving his armed forces the order to attack.

We turn next, with Barruel, to the early developmental growth of Illuminism, followed by its merger with Masonry, which had by that time joined forces with the Philosopher movement created by Voltaire. The French Revolution was to immediately follow.

Weishaupt, holding the position of Doctor of Laws at the University of Ingolstadt, founded his Order by the installation of two of his students on May 1, 1776. One of them, designated *Ajax*, in turn recruited Francis Xaverius Zwack, a fellow student, who was initiated on May 29, 1776. Zwack was given the name *Cato*, and showed such good promise that he shortly became second in command to Weishaupt, with the additional title of Inspector, meaning secret spy over any other Illuminee, and reporting directly to Weishaupt. Zwack was a master of the art of dissimulation, and was an excellent recruiter of new adepts, an activity which Weishaupt pressed above all else on his early adepts. He, in the meantime, worked hard on completing his Code for properly training up recruits to the higher positions in the Order where they could help govern it. He and Zwack were highly successful, with many lodges having been established in Bavaria, and adepts working toward others in Holland, Milan, Vienna, and elsewhere. In a letter of Nov. 13, 1778, less than three years after founding the Order, Weishaupt (p. 594) "...writes to *Cato* that he has more than a thousand adepts."

Barruel also notes that the two leaders nicely survived the Revolution (p. 599), and in 1797, as his book was being published, "...[just] as Weishaupt has found a protector in the person of the Duke of Saxe Gotha, so has [Zwack] been created a Privy Counselor to the Prince of Salm Kirbourg...." How curious that reigning monarchs would protect these men, when the Order's goal was to destroy all such monarchs!

The Order's early adepts were of two kinds, and worthy of note. First, one group of them was, on an absolute moral level, impossible. Weishaupt delivers to them a written tongue-lashing: "Judge yourselves what would be the consequence if [a desirable recruit were] to know what a *set of men, destitute of morals, what a set of debauchées, liars, spendthrifts, braggadocios, and fools replete with vanity and pride,* you have among you...." Weishaupt wasn't complaining that his men were immoral, but rather that many of them *gave the appearance* of being immoral, i.e., were not good enough at moral pretense. In reality, incoming adepts were well aware of why they were there: to acquire the wealth and other advances that the Order held out as lures to get them to come aboard. Weishaupt knew that he was going to *need* the commitment of his adepts to immoral means to accomplish his goals, so he deliberately sought out immoral or amoral adepts, and that's exactly what he got; he just needed the Order to look respectable to his more noble, or learned, or wealthy recruits.

A second group consisted of exactly those described as "noble, learned, or wealthy." Barruel deplores the success Weishaupt had in placing his men in ecclesiastic and state administrations where handling of property, jobs, contracts, etc., could be handled to the benefit of the Order. Upon reflection, future historians, he declares, "...will soon perceive the funds of the Sect swelled to an immense bulk by those shares which it preserves for its own use out of all the emoluments which it has procured for its adepts either in church or state." The same still applies today, for example, with profiting by pre-knowledge of the economic ups and downs manipulated by banking or currency-trading elites, or sharing in the profits of the monstrous drug commerce while pretending to fight it, etc.

Weishaupt early recognized what a great advancement it would be for his order if he could manage to form an alliance with Masonry. Accordingly, he managed to join a lodge in 1777, saw the possibilities, and then ordered all of his Areopagites to likewise join Masonic lodges. He soon became aware of all the Masonic secrets, while giving up none of his own. While he was debating with himself about how best to turn Masonry to his own ends, that problem was solved for him by the entry into his Order, in

July of 1780, of a Hanoverian Baron named Knigge, code-named *Philo*.

Knigge's father had dabbled in Masonry, permitting his son to likewise be exposed. The Baron Knigge was fascinated, and spent his youth probing and pushing into Masonry, trying to figure out its deeper secrets, and then later how to organize it into taking on more aggressive actions to achieve its goal of overturning all Thrones and Altars. Encountering an Illuminati recruiter, he was over-joyed to find a viable, going organization already working on so redefining Masonry, and he joined up.

Whereas Weishaupt was a man to carefully plan his next actions, Knigge was a man of action. Having a deep knowledge of Masonic byways, he plunged into recruiting for the Illuminati the higher-degreed Masons who knew something of the secret Masonic goals. He was so success-ful that Weishaupt himself saw that he could greatly shorten the long process of starting with and reeducating callow youth, and so ordered his recruiters to follow Knigge's methods.

By 1780, a call had gone out for an international assembly of Masons to be held in Wilhemsbaden during the first six months or so of 1782. Knigge, the consummate Mason, had been invited, and he hounded Weishaupt to let him take advantage of the opportunity for major recruiting among the deputies representing the million or so Masons around the world. He said, however, that Weishaupt would have to level with him about the Illuminati's final secrets for such recruiting to be successful. Weishaupt finally agreed, and admitted to Knigge that his Order, professedly so ancient, was still being finalized in his own head. He then asked Knigge to help him organize his higher degrees in such a way as to encourage mass defections from Masonry to Illuminism. Knigge enthusiastically responded, and threw himself into the task. Weishaupt, the master manipulator, had successfully executed a major coup.

Says Barruel (p. 625), "The chief point... was to know what rank should be given to the Freemasons [upon their entering] the Order, as a mode of facilitating the general intrusion [of Illuminism] into the [Masonic] Lodges." Knigge's views were accepted, and Masons above the three lower degrees were to be accepted as Major Illuminees, which were co-named "Scotch Novices." For those holding the Scotch and higher ranks in Masonry, rapid advancement could be expected to Directing Illuminee (co-named "Scotch Knight" as a parallel to the Masonic degree of Scotch Master), and to the degrees above that as appropriate.

Almost as important, the Code for the degrees Epopt, Regent, and above had not yet been finished by Weishaupt, and he and Knigge worked furiously to complete it before the Wilhemsbaden meeting. The completed Code covering the degrees of Epopt and Regent was signed by (at least) Knigge, Zwack, and Weishaupt on Dec. 20, 1781, and impressed with the grand seal of the Order. The conspirators were now ready for Wilhemsbaden.

They could hardly have been more successful. While the mass of disparate lodges fenced with each other over their myriad pedagogical differences, Knigge saw to the passage of a resolution to study the creation of a new Masonic code which would effectively enable the entry of Illuminati into any lodge. At the same time, he worked on proselytizing deputies outside of the conference on the great advantages of Illuminism to the whole world of Masonry. He was successful in both regards, and later writes, "In short, some of the deputies learned (*I know not how*) that our Illuminism was in existence. [Of such persons,] *almost all* came to me to entreat me to admit them.... *Most of them* appeared to be ready to follow any system that they judged conducive to give to [Masonry] that utility and activity that was the object of all their wishes." In a word, they were seeking strong leadership to energetically further their goals of Liberty and Equality, which, Knigge skillfully declared, was exactly what Illuminism offered them.

Upon termination of the conference, Knigge reports that deputies flocked to him begging admission into the Order, which he generously granted, even directly into the higher degrees. He writes (p. 648), "All of them *were enraptured* with our degrees of Epopt and Regent; all were enchanted with these *masterpieces*; for so they styled these degrees." In the period immediately following the conference, Knigge reports that he had Illuminized some 500 persons, nearly all of whom were mature Masons, ranging up to fifty years of age. The resulting spread of Illuminized lodges in late 1782 was apparent throughout Germany and Austria, with inroads being made as well in Italy, Belgium, Holland, and Poland. Weishaupt was, of course, highly gratified that Knigge's strategy was working so well, and he dispensed with the slow learning path through the Minerval schools, and urged the recruitment, as Knigge had done, of more mature men who could be quickly advanced to the higher degrees.

But Weishaupt and Knigge had even greater fish to fry. Barruel says (p. 656), "But the grand object that absorbs all [of Knigge's] attention is the means of consummating the intrusion [of Illuminism] into the Masonic Lodges, which is at once to enlist millions of men under the standard of his Areopage, and to effectuate his Illuminizing revolution." The Wilhemsbaden assembly had created a commission to propose a new Masonic Code, and Knigge undertook to cultivate and influence the leader of that commission, a man named Bode, to assure that the door would be opened wide to an Illuminati conquest. Knigge courted him, admitted him to the degree of Scotch Knight with the code name *Amelius,* found out that he hated Priests and Jesuits, and used that knowledge to skillfully extract from him promises "to labor for us, and, by means of the new System or Code to be formed for Masonry, to throw the [control] over the Lodges into our hands." Having made these and other valuable promises, Bode was quickly ushered into the higher degrees.

Simultaneously, Weishaupt had Knigge write a circular letter which was intended to be sent to all Masonic Lodges. The letter stated (p. 662) that several Lodges in Munich and elsewhere were willing to confederate with other lodges on the bases that: (1) the first three degrees granted in any lodge were to be mutually acceptable to other lodges; (2) each lodge may define its upper degrees however it wishes; (3) that all lodges shall be independent of each other; and (4) intercourse between lodges would be via correspondence and visits of the members. These innocuous sounding conditions were laid into a web of seduction, claiming that the grand goals of Masonry ("intended by God and nature to reclaim the rights of humanity oppressed, of virtue persecuted, and of science degenerated") had been deviated from, and that Illuminism alone was in possession of the real mysteries, and, retaining a zeal for the original goals, it desired to affiliate and lead Masons of every ilk who wished to regain Masonry's ancient splendor.

The seduction, plus the labors of Bode in convincing key Lodge Superiors and protectors, produced an avalanche of acceptances throughout Germany. In addition, Bode installed the Masonic Code changes that Weishaupt desired into the new Masonic Ritual (p. 671). Barruel quotes reactions from honest Masons appalled at the intrusion of criminal elements into Masonry. His own assessment is that the intrusion continued unabated until the Illuminati finally claimed that only one of the major lodges in Germany remained unaffiliated. Barruel then notes:

"This declaration does not imply that the greater number of the Brethren were already Illuminized, but only denotes that the Superiors, whether Masters, Wardens, or Treasurers, of almost every Lodge had entered into the federation with Weishaupt. But what an awful aspect does this subterraneous power present! A multitude of emissaries and agents dispersed throughout the [murky] recesses of Masonry. The Superiors once gained over, the Lodges would make but a feeble and short resistance."

Barruel next turns to the efforts made in the 1780's to expose the Illuminati, from which the Order emerged bloodied, but stronger (and more secret) than ever. In June 1784, the Elector at the court of Munich, acting on unknown sources, decreed the abolition of all secret societies not established by law. The untainted Masons closed up their lodges, but the Illuminati resisted, stayed open, and unleashed a flood of argument defending their probity. These arguments were apparently traced to their source, and in February 1785, Weishaupt was dismissed from his professorship at the University of Ingolstadt. He found refuge, however, along with his papers, in the town of Ratisbon, where he gave his full time to the Order's business.

About a month later, a lightning bolt struck dead one of Weishaupt's emissaries, and authorities recovered and inspected the papers he was carrying, thwarting the Order's practice of immediately obtaining and destroying any such papers upon a member's death. The examination resulted in the expulsion of fifteen of Weishaupt's former students at the University, and the firing of a number of public officials in Ingolstadt. In the months that followed, a number of former members were located and depositions taken from them, leading to raids, on October 11, 1786, on the homes of Zwack (*Cato*) and a second Illuminatus named Baron Bassus (*Hannibal*). The raids uncovered a huge store of the Order's archives, which were promptly published by the Bavarian Elector and made available to all under the title "*Original Writings of the Order and of the Sect of the Illuminees.*" These materials constituted Barruel's prime sources for his exposition on the Illuminati.

Inspection of the archives led to a death sentence for Weishaupt, but he fled to safety from Ratisbon to Gotha, where he was given refuge by his Highness the Duke of Saxe Gotha. Zwack likewise took flight to safety. About twenty other adepts were cited to appear before the court, and while some were given short prison sentences, many others were merely dismissed from public employment. In a word, except for Weishaupt, punishments for sedition were ridiculously light.

Further, practically no official actions were taken by other jurisdictions outside of Bavaria. Barruel marvels that the bulk of German officialdom could be so complacent, so lacking in concern even for self-survival. Of course, complaints are common even today about the public's complacency, but we know that in fact it is not complacency, but *manipulated ignorance* that produces disinterest and inaction. European peoples and their governing entities were victims of that manipulation over two hundred years ago, and the bulk of the world's citizenry remains so today.

Following these exposures, Zwack wrote a note, later found by authorities, saying that the Order should get rid of its malcontents, and work to restore its former vigor. Furthermore, says Barruel, "Weishaupt, six months after being fired from Ingolstadt, threatened those who dismissed him, saying in a letter of August 9, 1785 (p. 723), "Let our enemies rejoice. Their joy shall soon be changed into sorrow. Don't think that even in my banishment I shall remain idle." Clearly, Illuminism was still very much alive, in demonstration of which Barruel cites two of the Order's new projects.

The first involves a sudden deluge from familiar Illuminist/Sophist sources declaiming against the *Jesuits*, who were accused of secretly taking over control of non-Illuminist Masonic lodges. Whereas the Illuminati had previously claimed ownership of the true Masonic Mysteries, now they also claimed that they were the only ones immune from Jesuitical destruction. The result was that the two main Masonic holdouts from Illuminization – the Rosicrucians and the Lodge of the Strict Observance – flocked to the Eclectic lodges under the control of the Illuminati. "Thus," says Barruel (p. 706), "was the threat of Weishaupt accomplished, that he would either conquer the Strict Observance and the Rosicrucians, or destroy them." Weishaupt had in fact brought up the concept of Jesuit Masonry as far back as 1781, and several times since. Weishaupt, while apparently vegetating in the Saxe Gotha court, was, says Barruel, simply exercising "his favorite maxim of *appearing idle in the midst of the greatest activity.*" *Our* feeling is that it would take a remarkably twisted mind to think up such a perverse scheme for consolidating the Order's absorption of German Masonry, and Weishaupt's mind seems to us to have been just right for the job.

The second project was much more fundamental, being aimed exactly at maintaining the *manipulated ignorance* of the "prophane" populace. A recent recruit into the Illuminati was one Dr. Bahrdt, "a [Protestant] Doctor of Divinity at Halle," says Barruel, "but a man of such infamous morals that even *Philo*-Knigge was ashamed to see his name among Weishaupt's elect...." Dr. Bahrdt took on the generalship of a movement which created "The Germanic Union," the purpose of which, says Barruel (p. 715), "was nothing less than to reduce Germany, and by process of time the whole world, to the impossibility of receiving any other lessons, or of reading any other productions then those of the Illuminees." The Union was to be directed by a Council of Twenty-Two (analogous to Weishaupt's Areopagites), chosen from men "who by their functions, their knowledge, or their labors, had acquired a great facility in directing public opinion toward the errors of the Sect." Each of the twenty-two would have his own department, staffed by contributing brethren such as authors, librarians, booksellers, etc. Princes, court-followers, and public officials were to be excluded.

Selected activists amongst the brethren "were initiated into the secrets, the means, and the object of the coalition." Instructions given to such initiates, says Barruel, declared as follows: "To root out superstition, to restore mankind to liberty by enlightening them, to consummate the views of the founder even of Christianity without violent means, such is our object. It is for that purpose that we have formed a secret society [!], to which we invite all those who are actuated by the same views, and are properly sensible of their importance." A series of *literary societies*, or *reading clubs*, was set up throughout Germany to identify and recruit a continuing stream of new members. Once initiated, members were directed to contribute to the production of information agreeable to the Sect's objectives, using every known information media. Further, and of the greatest importance, booksellers, librarians, and other media controllers were to be put into place, and *used to prevent the publication or dissemination of books, articles, etc., which were inimical to the policies of the Order*.

Barruel summarizes (p. 717): "Such was the plan of the Germanic Union, Dr. Bahrdt's masterpiece. Never had the desire of tyrannically governing the public opinion invented a more perfidious plan." But was Dr. Bahrdt the plan's real author? He was himself soon arrested, briefly imprisoned, and reduced to near-poverty for his remaining days, but the plans of the Union continued on, with burgeoning literary societies looking more and more like

Weishaupt's Minerval Schools. "It is not known," says Barruel (p. 719), "how [much] Weishaupt had contributed personally to it; but it appears that he twice attended at the headquarters of the united brethren; that he spent several days with Bahrdt; and that the most zealous and active of the united brethren were also disciples of Weishaupt." We would add, of course, that antiestablishment access to the primary mass media remains negligble to this day, and *manipulated ignorance* continues to reign supreme.

Having firmly established itself within German Masonry, the Order now turned to doing the same in France. Barruel relates (p. 726) that Weishaupt and Knigge had discussed such plans as early as 1782, but had decided to wait until preparations elsewhere were complete, fearing that the "volatile and impetuous" French people, being unable to wait until other nations were properly prepared, would revolt prematurely. Certain French revolutionary leaders were early initiated into Illuminism, however, including Mayor Dietrich of Strasbourg (initiated by Knigge at Wilhemsbaden in 1782) and Marquis de Mirabeau (initiated by Knigge's disciple Mauvillon in 1784, during Mirabeau's diplomatic mission to Berlin for his monarch, Louis XVI).

Mirabeau, who was fully involved with French Masonry, understood the reasons for delay, but some time after his return to France he initiated a correspondence with Mauvillon, seeking to convince him that the time had now become ripe, and asking that appropriate teachers from the Order be sent to France to help Illuminize the French lodges. Barruel comments, "Certain it is... that Mirabeau's plan was adopted by the Areopage; and by a plurality of votes it was decided that France should be immediately Illuminized." The man selected for the job was Bode (*Amelius*), who had just done such an excellent job in helping Illuminize German Masonry and in getting the Masonic code rewritten and accepted. He was to be assisted by Baron de Busche (*Bayard*), another of Knigge's pupils, now a skilled Insinuator. Barruel calculates that they departed on their mission some time in early 1787.

To whom was the presentation to be made? Barruel describes the primary Masonic groups extant in Paris at the time. Briefly, there were three lodges which dominated. The first was The Grand Orient, with Grand Master Philip of Orleans the nominal head. It was subdivided into committees on Administration, Paris, the Provinces, and the Degrees, the latter being the directing and the most impenetrable component. The lodge acted rather like a Masonic parliament for all of France, issuing directives to subordinate lodges in some two hundred eighty-two French towns in 1787, with eighty-one lodges in Paris alone. Other subordinate lodges existed outside of France, in such places as Switzerland, Germany, Poland, Russia, all of the French colonies, and even in Portsmouth, Virginia. The Grand Orient, says Barruel (p. 729), could "ensure to the Illuminees as powerful an alliance as that formerly made by Knigge with the German lodges under the direction of Weishaupt."

The second of the powerful Parisian lodges was *Les Amis Réunis*, or United Friends. This lodge also had its own highly secret Central Committee, consisting only of those of the highest degree, i.e., Knights Kadosch. The lodge was subordinate to the Grand Orient, and was specifically charged with all Foreign Correspondence. The Central Committee of the United Friends was therefore the entity designated to host the German Illuminees, and to issue invitations to the French Masonic leaders who were to attend the secret conference.

The third notable Parisian lodge was presided over (p. 734) by one Savalette de Lange, meeting in the Rue de la Sourdiere. Savalette was in turn a member of the Central Committee of the United Friends. In the Sourdiere lodge were Mayor Dietrich, Secretary of the lodge and already an Illuminee, and the Philosopher's historian Condorcet, perhaps already initiated as well. The membership of this lodge was a savage mixture of French Martinists, whose cabalistic antecedents had called themselves Illuminees before Weishaupt ever came along, French *Theosophs*, who also called themselves Illuminees, and a scattering, says Barruel, of "Rosicrucians and other Masons both ancient and sophisticated." Despite the eclectic grouping, the core Mysteries of the lodge were indiscernible from those of Weishaupt, i.e., to seek the annihilation of all Priests, Kings, Altars, and Laws, and to regard as noble and meritorious any means used to accomplish those ends.

We can't help but stop to ask ourselves: Must we regard as *coincidental* this simultaneous creation and maturation, from groups unacquainted with each other, of identical programs for destroying society? Wouldn't it be rational to at least examine the possibility that some common hand might be orchestrating these movements?

The meetings then took place, in perhaps February and March of 1787. Barruel's account (p. 738) is brief: "Weishaupt's code was ordered to lie on the table, and commissioners were named to examine it and make their report.... All that my [sources further] say on the subject is that the negotiations took place; that the [German] deputies reported to their Areopage; that the negotiations lasted longer than expected; that it was at length decided that the new mysteries should be introduced into the French Lodges, but under a Masonic form; and that they should all be Illuminized, without even knowing the name of the Sect whose mysteries they were adopting. Only such parts of Weishaupt's code were to be selected as the circumstances would require to hasten the revolution."

Barruel notes that the success of the meeting was quickly evidenced by the changes made in the practices of the lodges. In 1787, the mysticity of the Martinists in the Parisian lodges disappeared, and new explanations were given for Masonic secrets. A new degree was introduced, and was transmitted to the hundreds of lodges subordinate to the Grand Orient. Adepts flocked to the new mysteries.

Barruel further records, "According to the agreement made with the Deputies, all the forms of Masonry were preserved in this new degree, ...but the groundwork of its mysteries was a discourse entirely copied from that pronounced by the Illuminizing Hierophant in the degree of Epopt.... In short, it contained all the principles of Equality and Liberty, and of natural religion, detailed in the degree of Epopt; and even the enthusiasm of style was preserved." The degree, which Barruel labels the *Masonic Epopt*, was rationalized merely as a deeper explanation of the origin and secrets of Masonry, though its obvious purpose was to more firmly bind its adherents to the goal of destroying all Priests and Kings. Nowhere, however, does a reference to Illuminism appear.

The last preparations for revolution are now made. Lodges throughout France multiply without precedent. Recruiting is heavily undertaken among the lowest classes of society, in order to acquire revolutionary foot-soldiers. Clubs and literary societies, as planned by the Germanic Union, sprout out. Everywhere are to be found clubs, regulating committees, and political committees which deliberate and pass resolutions. The Regulating Committee of the Friends of the Blacks, discussed earlier, sends its resolutions to the Grand Orient for dissemination. In short, a "French Areopage" is formed, containing such as Philip of Orleans, Mirabeau, Syeyes, Savalette de Lange, Condorcet, etc., all being Illuminati and/or Occult Masons. Secret messages are sent to the Lodge Venerables throughout France demanding reaffirmation of their vows to follow orders, from persons and for purposes unknown. Those who refuse to participate, and who quit their posts out of fear, are replaced by more zealous conspirators. Everything is now in place, and the date of July 14, 1789 is set for a "spontaneous" nationwide explosion.

The "French Areopage," as an organized group, was first called the Breton Club, which held meetings in Versailles. Since the bulk of the revolutionary activity was to be performed in Paris, Mirabeau brought the group to Paris, where it met in the church of a religious group called the Jacobins. "From that instant," says Barruel, "this temple is converted into a den of conspirators.... Soon does all Europe designate by the name of *Jacobin* the authors and abettors of the French Revolution."

Barruel concludes, "Thus, in this den of conspirators do we find everything in perfect unison with the Occult Lodges, to which it only succeeds. Adepts, object, principles – all are the same; whether we turn our eyes toward the adepts of impiety, of rebellion, or of anarchy, they are now but one conspiring Sect, under the disastrous name *Jacobin*. We have hitherto denominated some by the name *Sophisters*, others by that of *Occult Masons*, and lastly we have described those men styled *Illuminees*. Their very names will now disappear; they will in future all be described by the name *Jacobin*." Thus did Barruel see fit to carry that name into the title of his book.

Barruel very briefly describes the progressive course of the French Revolution, from the point of view of its pursuit of the goals defined by both the Jacobins and their ancient conspiratorial predecessors. The first step involved the convocation of a National Assembly which would serve to "authorize and direct" the changes in the steps to follow. Second, the Church was attacked, meaning church buildings and property were confiscated, along with the property and the very lives of priests, nuns, and other religious. Third, the Monarchy was overthrown (Louis XVI and his Queen both guillotined), and the property, wealth, and lives of as much of the Nobility as could be reached were claimed. Fourth, having stolen the property of the church and the nobility, a start was made toward annihilating *all* property by confiscating that of merchants as well. Full Equality was thus claimed to be near at hand.

A speech of the adept Babeuf denouncing private property is quoted (p. 770): "The Agrarian Law, or the equal partition of lands, was the momentary wish [of some]. We aim at something far more sublime, far more equitable: *Goods in common, or the community of estates!* No more individual properties in land, for the earth belongs to no-body. We demand and will enjoy the goods of the earth in common. The fruits will belong to all. Disappear now, ye disgusting distinctions of rich and poor, of higher and lower, of master and servant, of *governing and governed!* For no other distinction shall exist among mankind than those of age and sex." Further, the depopulation sought after by the Jacobins, as required by their return to primordial society, is voiced in a 1795 report of the Committee of Public Safety, addressed to those fearing for adequate food supplies: "Fear not; France has a sufficiency for twelve million inhabitants. All the rest [i.e., the other 12 million, says Barruel] must be put to death, and then there will be no scarcity of bread."

Thus were the worst, the most criminal, the most ghastly programs of the ancient Manicheans and the more modern Jacobins put into place. Our next review will contain much more of the Revolution's detail, written from more complete historical knowledge. However, Barruel does follow the developments *outside* of France up to the time his book was published (1798), which it is much worth our while to review. His emphasis is to show that it was not overwhelming military power or skill, but rather Masonic and Illuminist conspiratorial manipulations, which paved the way in Europe and the Near East for the conquests in those regions by the French Republican armies.

Barruel introduces his theme (p. 779): "We have seen [Jacobin generals] destitute of experience or merit baffling the wisdom and talents of heroes consummate in the military art.... Another [mystery] presses on our notice: These Jacobin conquerors are received like brethren by the vanquished nations.... To unfold these mysteries, let us boldly declare it: the Sect and its plots, its legions of secret emissaries, have everywhere preceded the armies and their thunderbolts of war.... Once prepared, traitors were to be found in the fortresses to open the gates, [and] were to be found in the armies and in the councils of Princes to render the plans of attack or defense abortive. Its subterraneous Clubs, Lodges, Corresponding Societies, Journals, and Propagandists had already disposed the populace and prepared the way.... So well did they know the importance of being masters of the public opinion that, to conquer it by means of their Propagandists, Journalists, and other writers, they spent no less than *thirty millions of livres* during the first year of their incursions, and during 1797 they lavished *twenty-one millions for the same purpose.*"

Thus, on the West Bank of the Rhine, the inexperienced French General Custine, with negligible military effort, conquered the German towns of Speyer, Worms, and Mainz, the latter through the conspiratorial cooperation of its "defenders;" shortly thereafter occurred the magical surrender of the entire West Bank, i.e., the area between the Rhine and the Low Countries. It was re-named for a time the Cis-Rhenane Republic, before becoming a simple province of the Parisian Republic. The Jacobins swarmed into its various ministries.

The French General Dumouriez similarly performed a cakewalk into Belgium, where he was joyfully accepted by the public as a result of propaganda conspiratorially applied after the successful manner of Custine, but expertly taking into account the specific fears and hatreds of the Belgian citizenry. Critical parts of the secret planning were accomplished by French adepts in London, who, when exposed to British officials, were nevertheless permitted to remain, "under close watch," as Barruel says.

Holland similarly fell to the French General Pichegru, mostly through the efforts of local Dutch adepts and a corrupt judiciary which, when conspirators were uncovered and tried, sentenced them to be exiled into the very towns through which the Jacobin armies were to enter Holland. The British army, for whatever reasons, and though presently at war with France, was ineffective in helping to defend its long-time Dutch ally.

Napoleon Bonaparte swept across northern Italy, picking up strength on the way, even though, says Barruel (p. 788), his armies were "more destitute of everything that can assure victory than those which had entered Germany under the command of Custine." Weishaupt, Knigge, and company had long since bragged of their recruiting exploits in those parts, and payoff time had come.

Malta was next to fall, or rather to welcome its conqueror, following which Napoleon set sail for Alexandria, Egypt, where he proceeded to take advantage of the preparations that the conspirators had made in buying their way into the good graces of the chiefs of the Ottoman Empire in Constantinople [now Istanbul, Turkey].

At this point, in mid-1798, time runs out on Barruel's chronological description of Napoleon's conquests, and he turns instead to a summary of what he knows of the preparations of the conspirators elsewhere around the world, discussing events in Spain, Portugal, the United States, Switzerland, Sweden, Poland, Russia, Austria, Germany, and finally England. We'll concentrate on his remarks about England.

There appear to be unique aspects of the English experience with the secret societies. On the one hand, Barruel documents many instances in which the British actively opposed attempts of the conspirators on the Continent to spread their intrigues back across the channel into Britain. On the other hand, he also documents a number of clear instances of British involvement in one way or another with the creation of, or assistance to, the revolutionary movements on the Continent. Even more pregnant is the existence, which he discovered only during his asylum in England, of a profound Masonic movement in Britain which dated from Cromwell and even earlier, thus substantially preceding the eighteenth century movements on the Continent. Let's look at each of these three aspects, and see if they can't somehow be fit together into a logical whole.

Barruel over and over acknowledges the existence of British Masonry, all the time insisting, however, that it is of a civilized, fully domesticated variety, generally limited to the first three rather innocuous degrees, with lodges populated by genial brotherhoods of likable chaps, never prone or permitted to criticize either church or state. Though all have sworn obedience to unknown Superiors, and a good many have risen to the Scotch and Rosicrucian degrees, the British "have not acknowledged" these degrees, and further, they might be said to have "rejected" the Grand Mysteries along with their "dangerous principles," and "found means of purifying Masonry," even of "transforming it into an association useful to their own society," as we have noted Barruel's words on previous pages. He further reveals (p. 806) his discovery of a pamphlet entitled "Freemasonry: A Word to the Wise," which supports the Grand Lodge of London in its complaints against the introduction of the higher degrees, specifically mentioning Rosicrucianism.

Further, Britain has taken several current actions to protect their Masonic status quo. A traveling German

Insinuator named Zimmerman claimed to have Illuminized a number of English lodges, but two that were thereafter examined were found to have abandoned Illuminism. Upon his leaving, he was replaced by one Dr. Ibiken, who in a short time was exposed as an Illuminist proselytizer, and was deported. A new emissary, named Reginhard, arrived from America, having just left certain Boston lodges which were corresponding with counterparts in London, where he expected to be received. He instead talked, and the English Illuminist lodges were exposed. Notwithstanding these small victories, the population of revolutionary lodges swelled, and came to include large numbers of low-life criminal aliens from Europe. The British thereupon passed their *Alien Bill*, facilitating the discovery and deportation of such illegals. In summary, the revolutionary movements in Germany and France never penetrated into Britain deeply enough to harm its governmental or social institutions.

But while Britain was defending its shores from European revolutionaries, it appeared at the same time to be helping along the revolution on the Continent, primarily by helping to form or to protect its leadership. The primary philosophers of religious and political revolution, Voltaire and Montesquieu respectively, each underwent early tours of indoctrination in England. Barruel does not identify Montesquieu's preceptors by name, saying only (p. 207) that Montesquieu, circa 1720, "stayed some time in England, and then returned to France full of those ideas which he has developed in the two works that have chiefly contributed to his fame." Voltaire's English educators were better known to Barruel: Collins and Bolingbroke, according to the "Philosopher's historian" Condorcet. As Barruel put it (p. 244): "The commencement of this conspiracy was when Collins, Bolingbroke, Bayle, and other masters of Voltaire," had, with Voltaire, commenced their anti-Christian conspiracy.

During the period of active Illuminati growth, Weishaupt ordered his adepts to seek control of all Masonic lodges except those constituted under English auspices (p. 465). Why? Zwack (*Cato*), Weishaupt's trusted lieutenant, was granted asylum for a year at Oxford, following the exposure of the Illuminati in Bavaria and the publication of its papers (p. 803). Why?

But most important, while in England Barruel discovered another work (p. 806), printed fifty years earlier (i.e., circa 1745), entitled *On the Origin and Doctrine of Freemasons.* He wished he had found it sooner. It detailed the Scotch degrees of Masonry extant at that time, leading to the degree of *Scotch Architect*, which he says fully encompasses the principles of the Knights Kadosch, and is, in its essence, "as bad as the Illuminees." Its grand object, revealed to new Architect adepts, is "to reduce all men to a reciprocal EQUALITY, and to reinstate mankind to its natural LIBERTY." Further, the order still exists in Great Britain, with the mother lodge called the Lodge Heredom of Kilwinning in Edinburgh, Scotland. The existence of the famed *Architects of Equality and Liberty* at this lodge explains the pre-eminence of the Scotch Lodges, to which the cabalistic French lodges (exemplified by the Parisian lodge of Savalette de Lange meeting in the Rue de la Sourdiere) maintained their affiliation, notwithstanding the influence of The Grand Orient of Paris.

Barruel had in fact earlier pointed out (p. 366) that the bulk of European Freemasons honor the Scotch Grand Lodge as the stock from whence Masonry spread through England to France, Germany, and other European states. He later (p. 827) castigates the British for being a party to Masonry's introduction onto the Continent, saying, "No longer than a century ago, the remaining part of Europe was nearly a stranger to your lodges and their mysteries. You made it the baneful present; the newly-erected lodges have filled with Jacobins, and from them the most disastrous scourge that has ever befallen the universe has rushed forth...."

The author of *On the Origin and Doctrine of Freemasons* attributes (p. 807) the restoration of Masonry, and perhaps its origin, to Oliver Cromwell and his Independents. Barruel comments that the document's author would not have mentioned *origin* had he known of the Oxford manuscript, dated circa 1460, which he earlier described (p. 386), and which related how the principles of Masonry had originated with the Manicheans, and were brought into England and elsewhere in Europe by Venetian merchants coming from the East.

He suggests that current *Architects* and their European adepts "...have discovered their progenitors ['Puritans, Anabaptists, and Independents'] in those same dens to which Cromwell had confined them, after having, through their means, dethroned and murdered his king, dissolved the parliament, and seduced the nation to his yoke." I.e., Cromwell *used* the early "Masons" to dethrone King Charles I, install himself in power, and then put them back down. Later history has Cromwell likewise losing power, the Stuarts returning, William III of Orange conquering, followed shortly by the start (in 1714) of an English branch of the Brunswick-Hanover dynasty (later renamed Windsor) in the person of the Hanoverian King George I, who spoke no English.

There is a great deal of history in those years with which most Americans are entirely unfamiliar, and probably even Britons also, if *true* history is what we mean. At any rate, Barruel is saying that Masonic predecessors came early to Britain, had a role in overturning the Stuart royal house, and ultimately survived in the Scottish lodges, where they had at least some role in the organization and prosecution of the revolution on the Continent. Barruel directly addresses the English (p. 816) to pay close attention to the 1794 Reports of the English House of Commons on plots underway in English lodges, in the light of which he sees the Mother Society of Edinburgh as having malevolent intentions equal to those of the *Secret Committees of the Grand Orient* under Philip of Orleans, the *Bavarian Areopage* under Weishaupt, or the *Holbach's Club* under D'Alembert.

How might these disparate circumstances fit together regarding Britain's role in the Jacobin Revolution? A logically inviting hypothesis is that an English shadow government already exists, engendering publicly known and publicly unknown events. Known and supported are efforts to keep the revolutionary rabble and their works out of Britain. Unknown is the at least partial control which profound adepts already have over the policies of the British government, which include the support of the secret societies in dismantling European altars and governments, and further entrenching the partial control they already have over the English ship of state. But to whose ultimate benefit?

We will, in our following reviews, continue to probe into the shadowy history of the secret societies, the better to be able to eliminate their direful effects on the lives of millions of ordinary people around our whole earth. Barruel, in the Conclusion of his *magnum opus*, presents his list of action items aimed at exposing and destroying the secret societies. I will merely list them, without going into his extensive rationale:

1. Destroy seditious written materials.
2. Prosecute consciously seditious writers for treason.
3. Form a league of anti-seditious writers.
4. Remove conspiratorial adepts from pulpits and classrooms.
5. Remove yourself from any lodge requiring secret obedience.

6. Proscribe all secret societies and lodges, especially in England.
7. Provide unquestioned police authority and ability to quell mobs.
8. Organize united action among nations to oppose Jacobin armies.
9. Make a personal return from "Reason" to revelatory Faith.

At the conclusion of our book, we will present our own program of action, as do most writers who are attempting to fight against our wannabe masters. You may at that time revisit Barruel's program, and test whether ours will encompass the intentions of his. Ours will of course presume today's modern means of communication, and will be written to specifically apply to the United States, with due care taken to protect the civil rights that are guaranteed to our citizens by our Constitution.

Chapter 2

"THE FRENCH REVOLUTION"

(By Nesta H. Webster. Orig. pub. 1919. Pub. 1988 by The Noontide Press, 1822½ Newport Blvd., #183, Costa Mesa, CA 92627. Available also from Omni Publications, PO Box 900566, Palmdale, CA 93590, 805-274-2240.)

We present this book next, out of chronological authorship order, because it so comprehensively puts flesh on the events of the actual revolution. Nesta Webster rightly complains that the French people have been unjustly defamed by over a century of being blamed in establishmentarian "received history" of bringing on the horrors of the Revolution in order to achieve their goals of a better life, etc. Webster says this is nonsense, and vows to prove the identity of the real culprits, and the consequent innocence of the great bulk of ordinary French citizens.

She starts by declaring that there were four behind-the-scenes movements seeking to influence the French public's attitudes and actions toward the church and/or the monarchy. They were the Orleanists, the Subversives (i.e., the Illuminati), the Prussians, and the English. Philip of Orleans hated Louis XVI and his queen Marie Antoinette, and personally coveted the throne for himself. Among his other exploits, he helped to *create* a grain shortage in order to drive the people to revolt. The Illuminati, leaders in rooting out religion, morality, and all property rights, and proclaiming that "good" ends justify any means, lay the psychological foundation for the Reign of Terror. The Prussians wished to break the friendly Franco-Austrian ties which opposed German expansionism, and blackened the name of the Austrian Marie Antoinette in order to promote a break between France and Austria. English coin was lavishly distributed to help pay for various revolutionary expenses, including the formation of Parisian mobs, coin which Webster says was derived from English accounts of Philip of Orleans and his revolutionary English friends, though not from the English government, which many suspected of involvement. Philip and others among the French revolutionary leadership frequently visited England, including such as Marat, Danton, Brissot, and Pétion, perhaps to visit certain persons whom Webster labels the "English Subversives," in which she included the Prince of Wales (the future George IV), Lord Stanhope, Dr. Price, Dr. Priestley, and others.

Webster sets about to prove the innocence of the French people by examining five major events of the Revolution in which the "public" played a major role. We will briefly outline those five events, not only to show the rightness of Webster's hypothesis, but to provide a flavor of what the revolution was really like, about which Americans and most others around the world have been dismally miseducated. We strongly urge readers to acquire this book, to get the full flavor of the horrible events which Webster so adequately presents.

1. The Siege of the Bastille. The Bastille was an ancient fortress, complete with guard towers and drawbridges, and used in more recent years as a state prison. On July 14, 1789, it was "besieged" by a mob of Parisians, which gained entrance over the drawbridges, swarmed in, and overcame its small force of guards, which had been ordered not to fire on the mob. The first major blood of the Revolution was then drawn in the massacring of the commander of the French guards along with the bulk of those under his command. The event was hailed by the Jacobins as their first victory over the authority of the King, whose

"weakness" in combating their efforts gave promise of easy victories in the future.

There is much to be added to that brief description, of which we will supply only those few tidbits which bear on *our* theme. First, by the preceding April, says Webster (p. 39), "The peaceful citizens [of Paris] saw with bewilderment bands of ragged men of horrible appearance, armed with thick knotted sticks, flocking through the barriers into the city." Eyewitnesses described them as neither workmen nor peasants, of no class other than bandits, as speaking a strange tongue, as "Marseillais – men of rapine and carnage, thirsting for blood and booty...." This contingent of imported "brigands from the South," as Webster calls them, was secretly "employed and paid for by the revolutionary leaders, a fact confirmed by authorities too numerous to quote at length."

The plan for attacking the Bastille was drawn up the day before the attack, as was admitted by revolutionary authorities (p. 73), and so was far from a "spontaneous" uprising of the people. In fact, says Webster (p. 95), only about 1000 of the 800,000 Parisians took any part in the siege, and the mob responsible for the worst of the atrocities consisted largely of those hired brigands imported from the South. Only seven prisoners were found in the Bastille, all incarcerated for non-political reasons.

Webster counts as the major result of the event of July 14 the exposure of Parisians to violent bloodshed. Thereafter, she says (p. 105), "the populace of Paris – the idlers, wastrels, and drunken inhabitants of the city – acquired a taste for bloodshed that made them the ready tools of their criminal leaders." A second result was the successful dress rehearsal of the Jacobin strategy of raising and using mobs, a strategy which was then used in all the later mass uprisings of the revolution. In this strategy, says Webster, the mechanism was threefold, consisting of actions by Instigators, Agitators, and Instruments. Only the latter two of these face any physical danger, since the Instigators prudently confine their role only to secretly planning and provoking the explosion, and not to getting blown up in it, the better to be able to plan the next uprising. Those unfamiliar with these tactics will find Webster's account very enlightening, and may thereafter be able to see the same strategy still being practiced all around the globe to this very day.

There is one other major lesson to be learned, having to do with the direful effects of conspiratorial actions within a legislative body. On June 17, 1789, the National Assembly was called into existence. It contained three opposing bodies. First were the Orleanists, who wished to replace Louis XVI by the Duc d'Orleans. Second were the Subversives, who wished to destroy all monarchy, religion, and law. Third were the "Royalist Democrats," later called "Constitutionals," who wished to create a more democratic Constitutional Monarchy. Webster shows that the latter program was close to the overwhelming recorded preferences of the French people.

The Orleanists and the Subversives, however, were *neither one* responsive to those desires, and hence their elections, as Webster says (p. 46), "had been secured on false pretenses, and their attitude from the outset was necessarily one of duplicity and imposture. Unable to avow their real policy lest they should be disowned by their constituents, ...they diverted attention from the real issues" by quibbles over trivia. We see the same in the U.S. Congress, e.g., quibbling over Lewinsky scandals while simultaneously supplying strategic armament capability to China. In the end, the French democratic reform effort, analogous to that of U.S. constitutionalism, was defeated by the two *antidemocratic* factions acting in concert, and the French Revolution proceeded apace.

The critical thing to be noted in the above is that the democratic reforms which would have prevented the revolution from occurring were defeated in the National Assembly because of the existence there of representatives who had *lied to their constituents* in order to get elected, and had acted in the legislature in support of the true agendas which motivated *all* their actions, to the vast sorrow of their constituents and all of France. We will assuredly come back to deal with such legislative immorality when we consider our own plan of action to cure the many societal ills of today's world.

      2.   <u>The March on Versailles.</u> The conspirators, seeing that they were in danger of being defeated in the Assembly by the constitutional reformers, with whom Louis XVI was cooperating, desired to assassinate the Queen if possible, and force the King to move himself and his household from his residence in Versailles to Paris, about 10 miles away, in order to take away from him the aura of regal mystery, or awe, surrounding the person of a rarely seen monarch. Once lodged in Paris, it was felt that he could be stripped of that aura, and then easily toppled from his throne. An excuse for raising a mob of marchers was needed, and was supplied by turning off the supply of grain to the Parisian bakeries, at first gradually, but then completely on October 5, the scheduled day of the march to Versailles. Leading the march of hungry and desperate Parisians were the same hired rabble from the South utilized three months earlier in the Bastille affair, this time with many of them dressed as women to make defending troops hesitate to use their firearms.

      Their strategy for gaining access to the royal Chateau in Versailles was successful (Webster provides lots of details), though the Queen escaped from her bed chamber to safety a few minutes before the mob managed to break down the doors, enter the chamber, and in their fury, slash her empty bed with their knives and other weapons. However, in the two-day confrontation, the mob was successful in bringing both the king and the queen back to Paris, where they were lodged, as virtual prisoners, in the palace of the Tuileries.

The primary reason for the plot's success, however, was (p. 160) that the King felt in his heart that the people had been "stirred up by evil men," and had acted wrongly, but that nevertheless "we must not bear a grudge against the people," who were to be pitied rather than blamed. For these heartfelt reasons, he had ordered his guards not to fire on the rabble breaking into the Chateau armed with clubs and pikes. Many of the palace guards thereupon met their deaths, and the king's forbearance was later regarded as simply weakness. However one chooses to regard it, his attitude ultimately sealed the fate of both the French monarchy and the reform movement of the non-conspiratorial legislators in the National Assembly, many of whom now chose to flee France rather than try to recover a position of strength without royal leadership. Webster points out that the king's fatal error was that he "failed to realize that the revolutionary mob which marched on Versailles was not *the people* at all, but an assemblage composed of impostors both male and female, and of hired rabble from the [lower class Parisian suburbs]." Queen Marie Antoinette's attitude better befitted a monarch determined to overcome potential or real enemies. Mirabeau so honored her a year later by saying (p. 130), "The King has only one man with him – his wife."

The culpability of the Duke of Orleans in creating and executing the above affair became common knowledge, within the Assembly at least. An investigation was mounted, accusing Mirabeau and the Duke, and was presented to the Assembly. Mirabeau could not and did not convincingly refute the evidence, but instead declaimed in the Assembly that the report was targeting not just two individuals, but the Revolution itself. This brought the Orleanists and the Subversives back together for the moment, and a majority of the Assembly then reversed the investigative findings and declared Mirabeau and the Duke to be innocent. That "innocence" was been written into our received history ever since.

But *true* history has also presented us with a hard lesson in reality which, if we learn it well, we may not be doomed to repeat it. Social grief *will come* if, in a duly constituted legislature, a majority arises which cares not at all about objective truth, or oaths of office, but only about what actions should be taken (including lying, cheating, stealing, or murder) to accomplish its secret goals. One might mentally compare their moral axiom – that the ends justify the means – with the Golden Rule, and then reflect on why the Conspirators were so adamant about destroying the Christian and all other religions *prior* to seeking the overthrow of established governments.

3. The Invasion and Siege of the Tuileries. Following the King's removal to the palace of the Tuileries, relative calm came to Paris, partly because Philip d'Orleans had been banished to England, and Mirabeau had recanted and come over to build up the royal authority (p. 175). Philip returned to France in July, 1790, and the agitation restarted. Mirabeau, identified as an Illuminatus by Barruel, died of "natural causes" in April of 1791, though poison was strongly suspected, in keeping with the Illuminati code.

In September of 1791, the King accepted the newly drafted Constitution, the flawed product of the Assembly with its Jacobin majority. The Jacobins had no intention of living under that Constitution, however. What they wanted was to dethrone Louis XVI and then the Constitution also. The first move was to abolish the Assembly as it existed and to form a "Legislative Assembly" to enact the laws under the new system. Robespierre offered up a proposal, quickly approved, which denied membership in the new assembly to those in the old assembly. This eliminated the "Royalist Democrats" while enabling immediate replacement of the Jacobin elements by their network of clubs and lodges throughout the country. The "Legislative Assembly" therefore represented almost exclusively the Jacobin conspirators, whose goals were in direct opposition to bringing peace and constitutional order to France, as was universally desired by the French people.

Webster specifically credits (p. 190) the Bavarian Illuminati as the thorough, systematic, methodical masters of organization which produced the many political committees and propaganda outlets which culminated in the formation of the hugely effective Jacobin Club, as compared to the deplorably weak and ineffective efforts of the royalists and constitutionalists. Webster also notes that the Jacobin Club, previously known as the Club Breton in Versailles, had moved to Paris following the forced move of the King on October 6, 1789. The building the club moved to was a Dominican convent directly across the Rue St. Honoré from the Tuileries, where the conspirators could keep close watch on their prey, the King of France. The convent was locally known as the Jacobins, after the street called Rue St. Jacques, where the order's main convent was located. The conspirators simply appropriated the name of the local convent.

Webster supplies lots of detail about the true aims of the several Assembly factions. The Orleanists are prominent, but likewise are elements (called the Girondins) supporting other possible successors to King Louis, including the Duke of York and the Duke of Brunswick, both from old German families. Aid to these factions came from both England and Germany. Webster writes (p. 198): "By the summer of 1792 a brisk correspondence had been started between the French and English Jacobins; a number of the latter came over to Paris – some, indeed, actually became members of the Club in the Rue St. Honoré – and, what is more important, English guineas were sent to finance sedition." Robespierre was in a class by himself – a cunning plotter who, after the King was dethroned, intended to maneuver the other factions into destroying each other, and then take power himself.

One other preliminary to the Tuileries riots of June 20, 1792, must be mentioned. On April 20, Louis XVI was finally maneuvered into declaring war on Austria, beginning the Napoleonic Wars that were to savage Europe for the following twenty-three years. Many Royalists hoped that by so doing the Austrian and other European monarchs would come to the rescue of Louis. The Jacobins had for years kept up a drumbeat of hatred toward the Austrian Marie Antoinette and her country, and so wished for the war, secretly hoping that Louis would fall into the trap of aiding the Austrians, permitting Louis to be tried for treason. Some of the Jacobins were hoping that the Duke of Brunswick, who was leading the joint forces of Austria and Germany, would fight his way to Paris and there take over the throne, ousting Louis XVI. The air was heavy with these plots and counterplots, and Louis, though strongly opposed to the war, finally gave in. Webster says (p. 210), "...there were tears in his eyes when on the 20th of April he formally announced the declaration of war against Austria."

The effort to dethrone Louis via these machinations brought forth no political fruit, and the conspirators settled instead on a call for a mob march on the palace. To this end, a new type of rabble had been imported (p. 210) consisting of raggedly-clothed young toughs who came to be called Sans-Culottes (literally "without breeches"). They and the other marchers were armed with pikes ordered up for the event by Philip of Orleans (p. 219), along with red "caps of liberty" to identify Philip's legions. The plan for the march was matured in the councils of the Orleanists, says Webster, "for it was they alone who could control the workings of the great revolutionary machine; it was they who chose and paid the mob leaders, they who distributed the roles, prompted the orators, and lavished gold and strong drink on the obedient multitude they held at their command. The Girondins could only suggest and perorate; the Orleanists knew how to lead from words to action." The disciplined preplanning which the Illuminati added to the conspiratorial mix was paying off.

The plan was to create the mob on whatever pretenses were available, but with announced goals not so savage as to unduly alarm the marchers. They were to be armed, plied with wine, and gotten moving in the right direction. Gates would get covertly opened for them, and nature was to take its course, including a hoped-for regicidal bullet or saber thrust. The planners were to take no physical part, to avoid blame and to be around to take control afterwards.

The day scheduled for the event, June 20, 1792, arrived. The Instigators who had done the planning absented themselves. The Agitators got the mob moving in the right directions, though with some difficulty (since the mob didn't know what they were ultimately supposed to do), and then mostly left the scene themselves. The Instruments, i.e., those composing the drunken mob, were ultimately successful that day in gaining access to the King's chambers, where a confrontation took place between the King and his close retainers and the portion of the mob that could fit into those chambers. But the nearly leaderless mob lacked the strength of will which was present in the Jacobin leadership. As a result, the King, after a four-hour confrontation, was finally able to dissuade the mob, and turn it away from the regicidal intentions of the Instigators.

In the following days, the Orleanists were publicly identified as the source of the uprising, and were denounced throughout the country, since the great bulk of the French citizenry was sick of civil disruptions, and supported the King and the brand new Constitution. But the Jacobins were still in possession of enough of the levers of government to turn aside the charges against them, and they vowed to make a better effort the next time. Further, the King failed to order his National Guards under the Marquis de Lafayette to attack, close down, and clear out the Jacobin Club on the Rue St. Honoré, which the Guard recommended and could easily have done. Louis seemed to remain frozen in his insistence never to mount any real attack against any other Frenchman, even in his own self-defense.

In the weeks that followed, it became apparent to the Jacobin leaders that the local public would not cooperate in efforts to dethrone the King. The conspirator Marat is quoted (p. 251) as saying that the Parisians were but "pitiable revolutionaries... Give me 200 Neapolitans [inhabitants of Naples] armed with daggers, and with them I will overrun France and make a revolution." This advice was acted upon, and a message was sent to Marseilles asking for "600 men who knew how to die." By the end of July, thousands of such men had arrived in Paris, "romantically described by historians," says Webster, "as 'the brave band of Marseillais, children of the South and liberty, singing their national hymn, *The Marseillais*'" These men were, however, the same "men of rapine and carnage, thirsting for blood and booty – the brigands from the South" who had been brought into Paris three years earlier to support the siege of the Bastille. With *these* men, and not the Parisian public, the conspirators were ready to make their next try.

SECRECY OR FREEDOM?

The second assault on the Tuileries was set for August 10, 1792. Its principle organizer, says Webster (p. 258), was Danton, who was quoted in fellow-conspirator Prudhomme's memoirs to say: "I [will] undertake to stir up the *canaille* of the Faubourgs St. Antoine and St. Marceau [Parisian working-class communities]. The Marseillais will be at their head. They have not come to Paris for plums." In the night prior to the assault, Danton, Marat, Robespierre, and the other Instigators "took the law into their own hands, and... the terrible council of the 'Commune'... came into being." Requests were sent to each section of Paris for representatives to cooperate with the Commune in the proposed insurrection. Many sections didn't respond, but enough did to permit the insurrection to proceed under a claimed color of law. A "responsible authority" having been created, the Instigators "retired into hiding."

The assault was successful, but at a terrible cost. The King had a force of some 3500 defenders, including 950 Swiss Guards. The force was commanded by the Marquis de Mandat, a determined and skillful military leader. Mandat was, however, lured to a meeting that morning with town officials, and murdered, leaving the King's forces leaderless. In short, the mob made its way into the outer court of the palace, where the defending battalions deserted their cannon, and the mob took them over. A delegation of municipal officers then came to the King's quarters and asked that he retire with his family to the adjacent Assembly, then in session, instead of staying and fighting the oncoming mob. The King rather quickly acquiesced, and upon leaving (p. 268), "gave strict orders to the Swiss not to fire on the insurgents, and to offer no resistance whatever happened,'" expecting that no further hostilities could then take place. He was tragically wrong, however, and when he and his family stepped foot into the Assembly, the bloodshed at the palace commenced.

The Swiss confronted the mob on the palace steps, a shot was soon fired, and a full-blown fusillade rapidly dispersed the mob, which fled in panic from the courtyard. A lying message was sent to the King in the adjacent Assembly saying that the Swiss were massacring the people. The King sent back a written message to the Swiss ordering them to lay down their arms and march to the Assembly. They did so, the mob saw that they could return with impunity, and the carnage began. Some of the soldiers safely reached the Assembly, but most were cut down and butchered in the Tuileries gardens and the adjacent courtyards. (Napoleon, who was present, is quoted (p. 277) as confirming this order of events.) The mob, led by the Marseillais, then entered the palace, found the wine cellars, gorged themselves, and set about on a rampage of killing nearly every living person that they could find in the palace. "Nameless indecencies, hideous debaucheries, ghastly mutilations of the dead, and again, as after the siege of the Bastille, cannibal orgies [were performed]." The mob had lost any aspect of humanity.

Unlike the aftermath of the June 20 affair, the August 10 rampage left France in a state of terror and shock, and the Jacobin power went almost entirely unchallenged. Lafayette protested, but most of his fellow generals went over to the Jacobins, and Lafayette fled to the frontier and was arrested and imprisoned by the Austrians. He later wrote (p. 285), "The preparations [for the assault] were denounced by the King. It was not he who had women and children massacred, who gave over to execution all those [known as Constitutionalists], who in one day destroyed the liberty of the press, of the posts, judgment by jury, ...everything that assures the liberty of men and nations." The people had lost their Constitution, and gained in its place a regime aimed at sweeping away all kings, nobles, clergy, government, religion, and even property, establishing, in a word, Anarchy.

4. The Massacres of September. With the King and Queen safely imprisoned, the immediate issue given priority by the conspirators was what to do with the nobles, clergy, and other political prisoners in the various Parisian jails. Should the imprisoned members of the two previously privileged estates, the nobility and the clergy, perhaps be released providing they agree to share their privileges and properties, and live with the common third estate on a more equal basis, and under the principles of the new Constitution? No way, say the conspirators. They are our enemies, they will always be our enemies, and they must and shall be liquidated!

The plans were formulated in secret councils of the "Comité de Surveillance" of the Commune, now become the highest visible public authority in France. Attending were Marat, Danton, Robespierre, and others whom Webster identifies. "Here," she says, "the whole scheme was mapped out with diabolical ingenuity. First of all, a number of fresh prisoners were to be incarcerated, principally wealthy people, for the massacres were to be not merely a method of extermination, but a highway robbery on a large scale. The Commune wanted money..." and the looting and pillage so far undertaken had not yielded enough for their needs.

Lists of wealthy citizen targets were thereupon created, along with the pretext to be publicly announced that a conspiracy was afoot between wealthy prisoners in the jails and the approaching armies of the Duke of Brunswick, and that additional suspected conspirators in the town would be sought out and arrested. Following the arrests, the prison massacres would begin, and would be represented to the people as the "irrepressible popular effervescence" of the people, who were justifiably fearful of the collusion between the invading armies and conspiring prisoners. The pretext may have been ludicrous, but was nevertheless deemed serviceable.

But how were several thousand people to be disposed of? This time no effort would be made to create a mob to do the dirty work. The Jacobins rightly figured that not even a mob could be created with the stomach to kill several thousand people, one by one. Rather, they sought out and selected a man, one Billaud-Varenne, ferocious enough and willing to undertake the organization of a band of assassins from among the Marseillais and other revolutionary elements in Paris, capable of doing the job. Their numbers could be supplemented, as was later found necessary, by criminals released from prison.

The plans having been completed, on August 29, 1792 the "domiciliary visits" – the knock on the door at night – began, and went on for three nights, while Paris trembled with fear. Estimates of the number arrested ran from 3000 to 8000. Money and every other form of valuable booty that could be found was confiscated.

On Sunday, September 2, 1792 it was officially proclaimed that the Prussians under the Duke of Brunswick were at the gates of Paris. Danton delivered a speech in the Assembly asking the people to form up and march to the frontiers, dig trenches, take up pikes, and prepare to defend the city "against the enemies of the country." Audacity, he declared, was what was needed to save France. That speech was the signal for the prison massacres to begin, and the assassin band went to work.

The killing went on for five, or possibly six, days and nights. We need not go into the detail which Webster, as a conscientious historian, found necessary. But we will repeat the summary which she tabulates. There were nine locations where prisoners were dispatched. Lumping them all together, 43 "Aristocrats and Officials" were killed, including 20 military officers; 245 "Priests" were killed; and

1080 "People" were killed. It is thus obvious that the nobility death rate was very small, the rate among the clergy was high, but the number of ordinary people killed was horrendous – people, says Webster (p. 330), "who had no connection whatever with the political situation."

When the conspirators observed the universal horror that the wholesale butchery inspired among the people, they disavowed any blame, and heaped it instead on the people, as they had planned. "It was a popular movement," Robespierre afterwards declared. Marat concurred: "The disastrous events of the 2nd and 3rd of September were entirely provoked by the indignation of the people at seeing themselves the slaves of all the traitors who had caused their disasters and misfortunes." Much of our received history reflects these sentiments. Of course it truly was not the people who did the killing, but rather an organized band of perhaps 300 murderers, the identities of whom were mostly found out and published (p. 332). The killings were clearly *not* the result of "irrepressible popular effervescence" of fearful Parisians, but rather of the secret deliberations of the conspiratorial Jacobins in the Commune.

Webster shows that certain of the English Jacobins were present in Paris during the killings, perhaps taking even an advisory role. A communication on September 4 back to Lord Auckland, the British ambassador at the Hague, stated, "Dr. Priestley is also there, and is looked upon as the great advisor of the present ministers, being consulted by them on all occasions. There are also eight or ten other English and Scotch who work with the Jacobins, and in great measure conduct their present maneuvers.... The names of some of them are Watts and Wilson of Manchester, Oswald a Scotsman, Stone an Englishman, and Mackintosh who wrote against Burke." Webster comments, "All these men, then, were in Paris during the massacres of September, and not one uttered a word of protest."

Two of the massacre sites were called the Abbaye and La Force. One witness at the Abbaye stated that "he saw two Englishmen plying the assassins with drink." Secondly, says Webster, "Prudhomme says that Englishmen were seen at La Force amongst the commanders of the butchery, and that 'these Englishmen were the guests of the Duc d'Orleans; they dined with him immediately after the death [on Sept. 3 at La Force] of the Princesse de Lamballe [the Superintendent of the Queen's household].'" Webster suspects that one of those guests might have been "Richard Sayre, or Sayer, the English agent in Paris who had been deputed by the revolutionary societies of England to supply arms to the Jacobins of France; [further,] the exceedingly compromising letters addressed by Sayre to Lord Stanhope... show clearly that the English revolutionaries in Paris, of whom Lord Stanhope was the leading spirit, were engaged in some guilty intrigue with the enemies of their country."

One speculation concerning that intrigue concerns the sequence of events which immediately followed. As reported by Webster's several historical sources, Billaud-Varenne, the organizer of the assassin band which performed the September massacres, left Paris with some few others of the Jacobins, reached the French army headed by General Dumouriez, and on Sept. 11 opened negotiations with Dumouriez, the Duke of Brunswick, and possibly Frederick William II, the King of Prussia. A bribe was offered to the Germans to halt their invasion, consisting of the two to three millions pillaged from the Tuileries palace on the preceding 10th of August. It was not enough. The conspirator Panis, a fellow member with Billaud of the secret "Comité de Surveillance" of the Commune, suggested, perhaps in jest, that they rob the crown jewels. Behold! On the upcoming night of the 16th and 17th, the depository of the jewels was broken into, and the Crown jewels were removed. The theft was committed, says Webster (p. 350), "by the orders of Tallien [another Comité member] and Danton, [and] produced, in different species, a sum of thirty millions."

Then on September 20 occurred the famous "cannonade of Valmy," says Webster, which "checked the advance of the allied armies on the capital, [and] is one of the enigmas of history which will perhaps never be entirely solved." On September 21 the Convention Nationale held its first sitting (p. 356), replacing the Legislative Assembly. The German armies during the following weeks were "driven" out of France, as is duly reported in our received history. Camille Desmoulins, one-time secretary to Danton, a year later wrote (p. 351), "In a word, Dumouriez led back the King of Prussia rather than he pursued him, and *there was not a soldier in the army who was not convinced that there had been an arrangement between the Prussians and the Convention by the medium of Dumouriez.*" Another memoir published in 1824 quoted the Duke of Brunswick as having said, "Why I retreated will never be known to my death."

Webster finally notes that, whatever the true facts may have been concerning the German motivation for quitting France, their "defeat" at Valmy "was a superb victory for Prussia. For to march on to Paris at this crisis must have [meant] to reestablish the Bourbons on the throne, and to leave the way open to a renewal of the Franco-Austrian alliance; by leaving France to tear itself to pieces, Frederick William worthily carried out the traditions of the great Frederick, and assured the future supremacy of Prussia.... Goethe, looking on at the famous fusillade, is said to have uttered these prophetic words: 'From this place and from this day forth begins a new era in the world's history, and you can all say that you were present at its birth.'" The events surrounding Valmy in fact confirmed France's conquest by the Jacobins, and laid her and all Europe open to the further depredations of Europe's conspiratorial revolutionists.

5. The Reign of Terror. With the external threat out of the way, the Jacobins set about to get rid of the monarchy, the Constitution, and the King. After that they could deal with who was going to rule the roost, and otherwise get on with their main program. Getting rid of the monarchy was easy – they simply passed a resolution in their brand new National Convention saying (p. 357): "The National Convention decrees that monarchy is abolished in France." No public hearings, no seeking the will of the people, no referendum. The Constitution thus became a dead letter, in contradistinction to the orderly establishment of the U.S. Constitution just a few years earlier. The Convention's philosophy? "The will of the people makes the law, *and we are the people.*"

Killing the King took a little longer – about three months, since it was clear to the Jacobins that the great majority of the people opposed his execution. A mob effort clearly wouldn't work, so a trial was finally contrived, to be run by the Convention, and for which its members voted themselves the functions of accusers, jury, and judges. The King was duly found guilty of a "long list of paltry charges," says Webster, even though no proofs of guilt were presented. A vote was taken on the penalty, and by a majority of one vote the King was condemned to the guillotine. The sentence was carried out on the morning of January 21, 1793. "All during the day that followed," says Webster (p. 377), "Paris was silent, almost deserted; people shut themselves up with their families to weep.... In the streets, people dared not look each other in the face...." Our received history of course has it quite otherwise.

Even before the King's trial, and in fulfillment of Goethe's prediction, the Jacobins declared their Revolutionary War on the rest of Europe. On November 19, 1792 they issued a proclamation saying (p. 380), "The National Convention declares in the name of the French nation that she will accord fraternity and assistance to all peoples who wish to recover their liberty..." and charged the French military to assist such peoples to that end. French armies under Custine and Dumouriez were at that time moving beyond the French borders into Germany, Belgium, and Holland, as described briefly in our review of Barruel's book. On December 15, says Webster (p. 384), "the Convention issued a further decree to each country entered by their armies, declaring that 'from this moment the French Republic proclaims the suppression of all your magistrates, civil and military, of all the authorities that have governed you, ...'" The other shoe had now dropped, and the Jacobins were announcing their demand that the countries they were invading should surrender forthwith.

In England, immediately after King Louis' execution on January 21, 1793, Prime Minister Pitt addressed Parliament, observing with alarm the French occupation of Belgium, and calling for preparations for war, while simultaneously seeking conciliatory talks with the Jacobins. But two days after his address, the Convention issued a declaration of war on England, to which the English Parliament promptly responded in kind, and the formal war was on. The war was to be "the greatest war of conquest the civilized world had ever seen," says Webster, a war precipitated by the invasions and war declarations engineered by the Jacobin masters of France, who therefore must bear "the full responsibility for the twenty-two years' conflict that followed." The French people, of course, were not consulted.

With their program of external aggression underway, the Jacobins next set about to settle the pecking order within their own domestic family. Who would end up being *numero uno*? The first major contestant to be eliminated was Philip of Orleans. This was an easy decision, since he was no longer useful as a noble figurehead, or money-raiser, or as a popular alternative to Louis XVI as the French monarch. Robespierre, says Webster, with his usual ingenuity, set the Girondin faction against Philip, and on April 6, 1793 Philip was banished from Paris, and would stand trial later in the year.

The faction surrounding Robespierre came to be called "The Mountain," and included such as Marat, Danton, St. Just, and others whom Webster lists (p. 358). The Mountain now took on the Girondins, who turned out to be no match. They fought back for a time in the Convention, but soon came to realize that the Mountain was in effective control of the revolutionary machinery. On June 2, 1793 the Girondin leaders lost their nerve and left the Convention to seek refuge in the town. Lacking their best leadership, the remaining Girondins were beaten down in the Convention, which the deeper conspirators had managed to have surrounded by several thousands of armed men, most of whom didn't know why they were there. Marat (pp. 403-404) read forth a list of Girondins to be proscribed; the Girondins and others who objected to voting on their own destruction while surrounded by bayonets, left the hall; their seats were filled by unknown and unelected strangers; the resolution ejecting the proscribed members from the Convention was then passed, a picture-perfect example of revolutionary due process.

The people of France played no essential part in the fight for Jacobin leadership. They were, however, aroused to fury, particularly in the countryside, at a distance from the perpetual disturbances in Paris. Their Constitution had been lost, their clergy was still being maligned and persecuted, the horrible September massacre had just occurred, and their King had been unjustly executed. "No less than 60 departments [provincial jurisdictions] had risen against the tyranny of the Convention," says Webster (p. 405). "At least three-quarters of the population was violently opposed to [the Mountain], and the remaining quarter was mainly terrorized into submission." The Jacobin leadership saw that consolidation of their victory was now called for, and with the aristocracy and the clergy substantially destroyed, attention must be turned to the rest of the people. The Terror was to begin.

Webster spells it out, in appalling detail. It was Weishaupt who had denounced the "mercantile tribe," and that "prosperous bourgeoisie" was to be attacked by waging war on manufacturing towns. In reality, says Webster, the whole industrial system was simply to be destroyed. Then educated classes were to be attacked. Libraries, museums, and art were targeted for destruction. Even civilized behavior was to be proscribed, or taken as a sign of anti-republicanism. The war was actually to be a war on *civilization*, and the return to a state of savagery, all in the name of seeking *absolute equality*.

Lyon was surrounded, besieged, starved, entered on October 9, 1793, and destroyed. The workers there were told that "commerce and arts should be unnecessary" to warrior people now able to enjoy their sublime equality. But at the same time, the population was mowed down by the hundreds. The guillotine, found to be too slow, was replaced by fusillades of rifle and cannon fire. The Rhone, having received over 2000 corpses, ran red with blood. Toulon, in the South, was similarly starved and crushed, and murders of no less than 14,325 men, women, and children were counted by the spring of 1794. In the small town of Orange, 318 fell. At Arras and Cambrai between 1500 and 2000. In the province of Anjou about 10,000. La Vendée, a Royalist stronghold, was "transformed into a desert," as called for by the Convention. At Nantes in Brittany, the work was especially savage, using the guillotine, clubs, sabers, muskets, and finally the famous technique of the *noyades*, or wholesale drownings, in which victims were placed on barges which were then sunk in the middle of the Loire River. Prudhomme estimates the number killed at Nantes at 32,000.

In all of France, the estimated death toll during the Terror was placed by Prudhomme (p. 419) at no less than 1,025,711, or approximately 4 percent of the French population. More important, says Webster, the deaths were *indiscriminate*, for "not only were the victims of the fusillades and noyades almost exclusively taken from amongst the people, ...but no attempt was made to discover their political opinions." How, she asks, can one explain "*the massacring of the people in the name of democracy?*" She proceeds to that task.

The Terror was in fact a policy deliberated and decided upon by the Jacobin leadership, and its rationalization is to be found in their own words, for some reason unreported by establishmentarian historians. Webster starts by referring (p. 421) to "the constantly recurring belief [of the Terror's leaders] in the impossibility of transforming France into a Republic." Marat is quoted as saying, early on, that a large State, such as France, must be monarchic, due to its extent, the multiplicity of its connections, etc. Webster explains that history has shown that democracy works "most harmoniously" in a small country, such as Marat's native Switzerland, but since the essence of democracy is "rule by the will of the Sovereign people," it will work well only if the "people" are in the main unanimous. The larger and more varied the people, the more difficulty will there be in maintaining unanimity. Thus Danton is quoted, "This country is not made for a Republic; one day it will cry 'Vive le Roi!'"

Robespierre early believed in monarchy, but later desired a dictatorship, no doubt clearly seeing that "equality" was only going to be attained by forcing everyone into the same mold. Thus in the "Institutions" drawn up by St. Just for the new government, the Republic was to be held together by virtue, after terror became no longer necessary. Webster writes (p. 422), "Everyone was to be austere, incorruptible, laborious, and, above all, public-spirited; for, according to the doctrine of the Illuminati, to which Robespierre belonged, the only way to make men happy was to produce in them a 'just and steady morality.'" St. Just further defined the best way of attaining uniform happiness and morality to be agriculture: "'A cottage, a field, and a plow' were to represent the summit of every man's ambitions. France was to be turned into a vast agrarian settlement."

Of course the leaders weren't to be counted among these equal citizens. Someone had to enforce the equality. In fact, says Webster, "It is doubtful [a major understatement] whether Liberty and Equality can exist together, for while liberty consists in allowing every man to live as he likes best, and to do as he will with his own, equality necessitates a perpetual system of repressions in order to maintain things at the same dead level." Thus in St. Just's Republic, the State was to be in control of the most minute activities of every equal human. No marriage. Children dress alike in cotton, and sleep on mats on the floor. At age five, boys become state property. Everyone *must* form "friendships" and report them to the state, creating a system by which the state can spy on the population. Etc., etc.

But the leaders doubted that a country of 25,000,000 could be thus transformed. Even worse, says Webster, "the plan of dividing things up into equal shares presented an insuperable difficulty, for it became evident that amongst a population of this size there was not enough money, not enough property, not enough employment, not even at this moment enough bread to go around, ...and instead of universal contentment, universal dissatisfaction would result. What was to be done? The population was too large for the scheme of the leaders to be carried out successfully, and therefore either the scheme must be abandoned or *the population must be diminished.*" (In 1798 this scheme was formally justified and codified by the English professor of political economy Thomas Malthus, and so has ever after borne the name "malthusianism." Isn't it odd that Pitt's England should have given employment to the man who produced the intellectual justification for subjecting whole populations to holocaust and carnage?)

The only issue among the French leaders was *by how much* should the population be reduced. Robespierre's papers, found after his death, revealed that the leaders "wished to annihilate twelve or fifteen millions of the French people." The Marquis d'Antonelle, a revolutionary intimate of Robespierre, actually explained the scheme in print (and was arrested for it), revealing the general feeling that the new order could not be attained until "a third of the population [i.e., about 8,000,000 people] had been suppressed." The socialist Babeuf also described the scheme in a 1795 pamphlet "On the System of Depopulation," identifying Robespierre as the primary author of the scheme, and outlining the process of first moving all property into the hands of the government, killing all the great proprietors, and then instituting the depopulation, since the French population "was in excess of the resources of the soil and of the requirements of useful industry.... A portion of the *sans culottes* must be sacrificed... and means must be found for doing it."

Not only were the guillotines, fusillades, and noyades discussed, but engineered famines and war itself were also examined as means of killing off the unwanted millions. The existence of the scheme was pronounced on the floor of the Convention in the spring of 1793 by Jean

113

Bon St. Andre, who declared (p. 428) that "in order to establish the Republic securely in France, the population must be reduced by more than half.... Herbois held that twelve to fifteen millions of the French must be destroyed, Carrier declared that the nation must be reduced to six millions, Guffroy in his journal expressed the opinion that only five million people should be allowed to survive, while Robespierre was reported to have said that a population of two millions would be more than enough."

Webster rightly points out (p. 429) that such monstrous crimes against humanity were made possible only by the acceptance of that pernicious doctrine which justifies lying, duplicity, treachery, murder, and any and all other inhumanities: The End Justifies The Means. "To hold this doctrine is not only to repudiate Christianity, but to strike at the very root of all morality." With our understanding from Barruel's work of the anti-Christian efforts made by the revolutionists from Voltaire on through Weishaupt, it is no surprise to find Republican France now in an orgy of anti-religious fury. Webster details the actions and the players. One of the prominent leaders was the Prussian baron Anacharsis Clootz, who (p. 433) John Robison in his *Proofs of a Conspiracy* says "was a keen Illuminati." Clootz hated Christianity, says Webster, and "the truth is that the whole of the anti-Christian movement [during the Terror] was the direct work of the Illuminati."

Webster then goes into the application of the Terror in Paris. The first to go were Queen Marie Antoinette and the Girondins who were ousted on June 2, 1793. They all met the guillotine on the following October 31st, and were followed a few days later by Philip, the Duke of Orleans. Robespierre then plotted the removal and execution of the remaining revolutionary factions that were not supporters of his plan of depopulation. Thus, a violent faction led by Hébert, and including the Baron Clootz, was condemned with the help of Danton's faction, and executed on March 24, 1794. Next to go was Danton and his whole faction, perceived by Robespierre to be interested only in personal enrichment. Robespierre and St. Just orchestrated the condemnation of the faction, the members of which were then guillotined on April 5, 1794.

"It was thus," says Webster (p. 451), "that in April of 1794 Robespierre and his colleagues, now in sole possession of the field, set to work with redoubled energy on their great scheme – the depopulation of Paris. It was now the people's turn to give their blood so that the ends of the plotters might be met. On June 10 an infamous law was decreed under which victims haled before the Revolutionary Tribunal "were denied all rights of defense; no advocates were to be allowed, no witnesses called, and the penalty imposed in all cases was to be death." It was, says Webster, Robespierre's bid for absolute power. He now held in his hands the absolute power of life and death, and over the next six weeks, says Webster (p. 459), "the period which constitutes 'The Great Terror,' no less than 1366 victims perished, and amongst these by far the largest proportion was taken from amongst either 'the people' or the *petite bourgeoisie.*"

Robespierre came a cropper, however, on that famous axiom of Lord Acton: Absolute Power Corrupts Absolutely. As the "judicial murders" of the public proceeded over the next month, Robespierre saw that he was losing some of his personal control to various of the confederates that he was using to manage the physical details of the Terror. Anticipating a struggle, he allied himself more closely with the Jacobin Club, which he must have seen as the fountainhead from which the real revolutionary directions emerged. He then let publicly drop that he was going to condemn and eliminate his erstwhile confederates, but they outnumbered him in the Convention, and they managed to turn the tables on him, outshout him in the "deliberations," and get the Convention to condemn and arrest him. He managed to obtain temporary freedom, but, in a final police chase, he was sorely wounded along with his last remaining supporters, and re-jailed. He was then himself denounced and sentenced to die without even a semblance of a trial. He mounted the guillotine on July 27, 1794.

Upon his execution, Robespierre's successors perceived that the people had had more than enough, and wanted peace and tranquillity more than anything else. The new leaders, not members of the innermost conspiratorial circle, and thus not ideologically bound to the depopulation scheme, were more than ready to return to peace, and bask in the security of their resulting acceptance by the people. The last of the local criminal leaders were rounded up, tried, and executed, and with the last execution, on May 1, 1795, the Great Terror officially came to an end. The *real* people, for the first time, had finally gotten their own way.

The End Results. Webster pauses to summarize. The *people* had never instigated or wanted any one of the five major events that she had described, notwithstanding what has been commonly attributed to them in our received history. The Revolution, far from being desired and cele-brated, had prostrated the French people and the whole of French society. People were starving; benevolence had vanished; the Treasury was empty, and no plan of finance or of any government existed; there were no food stores, and no public administration; hospitals and schools were without revenue or resources; roads and bridges and other commu-nication infrastructure were devastated; the French military was without discipline, provisions, pay, clothing, or equip-ment. The country was in a state of ruin, and was brought out of it only by the advent of a strong leader, bringing with him the Napoleonic dictatorship. An eighty year succession of unstable governments would follow.

Of Webster's four contributors to the Revolution, the Orleanists were momentarily defunct; the forces of anarchy were still active elsewhere around Europe and the world, but were now quiet in France; the Prussians, having obtained the breakup of the Franco-Austrian alliance, became momentarily quiescent. The British Jacobins, who Webster says continued a clandestine mutual support relationship with their French counterparts throughout the Terror, were regarded by the English public as traitors. On June 10, 1794, at the start of the Great Terror, the enraged public rioted and set fire to Lord Stanhope's house, perhaps protesting the inaction of English *officialdom* which seemed unable to see and/or act upon the sedition which was obvious to the public.

In her Epilogue, Webster gives us a quick hint as to what a study of the conspiracy in the 130 years following the French Revolution would show. First, the successive regimes following the end of the Terror were to be:

- The Directory. 1795-1799. This was the Executive authority created by the new 1795 Constitution, and summarily abolished by Napoleon Bonaparte because of its "tyranny, corruption, and mismanagement."
- The Consulate. 1799-1804. Napoleon declared himself First Consul, virtually the supreme ruler, under yet another new constitution.
- The Empire. 1804-1814. He then declared himself Emperor, a full-fledged dictator over all of his European conquests. He invaded Russia in 1812, was beaten back, and was then further defeated by a set of European allies. He abdicated and retired to Elba, briefly returned, was defeated again at Waterloo, and was finally exiled to St. Helena.

- <u>Louis XVIII</u>. 1815-1824. This brother of Louis XVI was enthroned, and after nine years died naturally. His was the first regime after the revolution not to end violently.
- <u>Charles X</u>. 1824-1830. This unpopular younger brother of Louis XVIII was overthrown by a fresh uprising of Orleanists.
- <u>Louis Philippe</u>. 1830-1848. An Orleanist now usurped the throne, but was soon displaced by yet another revolution.
- <u>Second Republic</u>. 1848-1851. Louis Napoleon, the nephew of Napoleon Bonaparte, was elected President, and shortly thereafter executed a coup d'état and dismissed the Assembly.
- <u>Second Empire</u>. 1852-1870. Louis titled himself Emperor Napoleon III, and reigned until defeated and taken prisoner by the Germans in the Franco-Prussian War.
- <u>Third Republic</u>. 1870-1919 and counting. Webster notes that this last regime has somehow managed to survive up to the time of her publication.

Writing in 1919, just after World War 1 and the Russian Revolution, she says (p. 491), "The scheme that [originated] with the Illuminati of Bavaria in 1776 is now being actively carried out by their successors. The plan of world revolution devised by Weishaupt has at last been realized.... Since at the present day it is still in secret societies and at meetings of spurious Freemasons that revolutionary doctrines [are being] propagated, can we doubt that these associations are also the direct continuations of the Illuminati, and that it is on the doctrines of Weishaupt, the inventor of 'world revolution,' that the thing we now call 'Bolshevism' is founded? ...The Bolshevik tirades against the bourgeoisie are copied almost verbatim from the diatribes of Robespierre. The danger that threatens civilization is therefore no new danger, but dates from before the

118

French Revolution.... Beginning with Weishaupt, continuing with Clootz, with Büchner and with Bakunin, hatred of religion, above all of Christianity, has characterized all the instigators of world revolution, since it is essential to their purpose that the doctrine of hatred should be substituted for the doctrine of love." Webster ends by quoting Barruel concerning the dire future faced by humanity if the conspiracy is not itself overthrown.

We have reviewed Webster's account of the details of the French Revolution because it was the first major try by a modern (as opposed to medieval) secret society to attain total power over an entire population. It was momentarily successful, and was ultimately beaten down in 1794 only by the slimmest of historical happenstance. We will find occasion to relate the events and techniques of this uprising with others which will follow. Unmistakable patterns will ultimately become clearly visible, as Webster has alleged above, and we will be led to actions which can be taken to strike back at the heart of the beast. But for now, we can learn one excellent lesson from Nesta Webster.

She asks herself (pp. 462-3), "Why did the people submit to this regime? How... are we to understand 'the blind docility of the most enlightened of nations in allowing itself to be taken piecemeal and butchered *en masse* like a stupid herd led to the shambles?' The answer is surely that the despotism of the demagogues was organized, whilst the people were composed of solitary units that could not coalesce. To form an effectual opposition it would have been necessary to meet in consultation to draw up some plan of campaign, and any such attempts would have been instantly crushed. The people therefore felt themselves helpless; no one dared to break the line, to take the first step, uncertain whether he would get a backing from his fellows...."

The lesson is that the only time that such a conspiracy may successfully be opposed without having to endure excruciating societal pain is *before* the conspiracy manages to accomplish its takeover. That is, society has a right, and an obligation to its descendants, to uncover and excise the cancer *before* it does its damage, by passing and energetically enforcing protective laws against sedition and conspiracy, specifically including conspiratorial efforts of secret societies. The goal of our book is first to identify who the conspirators are at the core, and then to break their system of secrecy and prevent their conspiratorial adherents from gaining public employment – as legislators, bureaucrats, or otherwise. We will, of course, have much more to say about that in upcoming chapters.

Chapter 3

"HUMANUM GENUS - on FREEMASONRY"

(By Pope Leo XIII. Encyclical Letter pub. April 20, 1884.
Pub. 1978 by Tan Books and Publishers, Inc., PO Box 424,
Rockford, IL 61105. Available also under the title *Freema-
sonry-Humanum Genus* from Amazon.com, PO Box 81410,
Seattle, WA 98108, or www.amazon.com.)

With this little pamphlet we jump about ninety years
ahead and look at the world as seen in 1884 by Pope Leo
XIII. In the next chapter we will examine the reprint of a
lecture given by Monsignor George Dillon in Edinburgh,
Scotland a few months after the issuance of the Pope's
encyclical, and will there learn a bit of the previous ninety
years of European history, at least insofar as it affected the
Catholic Church. Leo, however, confines himself to the
state of his present world, and the actions he urges on
priests, bishops, and other church leaders. Leo's main
points are compressed and paraphrased below.
    "To our Venerable Brethren, All Patriarchs, Pri-
mates, Archbishops and Bishops of the Catholic World."
    An evil combine, led or assisted by the Freemason
organization, is openly planning the destruction of the holy
Church [par. 2]. It is the Pope's duty to identify the assail-
ants, and to define a plan to defeat their attack [par. 3].
Predecessor Pontiffs have given the alarm, starting with
Clement XII in 1738, and continuing up to the frequent
warnings of our immediate predecessor, Pius IX [par. 4-5].
The papacy long ago denounced the sect and forbade
church members to enter it, and was supported in these
actions by many secular governments, such as in Holland,

Austria, Switzerland, Spain, Bavaria, and portions of Italy [par. 6]. These warnings were wisely given, since in the last 150 years Freemasonry has flourished to the point where it actually seems to dominate many governments, giving us grave reason to fear for their future [par. 7].

Freemason societies and their affiliates function openly, but are organized with a strict hierarchy of ranks and grades, with the lower grades, along with the general public, kept misinformed concerning the sect's purposes, particularly its secret goals, its leaders, its secret inner meetings, decisions, and planned actions. Candidates swear, under dire penalties including death, to reveal no sect secret to an unauthorized person, and to unquestioningly follow the orders of the sect's superiors [par. 9]. This pernicious system of lying both to the public and to prospective and lower ranking members concerning the goals of the sect, and of enslaving men to the will of unknown superiors, has enabled the sect to make such progress that its real goals can no longer be hidden – namely, the overthrow of the entire religious and political order produced by Christian teachings [par. 10].

"Naturalists" believe that human nature and human reason should be the guide to all human conduct. The Church, having the duty to teach divinely received truths as the most fundamental of guides, has thus been the target of attack by such Naturalists, including the Freemasons. The latter wish to reduce the church's authority and its wholesome influence to a nullity in the civil state, and to this end has declared that a wall should exist between church and state [par. 12-13]. Further, they have seen fit to attack the church by speech and writing, to limit its freedom of action in managing its own affairs and possessions, to hinder the growth of its clergy, and even to destroy not only the power of pontiffs, but even the Pontificate itself [par. 14-15].

New members are received without regard to their religion, and later are entered into contentious debates regarding whether or not a God really exists. Questioning God's existence implies questioning also the foundation of our principles of justice and morality. Where Christian education has been removed, as desired by the Freemasons, the sect has grown in influence, and the goodness and integrity of the people's morals have given way to a growing boldness of evil deeds. Further, human nature being naturally disposed more to vice than to virtue, our civil society has been easily drawn into worsening depths of vice by pamphlets, plays, works of art, and other enticements to pleasure. The Freemasons deliberately promote this vice, while also inhibiting Christian education, as they correctly observe that men satiated with vice, and unrestrained by Christian morality, are much more easily influenced to perform the immoral or illegal deeds which may be desired by the sect [par. 16-20].

Freemason doctrines have promoted a number of grievous social errors: Marriage should be a secular bond only, to be entered into or revoked according as the state alone deems lawful. The education of children should be in the hands of the Freemason sect, and never in the hands of the Church [par. 21]. Every man, being free, need obey only that authority which is within himself. All things belong to the free people, i.e., not to nobles or clergy. The State should not recognize any God. No religion should have precedence over any other religion [par. 22]. To realize the desired ultimate equality of all men, all goods should be held by the community, and every distinction of rank or property should be destroyed [par. 23].

This effort by the Freemasons to destroy religion and the Church, and to return to the manner and customs of pagans, is outrageous folly, and such studious efforts to destroy the foundations of justice and honesty will obviously tend to the ignominious ruin of the human race. Casting out marriage by permitting its arbitrary dissolution will destroy the family and the protections and dignity it gives to women and children. Removing God, the Author of human society, is not only disobedient to God, but is destructive of human society, which is needful of the leadership of its creator. As to equality, human beings, though possessed of common origins and common endings, are vastly different one from another in various abilities, in powers of mind and body, in manners, interests, and character. Requiring all to be "equal" while at the same time free, each following his own will, is an obvious impossibility. Substantial freedom under lawful leadership defines more appropriate requirements for a well-constituted State [par. 24-26].

The Freemason programs of irreverence, sedition, vice, and lawlessness will produce the changes and over-throws being deliberately planned by associations of Communists and Socialists, which are goals sought also by the Freemasons [par. 27]. The latter have lied to both people and princes, telling the people that both church and sovereigns have produced the people's unjust servitude and poverty, while telling princes that the Church is guilty of contending against the princes' sovereign power and authority [par. 28]. On the contrary, the Church is the friend of peace and concord, and embraces all with love; she teaches justice with clemency, authority with equity, and law-giving with moderation; individual rights and public order should be maintained; those in need should be relieved by public and private charity. Princes and people would do well to support the Church in fighting Freemason attacks, rather than joining in their attacks to destroy the Church [par. 29].

The duty undertaken by predecessor Pontiffs to counteract the evil of Freemasonry is reaffirmed, and their prior decrees to deter or withdraw men from the Masonic sect are ratified and confirmed [par. 30]. As befits the authority of the Pontificate, the following five-point program aimed at extirpating this foul plague is offered. First, by your sermons and pastoral letters, "tear away the mask from Freemasonry, and let it be seen as it really is;" instruct the people as to its artifices, its depravity, and its wickedness [par. 31].

Second, bring together the clergy and laity to mount a program of learning and understanding the sacred truths contained in the Christian philosophy, and of appreciating and loving the Church for its role in perpetuating those truths, in contradistinction to Masonic lies. Support the Order of St. Francis and its call for Christian liberty, fraternity, and equality of rights, as opposed to the Masonic perversion of those virtues [par. 32-34].

Third, work to restore the system of workmen's guilds, which in earlier times were used, under the guidance of the Church, to protect both the temporal interests and the morality of those who worked with their hands. Today, under the patronage of our Bishops, such guilds may be brought back into use to provide a wholesome alternative to the destructive sects which our working men are being drawn into by fraud, deceit, and immoral allurements [par. 35].

Fourth, look most especially after our young, the hope of all future human society. Keep them away from schools and masters breathing the poisons of the sects. Guide parents, priests, and other Christian instructors to teach the children about the true goals of these infamous sects, and the various fraudulent artifices used to ensnare adepts. Warn them never to so bind themselves without seeking the prior counsel of their parents or parish priests [par. 36].

Fifth and last, we must implore our Heavenly Master for the help which the greatness of the danger requires. The

sect binds its members in secrecy to give help to each other.
To meet that attack, we beseech all good men to form the
widest possible association of action and of prayer, that the
Christian name may prosper, that the Church may again
enjoy its needed liberty, and that those who have gone
astray will see the light and return. "By such prayer, we
hope that God will mercifully and opportunely succor the
human race, which is encompassed by so many dangers
[par. 37]."

"Given at St. Peter's in Rome, the twentieth day of
April, 1884, the 6th year of Our Pontificate. Leo XIII,
Pope."

Chapter 4

"GRAND ORIENT FREEMASONRY UNMASKED"

(Lectures in Oct. 1884 by Monsignor George F. Dillon, D.D., pub. 1885 by M. H. Gill & Son, Dublin. Available from Omni Publications, PO Box 900566, Palmdale, CA 93590, 805-274-2240.)

This little book was republished in 1950 by The Britons Publishing Society of London. We start by quoting from the Publisher's Note on page iv, which reveals the motivation of Britons: "All efforts to trace copies [of the Gill & Son book] through the ordinary trade channels had failed to find a single one.... The subject discussed is of world-wide importance and cannot fail to interest both Catholic and non-Catholic.... The warnings [Dillon] so concisely delivered [in 1884] when read in the light of [1950] current events may startle many into a realization of what is going on around them.... The appalling nature of international political intrigue, now so apparent, has [become more absorbing than fictional mysteries], so that the amateur detective is now replaced by the political investigator [of which I am one – ABJ]. It was one such investigator who volunteered the opinion that the book is 'the most exciting *thriller* I have ever read, because the whole plot is being enacted in living pages.'"

Britons notes that it is no longer just the Catholic Church, but "the whole of Christendom which is menaced by the forces of Communism and the secret societies behind it. Following the advice of the famous Pope Leo XIII to 'tear the mask off Freemasonry' we present this revised edition under the title *Grand Orient Freemasonry Unmasked as the Secret Power Behind Communism.*"

Dillon starts by stating his desire to respond positively to the call of Pope Leo XIII to unmask Freemasonry and the secret societies with which it is affiliated. He then begins, as did Barruel, with a discussion of the rise of Atheism in Europe. As leading lights in this movement, he briefly mentions Socinus and his nephew in the 16th century (about whom more will follow), Spinosa and Bayle in the 17th century, and in the early 18th century the several literary elites in Queen Anne's reign, including Bolingbroke and Shaftesbury. (All of these names are also mentioned by Barruel.) This leads Dillon directly to Voltaire.

Dillon seconds much of Barruel's account of Voltaire, but adds at least one very significant fact. Voltaire, having graduated from his Jesuit schooling, visited England from 1726-1727, returned to France, was soon jailed in the Bastille for publicly "ridiculing religion and royalty," was released on condition of exile later in 1727, and returned to England. There, says Dillon (pp. 5-6), "...he finally adopted those Infidel and anti-Christian principles which made him... what [historian] Cretineau-Joly justly calls 'the most perfect incarnation of Satan that the world ever saw.'" Most significantly, Dillon continues, "The Society of Freemasons was just then perfected in London, and Voltaire at the instance of his Infidel associates *joined one of its lodges; and he left England... an adept in both Infidelity and Freemasonry.*"

Barruel was apparently unaware of this fact, as he has Voltaire joining only in 1774 at age 80 (Bar., p. 368), apparently keeping his English membership a secret even from his French cohorts. It therefore seems possible that Voltaire was under the discipline of his English lodge during the whole time of his agitation in France against Church and State, perhaps even reporting to the "English" lodges in

France that Weishaupt had ordered his adepts not to visit without the permission of their Superiors (Bar., p. 465).

Dillon gives a clear summary (pp. 7-8) of Voltaire's plan of attack, which is very much worth repeating: "His policy [was] first to suppress the Jesuits and all religious orders, and to secularize their goods; then to deprive the Pope of temporal authority, and the Church of property and state recognition. Primary and higher-class education of a lay and Infidel character was to be established, the principle of divorce affirmed, and respect for ecclesiastics lessened and destroyed. Lastly, when the whole body of the Church should be sufficiently weakened and Infidelity strong enough, the final blow was to be dealt by the sword of open, relentless persecution. A reign of terror was to spread over the whole earth.... This, of course, was to be followed by a Universal Brotherhood without marriage, family, property, God, or law, [as was actually] attempted by the French Commune."

Dillon repeats and reinforces Barruel's view of Voltaire's ethics by quoting from Voltaire's letter to a disciple (p. 8): "Lying is a vice when it does evil. It is a great virtue when it does good. Be therefore more virtuous than ever. It is necessary to lie like a devil, not timidly and for a time, but boldly and always." Using secret societies to attain one's goals is of course consistent with such ethics.

Dillon, like Barruel, next has a go at identifying the source(s) of Freemasonry. He doesn't go back to Manes and the Manicheans, but does acknowledge the Templars, and brings up three previously unmentioned 16th century names: the Charter of Cologne, Laelius and Faustus Socinus, and the conference of Vicenza. We'll devote a few words to each, for future reference.

The Charter of Cologne, dated 1535, is a document existing in the archives of the Mother Lodge of Amsterdam, along with the Mother Lodge's own Constitution, dated

1519. While many Masonic lodges of the time showed no heresy or hostility to the Church, the Cologne Charter, "if genuine" says Dillon (p. 16), proves that there were numerous other lodges at that early time "having principles identical with those professed by the Masons of our own day.... It reveals the existence of lodges of kindred intent in London, Edinburgh, Vienna, Amsterdam, Paris, Lyon, Frankfurt, Hamburg, Antwerp, Rotterdam, Madrid, Venice, Goriz, Koenigsberg, Brussels, Dantzig, Magdeburg, Bremen, and Cologne; and it bears the signatures of well-known enemies of the Church at the period," whom Dillon then names. The document thus indicates the presence of anti-Christian Freemason lodges in both England and Scotland at the time of the Reformation, and therefore supports the evidence of the Oxford manuscript mentioned by Barruel (Bar., p. 386), which indicated the presence of such lodges in England by at least 1460.

Laelius Socinus was the uncle of Faustus Socinus. Both were of the ancient Sozzini family of Sienna, near Florence. Laelius, born in 1525, was, says Dillon (p. 11), "a heresiarch and founder of the sect of Unitarians, or, as they are generally called after him, Socinians." Our encyclopedia says that "in 1546 he was admitted [as] a member of a secret society at Vicenza," which is a town about 30 miles west of Venice. The society, possibly related to the Venice lodge referred to in the Cologne Charter, rejected the divinity of Christ and the doctrine of the Trinity (hence the name "Unitarian"). Laelius' papers, found after his death, showed that he "assisted at a 'Conference of Heretics' held at Vicenza in 1547, in which the destruction of Christianity was resolved upon...." Dillon quotes an authority who said of the conference, "They agreed upon the means of destroying [Christianity], by forming a society which, by progressive successes [might bring on] an almost general apostasy." The conspiracy was discovered by the Republic of Venice, several of its members were executed, but most escaped and fled, carrying and spreading their doctrines throughout all of Europe.

The younger Socinus, Faustus, was born in 1539, and also grew up in the bosom of heresy. When his uncle died in 1562, Faustus retrieved and studied his uncle's papers, and took up his uncle's causes, and with enormous success. His idea was to "raise up another temple into which any enemy of orthodoxy might freely enter" and form into a cohesive Brotherhood. He specifically welcomed Lutherans and Calvinists, but also anyone else who stood opposed to the Roman Church. He instructed his disciples to introduce "the rich, the learned, the powerful, and the influential of the world" into either Unitarianism [an open religion] or "the confederation formed at Vicenza" [a secret society]. That latter confederation, or Brotherhood, became known over time as "United Brethren," "Brother Masons," and finally "Freemasons."

The Socinian sect was most strongly established in Poland, from which proselytes were sent into Germany, Holland, and England, where they blended easily into preexisting apostate sects having origins from such as the Manicheans, the Templars, and the lodges identified in the Cologne Charter. The reason that these disparate apostate reform groups all so fortuitously ended up with the same name – Freemasonry – was no doubt due to the preexistence for many centuries of the guild of working masons, who desired most of all to guard the secrets of their trade. Their semisecret organization of Masonry was therefore fair game for those who wished to infiltrate and convert it into something subversive.

In 17th-century England, Freemasonry was given its final polished form via the attentions of one Elias Ashmole, an antiquarian who also played a major role in the founding of the Oxford Museum. Cromwell and his Independents had made their own use of English masonry, but Ashmole turned the sect, always strong in Scotland, to the support of the Stuarts and their return to the throne. After James II was in turn driven from the throne in 1688, the Jacobites, still in support of the Stuarts, formed Scotch, English, and Irish constitutions of the lodge. The English branch went through some gyrations, and settled in 1717 as The Grand Lodge of London. It threw off auxiliary lodges in Dunkirk (1721), Paris (1725), Ireland (1729), Holland (1730), Germany (1736), and later in Italy, Spain, and generally the rest of Europe. The growth of these European lodges matched the period of growth of European Atheism, exemplified by the career of Voltaire.

In France, Philip of Orleans became head of the Paris lodge, and, seeking more local cohesion, separated it from the Mother Lodge of England, and formed the Grand Orient of France, of which he was elected the Grand Master. He established "Androgyne" lodges for women, appointing his sister, the Duchess of Bourbon, as their head. They very successfully invaded the domestic circles in the French and all other European royal Courts, where they provided critical assistance to the spread of Freemasonry.

The movement was aided yet further by the intro-duction into the Lodge of Lyons, by the Portuguese Jew Martinez Pasqualis, of the first French "Illuminism." It was "perfected" by St. Martin, from whom the sect took the name Martinists. Its Illuminism, says Dillon, "was simply an advance in the intensity of immorality, Atheism, secrecy, and terror, which already reigned in the lodges of France." Even before the advent of Weishaupt, Freemasonry had grown so strong (p. 20) that "it began already to extend its influence into every department of state. Promotion in the army, in the navy, in the public service, [and] in the law... became impossible without its aid." In fact, it became powerful enough to successfully intrigue against the Jesuits, and in 1773 Pope Clement XIV dissolved the order, which was one of the goals long-sought by Voltaire.

Dillon then gets to Weishaupt. He was a man, says Dillon (p. 22), "who, more than any of the Atheists that have arisen in Masonry, has been the cause of the success of its agencies in controlling the fate of the world since his day." The Philosophism of Voltaire contained "only a mitigated antipathy for monarchy." On the contrary, not only a hatred of religion, but also the "determination to found a universal republic on the lines of Communism was [for] Weishaupt a settled sentiment. Possessed of a rare power of organization, an education in law, ...an extended knowledge of men and things, a command over himself, a repute for external morality, and finally a position calculated to win disciples, Weishaupt employed for fifty years after the death of Voltaire [in 1778] his whole life and energies in the one work of perfecting secret associations to accomplish by deep deceit, and by force when that should be practical, the ruin of the existing order of religion, civilization, and government...."

Dillon describes in a few pages the form of the society Weishaupt created, and its methodology for elevating the most criminally adaptable of adepts to the highest levels of leadership within the Order. He repeats Weishaupt's admissions to his high-level adepts that he has lied to them about the Order's religious tolerance, that all religions are in fact tyrannical and are to be destroyed, and that to lie about such matters was truly moral, since the good ends of the Order justify the use of any means, including lying, cheating, stealing, etc. We have covered all this in our detailed review of Barruel's work, but a portion of Dillon's summary (p. 26) is worth repeating: "[Weishaupt] contemplated placing the thread of the whole conspiracy, destined to be controlled by the Illuminati, in the hands of one man, advised by a small council [the Areopage]. The

Illuminati were to be in Masonry and of Masonry, so as to move amongst its members secretly. They were so trained that they could obtain the mastery of every form of secret society, and thus render it subservient to their own Chief. The Chief himself was kept safe by his position, his long training, and by his council."

Dillon then adds a few words about the scope of Weishaupt's upcoming career: "Weishaupt, after being deprived of his professorship in Bavaria [in 1785], found an asylum with the Prince of Coburg-Gotha, where he remained in honor, affluence, and security, until his death in 1830. He continued all his life the Chief of the Illuminati, and this fact may account in large measure for the fidelity with which the Illuminati of the Revolution, the Directory, the Consulate, the Empire, the Restoration, and the Revolution of 1830, invariably carried out his program of perpetual conspiracy for the ends he had in view. It may also account for the strange vitality of the spirit of the Illuminati in Italy, Switzerland, Germany, and Spain, and of its continuance through the 'Illuminated' reigns of Nubius and Palmerston, the successors of Weishaupt to our own day [1884]." These two successors will be dealt with presently.

Returning to 1781, Dillon recounts the international Masonic conference at Wilhelmsbad (Barruel's Wilhemsbaden), where Weishaupt executed his master stroke of penetrating Masonry on a world-wide basis, and attaching Illuminism as the secret controlling organism within Freemason lodges all over the world. Dillon alleges that the conference was in fact *conceived* by Weishaupt, who then worked out a way for getting the conference called, under the nominal leadership of the Duke of Brunswick as "Supreme Grand Master." The conference put in place the fundamental enabling measures for bringing about the World Revolution which is still going on around us.

Dillon goes next to the French Revolution, and contents himself with merely quoting his sources to show how completely the lodges were in control of the levers of society before the revolution started. Europe was formally warned of the impending clash, both by the public discovery of the Illuminati and its papers, and by warnings from the Vatican. But most of the centers of temporal power were themselves infiltrated, and negligible effort was made to crush the movement when such was still possible. In 1787, when the Illuminati felt the time had become ripe, another convention was held, this time between the French adepts and a few German Illuminati who were deputed to complete the French Illuminization and get the French organized to start the Revolution. We have covered Barruel's description of these events.

The Revolution did then proceed apace, with the secret Illuminati leaders always on the same page, and with Weishaupt, with his German Illuminati, helping wherever he could, but always secretly, and from a safe distance. Dillon quotes from John Robison's *"Proofs of a Conspiracy"* to show that, in 1797, well after the French conflagration had subsided, the connection between the Revolution and Free-masonry was well understood in Europe, as various Masonic writers have themselves not only admitted, but even boasted of.

Napoleon was a military careerist who supported the Jacobins during the French Revolution, since, being also a Freemason, he could easily guess who his future bosses were going to be. He therefore did their bidding, and gratefully accepted their help in winning his military victories throughout Europe and the Mediterranean region. The Jacobins, for their part, needed to give the French people a rest, but decided to use Napoleon to conquer as much real estate for the Illuminati as possible, while at the same time seeking the destruction of the papacy.

Concerning Napoleon's empowerment, Dillon notes (p. 38), "When Napoleon obtained power, it was, we know, principally by means of the Illuminated Freemason Talleyrand.... The supreme hidden directory [of the sect] saw that a reaction had set in, which, if not averted, would speedily lead to the return of the exiled Bourbons.... As a lesser evil, therefore, and as a means of forwarding the unification of Europe which they had planned by his conquests, they placed supreme power in the hands of Bonaparte, and urged him on in his career, watching, at the same time, closely, their own opportunities for the development of the deadly designs of the sect."

To soothe the French public, official help in restoring the French church was announced, though such help was ultimately given (p. 34) only "grudgingly, parsimoniously, and meanly." Having put themselves into positions of ministerial power, the Freemason conspirators promoted secular over church education, and otherwise minimized the recovery of the Church. On issues external to France, they caused dissension between the Pope and the Emperor, and let Napoleon treat the Church as brutally as ever. In Napoleon's first campaign in Italy, "He suppressed the abodes of the consecrated servants of God, sacked churches, cathedrals, and sanctuaries, and reduced the Pope to the direst extremities.... " In a word, the Papal States were occupied and plundered, and Pope Pius VI was carried away into France, where he died in 1799. In 1808, dissension again arose, leading to the reoccupation of the Papal States, their annexation into the French Empire, and the imprisonment (until Bonaparte's overthrow) of Pope Pius VII.

Napoleon, however, was not a member of Illuminism's inner circle, so he encountered trouble as soon as his personal interests diverged from their ideology. Having experienced close to absolute power, he perhaps felt he could successfully follow his own ambitions. He divorced his wife Josephine and married Marie Louise of Austria, who promptly bore him a son and heir to his throne. Masonry, of course, wanted to choose their own leader for their newly created "Universal State." Napoleon showed a new coldness toward the sect, and his opposition to the promotion of its aims. Behold! The sect turned against him, and of a sudden his military and political actions were everywhere thwarted. He was intrigued into an unwinable and disastrous war in Russia, upon his return from which he was confronted with united European armies against him. In fine, his former friends, always much more powerful than he was, secretly betrayed and ultimately destroyed him. As noted above, he spent his last days in confinement on the island of St. Helena.

During the whole course of Napoleon's reign, Weishaupt directed the Illuminati from the safety of the Court at Coburg-Gotha, while his confederates were to be found in ministerial positions in every Court of Europe, including Berlin, Brunswick, Vienna, Russia, and of course France. In the latter, seeing that Napoleon had to go, they tried first to replace him with the Protestant and Masonic King William I of Holland. Failing that, they agreed to go along with the reinstatement of the Bourbon King Louis XVIII, whose counsels and Parliament they quickly came to dominate. The King acquiesced to the return of press freedom, which produced a deluge of propagandistic writing against church and monarchy, leading in 1830 to the overthrow of King Louis' Bourbon successor Charles X, France's last legitimate monarch. The usurper whom the Illuminati enthroned was someone closer to their pick this time, namely Louis Philippe, the son of the former Duke of Orleans and Grand Master of the Grand Orient.

Dillon now turns his attention to the post-Napoleon strategy of Illuminized Masonry. After Wilhelmsbad, the Illuminati had the mechanisms in place to control any

Masonic lodge that they wished, essentially world-wide, no matter under what name it may have been constituted. Further, Napoleon's armies, upon retreating into France, left behind in the invaded countries a cancerous infection of Atheist conspirators seeking to advance Weishaupt's program. However, the great majority of the peoples of Europe had come to yearn for peace, stability, and Christianity rather than the "Liberty and Equality" of French Republicanism. The Congress of Vienna, convened after Napoleon's exile, returned the Papal States to the papacy, since the princes leading that Congress perceived that if the Church's property holdings were to go, those of local princes would not be far behind.

The Illuminati perceived the same, says Dillon (p. 48), understanding that they could never conquer the conservative kings and their peoples without first destroying the foundation of Christian morality upon which the existing society was built. The moral core of the society was embodied in the temporal and spiritual authority of the Pope. Destruction of his temporal authority was seen as the easier task, and would shortly lead to destruction of his spiritual authority as well. Thus, the temporal power of the Pope was selected as the next strategic target, and would be attacked by generating political discontent among the various states located on the Italian Peninsula. The pretext was to be the creation of a "united Italy," but a new organization would be needed, with no visible connections to the hated Napoleon or to French Masonry. The organization created was called the Carbonari.

The ploy of the Illuminati was to create an organization which had the needed attributes of oaths of secrecy, the death penalty for a breach of secrecy, ascending degrees, and blind obedience to unknown masters, by means of which the core conspirators could easily gain and maintain ultimate control. Its announced goals, however, were not Atheism and anarchy, but rather the enthusiastic and vigorous support of national sovereigns, Catholicism, the Pope, and Jesus Christ Our Lord, who was proclaimed the Grand Master. The society was formed during the occupation of Napoleon, and its goals being acceptable to the great bulk of the Italian population, it thrived mightily. Its secrecy was accepted because of the strength of the hatred felt toward Napoleon and the French, and because the order's "secret" goal of regaining Italian national freedom was deemed highly patriotic.

Upon Napoleon's downfall, however, the higher degrees of the Carbonari turned to the vigorous pursuit of the secret goals conceived by Weishaupt for the group. The effort was highly successful, the Italians outstripping even the Germans in manipulative skills. By the time of Weishaupt's death in 1830, says Dillon (p. 50), "the supreme government of all the secret societies of the world was exercised by the *Alta Vendita* [i.e., the "highest lodge"] of the Italian Carbonari. The Alta Vendita ruled the blackest Freemasonry of France, Germany, and England; and until [about 1838] it continued with consummate ability to direct the revolutions of Europe." Its specific *primary* goal, however, remained the planning and the institution of the process for destroying the papacy, while leaving the more political matters within each of the several European states to the local Masonic movements within each state.

The leader of the Alta Vendita (p. 57) was for many years a corrupt Italian nobleman, of unknown true identity, who had taken the name *Nubius*, just as Weishaupt had taken the name *Spartacus*. Weishaupt had appointed Nubius to head the Carbonari, and his leadership was so successful that, according to Dillon, he was elevated to Weishaupt's role as Grand Master Conspirator upon, or perhaps just prior to, Weishaupt's death. In about 1838, Nubius himself died, perhaps assassinated by poison, but the

139

circumstances of his impending demise apparently led him to take actions resulting in the exposure of the Carbonari's archives (p. 68), to our great benefit. The torch of leadership had necessarily to be passed once again, as we shall momentarily discuss. But first, Dillon quotes from two of the archived Carbonari documents.

The first document is a "Permanent Instruction" written to high-ranked Carbonari as to how the Pope's authority was to be destroyed. It became, says Dillon, "the Gospel of all the secret societies of Europe." We have severely compressed and paraphrased that Instruction as follows:

"Our goal, with that of Voltaire and the French Revolution, is the obliteration of Catholicism and the very concept of Christianity. Our means is to acquire, perhaps in a hundred years, the leadership of the Church, up to and including the papacy. With this power, the people can be influenced as we would desire. To get there, we must not try to convert the Pope or the old clergy, which would result in our own exposure and destruction. Rather, as our first priority, we must work to secretly influence and bend to our ends the minds of young men entering the clergy. These men, while admiring and respecting us as advisors, will in the fullness of time be the persons who will govern and administer the church, and will be called upon to choose the Pontiff who will reign. That Pontiff, with his subordinates, will be imbued with the principles which we are about to put into circulation. We will, in short, maneuver into the Church's highest ranks clergy who are marching under our banner while believing they are marching to the drums of the Apostles."

This Instruction must have been written at least by 1822, since a letter dated 1822 written by a Nubius agent code-named *Piccolo Tigre*, and addressed to Carbonari

140

lodges in northern Italy, made unmistakable references (p. 61) to the Instruction's demand that the first priority of importance be the long-term attack on the papacy. The Instruction makes it clear that Weishaupt learned from the French Revolution and its aftermath that killing priests en masse and deposing the Pope could not by themselves obliterate Christianity and its moral code. A much longer-term program would be needed to pervert Christianity enough to either destroy it or enlist it in the service of the Conspiracy.

A second document which Dillon quotes at length was written on August 9, 1838 to Nubius by an agent code-named *Vindex*. It is remarkable for the clarity with which it spells out the conspiracy's intent and purpose for corrupting the morals of both clergy and the people, entirely consistent with the direction given in the Weishaupt-Nubius Instruction. The Vindex letter states in part:

"Catholicism has no more fear of a well-sharpened stiletto than monarchies have, but these two bases of social order *can fall by corruption.* Let us then never cease to corrupt.... Let us not make martyrs, but let us popularize vice amongst the multitudes. Let us cause them to draw it in by their five senses; to drink it in; to be saturated with it; [they are already] disposed to receive lewd teachings. Make vicious hearts, and you will have no more Catholics. Keep the priest away from labor, from the altar, from virtue.... Make him lazy, a gourmand, and a patriot. He will become ambitious, intriguing, and perverse....

"It is corruption en masse that we have undertaken; the corruption of the people by the clergy, and the corruption of the clergy by ourselves; the corruption which ought, one day, to put the Church in her tomb.... The best poniard with which to strike the Church is corruption. To the work, then, even to the very end."

Dillon comments, "The horrible program of impurity here proposed was at once adopted." We would comment that a careful look at today's society about 160 years later would suggest that the program is still in full operation.

As noted above, a disruption in the Alta Vendita's leadership occurred in 1838, brought about by one Giuseppe Mazzini, a vigorous Carbonari activist who favored violent direct action, specifically assassination, against whomever he considered to be an enemy. He was excluded from the Alta Vendita group, who deplored his tactics, or perhaps feared them, but in 1838 Nubius mysteriously died, with many suspecting poison from the hand of, or to accomplish the elevation of, Mazzini. This heralded a new era for the Freemason Conspiracy, with Mazzini taking on the role of at least co-leader.

The organization, in fact, redefined itself. The Alta Vendita, which constituted a Supreme Directory of the "Invisible Forty" – the number beyond which it was never permitted to go, says Dillon (p. 68) – remained the leadership group, the successor to Weishaupt's Inner Circle, or Areopage. After 1838, the group moved to Paris, and then, it is believed, to Berlin. A single chief, like Weishaupt or Nubius, was always to be recognized as leader, though unknown to the rank and file in the lodges. Under the Directory were created two operative bodies which Dillon calls the Intellectual Party and the War Party, each having specified roles, the former's involving planning, propagandizing, agitation, etc., and the latter's involving direct physical action. The former will aspire to political power, and try to protect and defend the latter if it gets into trouble with the public (e.g., will behave as anti-anticommunists), while the latter will seek positions of physical authority, such as generals, admirals, and police chiefs.

In 1837, shortly before Nubius' death, Mazzini moved his permanent abode to London, and later emerged as the head of the War Party. But who emerged as the Grand Patriarch succeeding Nubius? Dillon drops his bombshell. It was none other, he says, than Lord Palmerston, then the British Foreign Secretary, and soon to be Home Secretary and then Prime Minister.

Dillon hastens to his proofs, from his own personal knowledge, and from that of his most trusted sources, of which we will repeat a portion. He didn't want to believe it at first, he says (p. 72), "But the mass of evidence collected by Father Deschamps and others to prove Lord Palmerston's complicity... is so weighty, clear, and conclusive, that it is impossible to refuse it credence.... In 1830 he accepted the position of Foreign Secretary in the Whig Ministry of Earl Grey." Whereupon, says Dillon, "Palmerston at once threw the whole weight of his energy, position, and influence to cause his government to side with the Masonic program for revolutionizing Europe." He was no figurehead, insists Dillon. "He was admitted into the very recesses of the sect. He was made its Monarch, and as such ruled with a real sway over the realms of darkness." The 1848 revolutions in Europe put the Carbonaro Louis Napoleon on the throne of France, who executed a coup d'état in 1852 and declared himself Emperor. Palmerston supported Louis in 1848, but also unilaterally sent a letter in 1852, as the English Foreign Secretary, proclaiming England's recognition of him as Emperor, *without consulting, and against the wishes of, the Queen, the Cabinet, and Parliament.* Queen Victoria thereupon dismissed Palmerston, but his recognition of the French regime stood, and he himself was strong enough to return to power within a year as Home Secretary, and by 1855 as Prime Minister. Even the English people gazed with awe at this display of his personal power.

Accompanying Mazzini to London in 1837, says Dillon, were "several Counselors of the 'Grand Patriarch,'" presumably a reference to Nubius, whose life, in the follow-

143

ing year, came to an abrupt end. Palmerston was briefly out of office from 1841 to 1846, freeing him up to plan ahead for the Conspiracy. During this time, says Dillon, "plans were elaborated destined to move the program of Weishaupt another step toward its ultimate completion. These [plans] were:

- "To create, by the aid of well-planned revolutions, one immense Empire from the small German states, in the center of Europe, under the house of Brandenburg;
- "Next, to weaken Austrian dominion;
- "Then, to annihilate the temporal sovereignty of the Pope, by the formation of a United Kingdom of Italy under the provisional government of the house of Savoy;
- "And lastly, to form of the discontented Polish, Hungarian, and Slavonian populations, an independent kingdom between Austria and Russia."

Is it reasonable to believe that these plans all came out of Palmerston's own, personal, private deliberations? How might he personally benefit? We ask once more, as we did earlier concerning Weishaupt's motivation, "Cui bono?" Who or what is providing the continuity of planning as leaders die and are replaced? What *are* the final goals the conspiracy is after? *Who* is going to end up in power over the whole world? Let us remain aware of these questions while we follow the development of Lord Palmerston's secret plans of the mid-nineteenth century.

Palmerston died in 1865 (about six months after Lincoln was assassinated), while holding the office of Prime Minister. During his "reign," and while Grand Patriarch of the Freemasons, both of the two operative sections of the conspiracy made their advances. The Intellectual Party pressed, throughout all of Europe, the advance of immorality as prescribed in the Weishaupt-Nubius "Permanent Instruction" and in the advices of Vindex, deluging Europe

144

with immoral and immodest novels, pictures, and all manner of literature. Proposals were made to legalize prostitution. Marriage and divorce laws were liberalized and secularized. Schools were pressed into the "secular, compulsory, and free" mold. Hence France, under the Emperor Louis Napoleon (p. 78) "became a very pandemonium of vice," while Italy "became systematically corrupted on the very lines laid down by the Alta Vendita."

On the War Party front, Mazzini organized a series of revolutionary sects generically named Young Italy, Young Poland, Young Europe, etc. With them he initiated in 1848 a number of simultaneous uprisings in the various countries and kingdoms within Europe, commonly labeled the Revolution of 1848. Most of the uprisings were put down without excessive difficulty, and were regarded as failures. In the process, however, Louis Philippe was deposed, and the Second French Republic was declared, with Louis Napoleon elected President. This new Republic lasted only three years, ended by the coup d'état in 1852 which created the Second French Empire, now under *Emperor* Napoleon III.

The longer-term plans of Palmerston, however, proceeded like clockwork. Austria was the primary protector of the Pope in Italy. Austria had a treaty of mutual aid with Russia. Palmerston sought to break that treaty and weaken each of Russia and Austria, exposing the Pope. Palmerston and the Carbonaro Napoleon III joined forces, and England, France, and Turkey threatened what became the Crimean War against Russia. They also threatened to start a Balkan war aimed at creating a Polish-Hungarian Kingdom. They then promised Austria to give up that latter project provided Austria would not interfere with their projected Crimean War. Austria (to its later sorrow) agreed, and broke its treaty with Russia. Prussia also succumbed to a diplomatic bribe, being promised to get, in due time, the Empire of United Germany. The Crimean War then proceeded, ending with Allied victory in 1856. France then engaged Austria over their Italian holdings, Austria was ejected, and in 1861 Victor Emmanuel II was proclaimed King of all Italy. Victor Emmanuel, an ardent Freemason, was of the centuries-old House of Savoy based in the Italian principality of Piedmont in the northwest corner of Italy.

Palmerston died in 1865, but the Conspiracy continued his program, albeit under some new leadership arrangement. Shortly before his death, Otto von Bismarck of the house of Brandenburg attained undisputed power in Prussia, and accepted the help of Masonry to attain the leadership of a United Germany. He made war on Austria, finishing her off in 1866 as a significant independent European power. He then turned on France, and proceeded with the Franco-Prussian War, with the Masons now deserting Napoleon III and siding with the Germans. The southern German states joined Prussia, Napoleon III was thoroughly defeated, and in 1871 all of Germany was included in the new German Empire. In September, 1870, the defeated French withdrew their last troops from Rome, and in the following month Victor Emmanuel, Bismarck's ally, annexed the Papal States to his Kingdom of Italy, and completed the unification by making Rome his capital. Also in 1870, the French, with their emperor Napoleon III defeated and captured, twisted once more in their historical agony and created their Third Republic. Mazzini died in 1872, and Napoleon III a year later, in 1873.

Immediately upon Bismarck's victory, says Dillon (p. 86), "he hastened to pay to Freemasonry his promised persecution of the Church." Thus, religious orders were suppressed or banished, followed by Catholic education, Catholic properties, and Catholic clergy themselves. "All but the existence of Catholics was proscribed," says Dillon.

The "dark Directory" succeeding the regimes of Weishaupt, Nubius, and Palmerston sits "almost openly" in Paris and Berlin, eating away without significant opposition at whatever remaining structures were visible to them of the old society.

The Freemasonic power in Italy was equally pervasive and damaging. Says Dillon (p. 89), "The whole property of the church was seized upon.... The change simply put hungry Freemasons, and chiefly those of Piedmont, in possession of the Church lands and revenues." All native princes were driven from their thrones, and the peasantry was taxed, in their lands, their rents, and their produce, as never before. Legions of Freemasons filled unneeded civil service billets, making the people "more wretched and miserable than any Christian peasantry... on the face of the earth." The portion of the Conspiracy's grand plan assigned to Palmerston was thus substantially completed.

New organizations had by this time been formed, in preparation for the next steps. Dillon briefly mentions the *International*, which later history came to call the First International. It was formed in London in 1864 in support of the socialist principles espoused by Karl Marx and Friedrich Engels. The thrust of the new movement was rather different, however, in that it demanded that the bourgeoisie, who had flocked to Freemasonry for the economic benefits which it offered, must now relinquish such benefits and distribute them to working men everywhere. Everyone was to be leveled downward to the lowest class, except, of course, those few who were to remain on top to enforce the leveling down.

The International had three degrees, organized as distinct hierarchical societies (p. 92): the International Brethren, the National Brethren, and various Workmen's Societies. The higher two degrees "are formed strictly upon the lines laid down by Weishaupt." The lower degrees

147

know nothing of the degrees above them, though the upper degrees secretly direct the activities of the lower. As in the Illuminati, "The death penalty for indiscretion or treason is common [to] every degree." The Masonic emphasis on recruiting princely adepts was continued, obtaining, for example, "a Russian Prince of high lineage, a representative of the wealthiest, most exclusive, and perhaps richest aristocracy in the world [namely, Prince Kropotkin]."

Simultaneously with the International came new groups dedicated to intrigue, violence, and terror, such as the Black Hand and the Nihilists. Dillon mentions several events which smack of their efforts, including the assassination in 1882 of Leon Gambetta, a French premier (of the Third French Republic) driven from office for his reformist efforts (p. 91), and the assassination in 1881 of the reformist Emperor Alexander II of Russia (p. 94). Obviously, the ends of the Conspiracy are still presumed to justify such means.

Finally, Dillon deals briefly with England and then the conspiratorial strategy in Ireland. We will confine our review just to England. He first reiterates the commonly accepted notion that English Masonry was non-threatening, remaining loyal to both Monarchy and Church. However, it *was* the source of Continental Masonry, which at least some English Masons aided and abetted in its destructive rampage. Further, even the innocuous bottom three degrees of English Masonry required their candidates to swear to carefully keep any sect secrets which may be revealed to them, and to expect death as the penalty for any violation, an action beyond the pale for a fun social group, but not inappropriate for one with dark and deadly secrets not yet revealed.

But of much greater significance, he points to one of the groups which helped Palmerston successfully guide the affairs of Europe from his base in London. Dillon notes (p.

106), "...there have been at all times, at least in London, some lodges affiliated to Continental lodges, and doing the work of Weishaupt. Of this class were several lodges of foreigners and Jews, which existed in London contemporaneously with Lord Palmerston, and which aided him in the government and direction of the secret societies of the world, and in the Infidel Revolution which was carried on during his reign with such ability and success."

Yes, such lodges might certainly have housed the leadership of the World Conspiracy, and facilitated communication of directives to subordinate lodges everywhere. Also to be observed is that the "innocuous" English lodges are also governed via higher-degree members who are subject to Palmerston and his high inner circle. Thus, if Palmerston orders that no significant revolutionary activity shall occur in and against England, then none will occur. The rationalization for such an order is obvious. England, having been secretly taken over at the highest political level, must be kept politically stable in order to provide a secure home base for the Conspiracy, and to facilitate the use of British force and leadership in bringing about the secret aims of the Conspiracy. We will continue to test the hypothesis which we have finally put into words as we proceed through the rest of our reviews.

Chapter 5

"FREEMASONRY IN THE LIFE AND TIMES OF POPE PIUS IX"

(By Fr. Leonard Feeney, pub. ~1950. Available from Omni Publications, PO Box 900566, Palmdale, CA 93590, 805-274-2240.)

Monsignor Dillon, in our preceding review, described the grand strategy by which the Freemason conspirators sought, as their highest priority, to strip the papacy of its property and its temporal power, in their belief that the Pope's spiritual authority and Christianity's moral foundation would in turn be fatally damaged and ultimately destroyed. Wars involving Britain, Russia, France, Germany, Austria, and Italy were planned and executed to accomplish that purpose. Fr. Feeney, on the other hand, looks at the same series of events as seen by the primary target of the Freemasons, Pope Pius IX, who sat as the leader of the Catholic Church from 1846 until his death in 1878 at the age of 86.

Feeney leads up to his subject by recounting names and events most of which are now familiar to us, including Voltaire, Rousseau, Frederick the Great, Weishaupt and his Illuminati, the Illuminization of Masonry at Wilhelmsbad, the French Revolution and its demonic leaders, the rise of Napoleon, etc. We'll mention a few of his observations not previously covered.

Concerning the reconstitution of modern English Masonry in 1717, Feeney says (p. 3), "*Modern* Freemasonry – for such is the scourge – came into being in England in 1717, when the ancient Catholic guild of working masons,

Protestantized long since in England, but existing in Great Britain and Europe for many centuries, was revised. Its professional, laboring character was dropped, and it emerged a philosophical, pseudo-religious secret society, [of which] its Grand Master, in 1722, was the profligate, thoroughly immoral Duke of Wharton, who everywhere was reputed to be 'from no vice exempt.'" This was the English Freemasonry which Voltaire joined in 1727.

After the French Revolution, the American public was well-aware of what had gone on in France, though that truth is obviously not being taught in our schools today. In 1798, Timothy Dwight, President of Yale University, addressed the people of New Haven as follows (p. 8):

"No personal or national interest of man has been uninvaded [by the French Revolution]; no impious sentiment of action against God has been [unproclaimed]; no malignant hostility against Christ and His religion has been unattempted. Justice, truth, kindness, piety, and moral obligation universally have been not merely trodden underfoot... but ridiculed, spurned, and insulted.... For what end shall we be connected with men of whom this is the character and conduct? ... Is it that our churches may become temples of reason, our Sabbath a decade, and our psalms of praise Marseillais hymns? ... Shall our sons become the disciples of Voltaire and the dragoons of Marat, or our daughters the concubines of the Illuminati?"

When, in 1802, Napoleon legalized Catholic worship in France (p. 10), his Concordat (agreement with the Vatican) contained, as additions not agreed to by Pope Pius VII, the *Four Gallican Articles* of 1682, by means of which Louis XIV had denied to the Pope any substantial jurisdiction over the French Catholic Church. In 1809, Napoleon reoccupied the Papal States, and declared them to be joined to the French Republic, whereupon Pope Pius VII excommunicated him, for which the Pope was arrested and exiled until 1814, when Napoleon was himself finally deposed. Napoleon's goal was obviously not to restore a healthy Catholicism, but rather to assure that French Catholicism would be *entirely under the control of the French State.* The revolutionary slogan "Separation of Church and State," which to the revolutionaries really meant "Control of the Church by the State," was so successfully popularized that Catholics came to regard it almost as dogma. In today's world, the slogan is used by collectivists to assure that the Christian Church and its clergy shall have no influence or authority in any temporal matter of interest to collectivists, such as public school education.

Pius IX, elected Pope in June of 1846, was conservative in his faith, but liberal in his politics. During the eighteen months before the 1848 revolutions began, he was repeatedly warned about his politics by many around him, including the experienced old Chancellor of Austria, Prince Metternich. The Prince had almost single-handedly, says Feeney (p. 13), "...ever since the Congress of Vienna in 1815, staved off the enslavement of the Catholic Church and the countries of Europe, even though he was called a 'reactionary' for doing so...." The Pope, however, had not taken seriously that the Freemasonic goal was to destroy Christianity, and that the conspirators could never be reasoned with, or converted, or moved from their moral bedrock that the Ends Justify the Means. He remained politically "liberal" – emptying jails of thousands of political prisoners, appointing a notoriously liberal Secretary of State, arming a local "Civic Guard" which Metternich deplored as tantamount to arming the revolutionaries – until the 1848 revolutions began to catch up to him personally.

In January, 1848, revolt broke out in Sicily, moved up the peninsula, and soon encompassed practically every sizeable Italian city (p. 16). The Paris revolution began in

February. In March it came to Vienna, putting Metternich to flight after 33 years of successful opposition. On March 15, the Pope granted a constitution to the Papal States. In April, a Piedmontese army general unilaterally proclaimed the Pope to be at the head of a United Italian war against Austria and all other foreigners, "...with the end that Italy should become a united republic with the Pope as President!" The Pope's lay ministers supported such a war, but his Cardinals opposed it. The Pope, obviously opposed to being responsible for starting a general war, sided with his Cardinals, and his ministers then resigned. This was the signal for mobs to get busy, and they, joined by the Pope's treasonous Civic Guard, filled the streets around his residence, virtually imprisoning the Pope. The press and local Masonic clubs, resembling the Jacobin clubs which preceded them, "openly discussed an alliance with the Piedmontese Government and the necessity of abolishing then and there the papal rule!"

It was only then, says Feeney, that "the scales fell from the eyes" of the hitherto liberal Pope, who "was never again the same." On April 29 he published a response in which "he disavowed any connection with Mazzini's sly schemes for an Italian Republic," and he warned Italians against, in the Pope's own words, "the perfidious designs and counsels of men who would detach [Italians] from the obedience due their respective sovereigns. As to ourselves, we declare in the most solemn manner that all our thoughts, our cares, our endeavors, as Roman pontiff, aim at enlarging continually the Kingdom of Christ, and not at extending the boundaries of the temporal principality which Providence has bestowed on the Holy See..."

Feeney accuses Lord Palmerston of being the responsible revolutionary leader (pp. 15-16): "Throne after throne toppled in the year 1848. Catholic ruler after Catholic ruler... was forced to flee. For the order had been sent out, the fuse had been lighted by the supreme, secret head of Freemasonry, who at this time was none other than [the] highly respectable, exquisitely appointed, last man in the world to suspect, British Prime Minister, Lord Palmerston. It was Lord Palmerston who made and broke the Masonic rulers of Europe. It was he who set up and hurled down the Freemason Emperor Napoleon III of France, the nephew of Napoleon Bonaparte. It was Lord Palmerston who made and broke Mazzini, ... the head of the dreaded secret society of the Carbonari, the lone founder of the bitterly anti-Catholic Young Italy, and the successor of the corrupt Italian nobleman who went under the assumed name of Nubius, ...who was the Grand Master of the Alta Vendita....

"It was Lord Palmerston who aided the extraordinary rise of the Prussian Chancellor Prince Otto von Bismarck, and set the stage for his victory over Napoleon III in the Franco-Prussian War, the war which brought into being the German Empire of the Kaisers at the expense of the defeated Catholic Austria and France. It was Lord Palmerston who provided the Freemason [Count Camillo] Cavour, Prime Minister of Sardinia, with *the money* [our emphasis] whereby that poor little Italian state, comprising Sardinia and Piedmont, would later war on [Pope Pius IX] and annex the Papal States, all Italy, and finally Rome itself, and [then] set up in the place of the Pope-King the rotund, bewhiskered little man, Victor Emmanuel...."

The seven months following his April 29 declaration was a nightmare for the Pope. "Violence followed upon violence," says Feeney, as soon as the revolutionaries saw that the Pope had become their serious enemy. "Young Italy and the secret societies under Mazzini raged, conspired, and plotted. So did Cavour, the Prime Minister of Sardinia, for the interests of the Piedmontese. Lord Palmerston worked openly through his special envoy in

Rome, Lord Minto, whose policy it became to encourage the most dangerous revolutionaries in Italy." In September, the Pope appointed the brave and competent Count Rossi as Prime Minister of the Papal States. Recognized as a major stumbling block, Rossi was targeted for assassination, which was carried out by a dagger to the throat on November 15 upon the opening of the Parliament of the Papal States. Feeney gives the details.

A mob then formed around the papal residence, and the Pope's protection was reduced to the foreign diplomatic corps (excepting that from Great Britain, Sardinia, and *the United States!*), one hundred Swiss Guards, two Cardinals, and a few priests and servants. The mob leaders, who were leaders also of Mazzini's Young Italy, presented the Pope with written demands amounting to his surrender to the dictates of Mazzini's regime. The Pope refused to sign, whereupon the mob stormed the palace, bullets flew, and various of the Swiss Guards and the Bishops were killed. Cannon were then brought up and trained upon the front gate, and an ultimatum delivered to the Pope demanding his surrender or every living person found in his premises would be put to death excepting only the Pope himself.

The Pope still did not sign, but did quiet the revolutionaries by acquiescing to the appointment of Mazzini's choices as ministers of the Papal States, including a Prime Minister named Galletti, who was "a close personal friend of Mazzini." Three days later, the new "government" dismissed the Pope's Swiss Guards, leaving the Pope physically defenseless. The Pope was nevertheless, on November 24, spirited out of his residence, out of Rome, and to the safety of the Kingdom of Naples, in a flight organized by the French and Bavarian ambassadors, and larded with flim-flam and derring-do worthy of the fictional British Agent James Bond. Feeney's account will have you holding your breath.

SECRECY OR FREEDOM?

As described in our previous review, the 1848 revolutions were rather shallow, and Mazzini's "triumphs" were rather quickly turned around. The Pope returned to Rome in 1850 under the protection of the French army, and Mazzini's plan gave way to the longer-term, more substantial and integrated plan of Lord Palmerston. The Crimean War was over by 1856. By 1861, France had ejected Austria from Italy, and Victor Emmanuel, with the help of Palmerston and Napoleon III, had gobbled up the Papal States and proclaimed himself King of Italy, with his capital temporarily in Florence. The Pope was left (p.23) "with only the old duchy of Rome, the ancient Patrimony of St. Peter."

By 1866, Bismarck had warred on and defeated Austria, and had then turned on France. Thoroughly defeated, the French withdrew their forces from Italy, enabling Victor Emmanuel, on September 20, 1870, to march substantially unopposed into Rome. The Holy Roman Pontiff was stripped of all his possessions, was proclaimed a "guest" of the government, and was permitted to use the Vatican Palace as his residence. He remained there, a virtual prisoner, until his death on February 7, 1878.

Though defeated by military forces and the Freemasonic plotting of Palmerston and his successors and subordinates, Pope Pius IX never acknowledged the legitimacy of Victor Emmanuel or his government, and remained implacably opposed while the State went about its standard anti-Christian program of confiscating monasteries and convents, abolishing religious teaching in the schools, interfering with seminary training, legislating on marriage, etc. During the tumultuous years of his reign, he remained true to the Faith, and continued to provide energetic Catholic leadership. For example, in 1850 he reestablished a Catholic hierarchy in England, and the same a little later in Holland, to the tune of anti-Catholic demonstrations in both countries. Between

1847 and 1853, he established archbishoprics in many cities in the U.S., including St. Louis, New York, Cincinnati, New Orleans, and San Francisco. In 1854 he defined the divine dogma of the Immaculate Conception before 170 Bishops and many other pilgrims in the Basilica of St. Peter's, to which the Catholic faithful around the world rejoiced. In 1860 and 1862, he serenely beatified Christian martyrs even while being threatened with destruction by Victor Emmanuel. In 1864 he issued a compendium of encyclicals, allocutions, and letters generated during his pontificate concerning the errors and false teachings of Liberalism which were eating away at the foundations of the Church and of Christian morality, an action which produced a storm of hatred and vitriol from liberals worldwide.

"On six different occasions between 1846 and 1873," says Feeney, "he condemned Freemasonry and its kindred secret sects. 'You are from your father the devil,' he said to them [in one writing], 'and it is the works of your father that you wish to do.'" He gave author Jacques Cretineau-Joly access to the papers of the Alta Vendita which had been acquired during the earlier reign of Pope Gregory XVI, and which revealed the Freemasonic program and its planned methodology. And then in June, 1868, he issued a call, to the fury of his enemies, for an ecumenical council to open at the Vatican Basilica in December of 1869, the first such council in three centuries. Over seven hundred priests attended, with some eighty thousand persons jamming into the area around St. Peter's. In July, 1870, at about the time that Bismarck declared war on France, the council voted and adopted as dogma a declaration defining Papal Infallibility, "despite the overwhelming, hysterical, and desperate protest in the press all over the world," says Feeney. The Vatican Council continued until October, 1870, about a month after the seizure of Rome by Victor Emmanuel.

Though his property had been taken from him, along with his temporal power over the Papal States, his spiritual authority remained strong (as shown by the Vatican Council), as did his voice for the maintenance of Christian morality. In accordance with the love and gratitude shown to him during and after the years of his reign, by millions of Catholics around the world, he was started down the road to beatification in February, 1907, by Pope Pius X, the successor to the great Leo XIII, whose work *Humanum Genus* we previously reviewed. The goal set by Weishaupt-Nubius many years earlier – to destroy the moral authority of the Pope – remained unaccomplished.

Recall, however, that the removal of the Pope's temporal authority was only the shorter-term portion of the overall plan of the conspirators. The longer-term effort, as Dillon revealed in his book, was spelled out in the Weishaupt-Nubius "Permanent Instruction," which called for the infiltration into the Catholic clergy, and the ultimate takeover of the papacy itself, in perhaps one hundred years, by agents of the conspiracy dedicated to that purpose. A great deal of that program, laid out as early as 1822, was in fact accomplished during the 20th century, as evidenced by the Vatican II Conference in the 1960's. But instead of pursuing that, we shall next look further backwards for more historical underpinnings which will bear on our developing theme.

Chapter 6

"WORLD REVOLUTION"

(By Nesta H. Webster, pub. 1921. 7th ed., pub. 1994 by Veritas Pub. Co., PO Box 42, Cranbrook, Western Australia 6321. Available from Omni Publications, PO Box 900566, Palmdale, CA 93590, 805-274-2240.)

We review this book because it helps corroborate some of the 19th century history we have covered, and then continues that history through the Russian Revolution. Webster starts earlier, however, by describing the appearance in the 18th century of Weishaupt and his Illuminati, and then the cataclysm of the French Revolution. The Illuminati was covered in much more detail in Barruel's book, however, and Webster herself devoted a whole book to the French Revolution, both of which we have reviewed. We will therefore move ahead to Webster's post-revolution topics, starting with Francois Babeuf.

This gentleman was born in 1762, and worked as a revolutionary bureaucrat early in the French Revolution. Among the Illuminati, he sported the name *Gracchus*. Though originally opposed to the depopulation scheme of Robespierre, that tyrant later became his hero. After Robespierre's execution, Babeuf organized his own revolutionary band aimed at overthrowing the Directory and carrying out Robespierre's unfinished program. Babeuf's plan was reduced to writing in a proclamation entitled "Manifesto of the Equals." It was, however, never delivered to the people, because Babeuf's own brain trust felt that it revealed too much that the people wouldn't buy. It was therefore rewritten under the title "Analysis of the Doctrine of

Babeuf." Before either could be delivered, however, the conspiracy was uncovered, and he was arrested on the day before his uprising was scheduled. Though he protested that he was only the agent of other unnamed conspiratorial leaders, he was nevertheless condemned, and on May 28, 1797, mounted the scaffold to meet his maker.

The Manifesto and the Analysis documents were, however, very illuminating. They called for compulsory equal hours of work from everyone for equal pay in kind or via barter (money was to be abolished); boys would be trained for tasks that were "needed" rather than professions they might want; most would be sent to till the fields; their education would be such as to convince them of the wisdom of the state institutions under which they lived; all other avenues of knowledge were to be closed; etc., etc. One author is quoted as describing the Analysis document as "the veritable Bible or Koran of the despotic system known as Communism." Webster observes (p. 81), "The fact is that... *Babouvisme and Bolshevism are identical*; between the two creeds there is no essential difference. The Third International of Moscow [in about 1919] rightly traces its descent from Babeuf," whose written effusions preceded Karl Marx's "Communist Manifesto" by about 50 years. The renowned Karl Marx is thus seen to be little more than a plagiarist of much earlier Illuminati doctrine.

During the first half of the 19th century, a large number of attempts were made at founding settlements based upon communistic principles, no doubt to create showplaces to demonstrate how well communist theory could be put into practice. Webster follows several of these experiments, all of which ended as abject failures. As an interesting footnote, she succinctly summarizes why they *must fail* (p. 16): "The only form of Communism, in its true sense of holding everything in common, which it has ever been possible to carry out successfully is that practiced by religious communities. Monasteries and convents of course practice Communism, but the fact which enables them to do this peacefully is that they are composed of people who have renounced all interest in earthly things, and center all their thoughts and desires on the Kingdom of Heaven. Secular Communism, by its insistence on materialism, eliminates the only factor which makes the system feasible – belief in God and a Hereafter."

Communist theory was nevertheless kept publicly alive throughout this period, says Webster, in part by the production in 1828, and its wide distribution among the French proletariat, of a book entitled "History of the Conspiracy of the Equals." It was written by a co-conspirator of Babeuf named Buonarotti, who the French Directory failed to execute with Babeuf. Buonarotti, says Webster, was clearly acting to further the program that the Illuminati had given to Babeuf to administer. She quotes socialist sources who admit to the transmission of the principles of communism via the darkness of the secret societies during this time period, an activity into which Buonarotti's work precisely fits.

Webster quotes Piccolo Tigre writing in 1846 concerning the readiness of the conspiracy to commence with the main event for all Europe. In the same year, says Webster (p. 134), "A great Masonic Congress was held… at Strasbourg. Amongst the French Masons present were the men who played the leading parts in the subsequent revolution – Louis Blanc, Caussidière, Crémieux, Ledru-Rollin, etc." Caussidière was also the Paris police chief during the 1848 uprising, and he wrote in his memoirs about the secret society plans for that event, memoirs which Webster gratefully quotes.

Webster then spends considerable words detailing the Parisian uprising. On a pretext, a mob was raised on the morning of February 24, 1848; it acquired arms, set up barricades, encountered little resistance, and advanced on the Tuileries Palace. The usurper Louis Philippe saw the handwriting on the wall, and fled with his family before the day was half gone. The Second Republic was declared, but Louis Blanc and the other leaders found within a day or so that they had no program to provide instant gratification to the workers they had conned into mob action. There followed four months of violent argumentation, climaxed by a riotous confrontation between unemployed workers and the army, generating casualties of about 10,000 killed or wounded. The victorious commanding general declared a military dictatorship, Louis Napoleon was elected President in December, 1848, and by coup d'état promoted himself to Emperor Napoleon III in December, 1852, ending the Second Republic. His regime was one of absolute repression. The socialist leaders were arrested, some 25,000 prisoners were taken, and a great many deported without trial.

Uprisings in the same year of 1848 occurred in various cities in Austria, Germany, Spain, Italy, and Russia. Our received history reports the dates, but ignores the causes, says Webster (p. 156). "That the European Revolution of 1848 was the result of Masonic organization," she continues, "cannot be doubted by anyone who takes the trouble to dig below the surface. We have already seen how Mazzini and the 'Young Italy' movement, ...operating through the lodges, had prepared the ground in every country." In support of her case, she identifies a half-dozen leaders of the German revolution who had attended the Masonic Congress in Strasbourg, and quotes also the French socialists Lamartine and Crémieux, each acknowledging, while still in power during the four months of Provisional Republican government, the role of the Freemason lodges in creating the explosion.

The Prussian monarch during the 1848 Revolution was Frederick William IV, who reigned from 1840 to 1861. He was apparently opposed to the subversive efforts of his predecessors, and instead was supportive of Austria. However, he was replaced after his death by William I, whom Webster describes (p. 165) as "the protector of Masonry." Bismarck became the Prussian Chancellor, and Palmerston's anti-Austrian efforts commenced, as Dillon has described. Austria was defeated by Bismarck at the Battle of Sidowa in 1866, and Prussia remained for the moment a committed tool of Palmerston's strategy.

Five years before the European Revolution of 1848, a young German by the name of Karl Marx graduated from Berlin University with a degree in philosophy, got married, and moved to Paris, where he took up the profession of Socialism. He joined forces there with Friedrich Engels, who worked for an English textile firm, and who likewise was drawn to Socialism. Marx was deported from France for revolutionary activities in 1845, and he and Engels moved to Brussels where they reorganized the Communist League, and where, in 1847, they published their famous *Communist Manifesto.* In 1848, Marx returned to Germany, took part in the 1848 Revolution, and headed, says Webster (p. 168), "a secret Communist society wielding the powers of life and death. For this it is said that he was condemned to death, but succeeded in escaping to London, where he settled down for the rest of his life, and where at this moment, according to the strange British custom, *revolutionaries from all over Europe had been allowed to foregather* (our emphasis)."

Whereas Marx spent many years in producing his magnum opus *Das Kapital*, the first volume of which was published in 1867, the much shorter Communist Manifesto took only a few days to write, and was mostly the work of Engels. Whereas working men must have found Das Kapital for the most part unintelligible, says Webster, the Communist Manifesto was plain enough, but contained *nothing* that was original with Marx or Engels. "Here," she says, "are all the diatribes against the bourgeoisie and capitalists with which Marat, Hébert, and Babeuf had familiarized the people, and here in plain language are set forth the doctrines laid down in the code of Weishaupt – the abolition of monarchy and all ordered government, of property and inheritance, of patriotism, of marriage and the family, of all religion, the institution of the community of women, and the communal education of children by the State."

Webster, in analyzing the two works attributed to Marx by history, finds his works not to contain a single idea that had not been previously put forth by others, whom she takes pains to identify. "Marx," she says (p. 172), "was an impostor from the beginning. Posing as the prophet of a new gospel, he was in reality nothing but a plagiarist without the common honesty to pay tribute to the sources whence he drew his material. For after pillaging freely from all the earlier Socialists, Marx dismisses them with a sneer." He was apparently a man whose ego could not stand competition in intellectual matters over which he deemed himself the Headmaster. Thus Ferdinand Lassalle, Louis Blanc, and other socialists in his peer group were held in contempt, as were likewise any of the working proletariat, who were regarded as so much raw material to be remolded by his revolutionary machinery.

The other social development to which Marx adhered *after* it was created by others was the International, called by later history the First International. It was conceived of by French and English working men who were seeking ways to strengthen the clout of trade unions to protect the interests of workers. Their non-revolutionary reforms were supported in France by Napoleon III. The European Freemasons were not interested in real reform, however, and set about to take over the movement. At a London organization meeting on September 28, 1864, a draft of the statutes of the association was presented by *Mazzini's* Polish secretary, a man named Wolff. Before the meeting was over, Marx had suggested a number of amendments, which were accepted by the organization committee. The document was returned to France and similarly accepted there.

Thus the secret societies had been involved in the preparatory work of the International Association of Workingmen well before Marx's involvement – beginning at least by 1862 according to the Association's Swiss historian James Guillaume. Further, the secret societies throughout Europe and North America then targeted and invaded the new organization, and by 1865, they were in substantial control. Elements of French Freemasonry, the secret societies in Russia and Poland, the Carbonari, and the Fenians of Ireland were all involved, and instead of a working-class organization dedicated to the protection of workers, it became a subversive, revolutionary group organized on the lines of the Illuminati, with unknown masters and secret goals privy only to higher level adepts, etc.

Congresses of the International were held in 1866 (Geneva), 1867 (Lausanne), 1868 (Brussels), and 1869 (Basle). The last of these managed to incorporate into its goals the abolition of private ownership of land and the abolition of inheritance. "The program of Weishaupt," says Webster (p. 194), "had thus been accepted almost in its entirety by the International." The organization conceived by the workingmen had been killed and turned into a new machine for revolution. Webster concludes:

"All talk of conditions of labor, all discussions of the practical problems of industry had been abandoned, and the International had become simply an engine of warfare against civilization. By its absorption of the secret societies and of the doctrines of Illuminism, all the machinery of revolution passed into its keeping. Every move in the game devised by Weishaupt, every method for engineering disturbances and for spreading inflammatory propaganda, became part of its program. So just as the Jacobin Club had openly executed the hidden plan of the Illuminati, the International, holding within it the same terrible secrets, carried on the work of World Revolution in the full light of day."

The last act of Palmerston's plan was now set into motion. After defeating Austria in 1866, Bismarck negotiated a military alliance between Prussia and the southern German states, in which they jointly promised to support each other upon any "French aggression." He then initiated a ploy involving his sending an insulting diplomatic missive to the French, whereupon the easily aroused French public demanded satisfaction. On July 19, 1870, France foolishly moved to declare war on Prussia. (By August, French troops were leaving Italy to fight the Prussians, exposing the Pope in Rome. In September, Victor Emmanuel forced his way into Rome, virtually imprisoning the Pope in the Vatican, as has been described by Dillon and Feeney above.)

Bismarck now had both the northern and the southern German states under his command. He overwhelmed the French forces, concluding the bulk of the fighting in about six weeks, with the major French army surrendering at Sedan (near the Belgian border) on September 1, and with Louis Bonaparte himself being captured in the action. Our encyclopedia notes the following about the war: "The French were the first at getting their troops to the frontier, ...but it soon became clear that the French army, instead of being in a complete state of preparation for war, was defective in almost everything essential to the equipment of an army. German preparation was a contrast. There, the arrangements for mobilizing the army, which had previously been tested in Prussia in 1864 and 1866, were again found to work admirably." Napoleon Bonaparte had earlier experienced how his army was first helped and then hindered according to whether the Illuminized Freemasons wanted him to win or lose, and now Louis Napoleon was clearly being treated to a replay of his uncle's experience.

On September 4, 1870, three days after their defeat at Sedan, the French declared their Empire overthrown, and set up the 3rd French Republic. It continued to prosecute the war until January 28, 1871, when Paris surrendered under siege. A few days earlier, on January 18, 1871, King William of Prussia was crowned as Emperor William I of all Germany, realizing the plans made many years earlier by Lord Palmerston.

For the next four months, the streets of Paris were once more taken over by socialist and anarchic revolutionaries, who somehow felt that France was needful of their solutions. They manned the barricades, and fought until the city had exhausted itself with profitless carnage. Webster describes the outcome (p. 211): "When the struggle between the revolutionary army of the Commune and the forces of law and order had ended in a victory for the latter, thousands of victims strewed the streets of Paris. According to Prince Kropotkin, no less than 30,000 men, women, and children perished in the fray." Perhaps the hidden masters of the French, who were experts in the creation of local riots, wanted no more than simply to absorb any remaining French energy, to assure that the French would not try to interfere with Victor Emmanuel's handling of the Pope in the Vatican.

Webster notes that from the correspondence between Marx and Engels, both were clearly on the side of the German Bismarck during this war. "In 1870 Marx faithfully served the cause of German Imperialism," she says (p. 202). "In this attitude he was naturally supported by Engels – 'Marx's evil genius,' as Mrs. Marx was wont to describe him

– a constitutional militarist." A more likely explanation, we believe, is that Marx and Engels were in on the real purposes of the plot, or were at least sure they were following the conspiracy's high-level orders, which were to assure that France would be defeated by Bismarck, in accordance with the plans made years earlier in London.

Marx's support of Bismarck, and of his clear ideological support of State Socialism, rankled in the hearts of the Anarchists who had just been so sorely defeated in the streets of Paris. The split widened into a chasm (p. 215), and in 1872 the anarchic Bakunists were excluded from the 1872 Hague Congress of the International. The anarchists thereupon moved the headquarters of their open organization called the Jura Federation out of Europe to New York, whence it quietly expired four years later in Philadelphia. This public rancor and split spelled the doom of the First International, as workingmen's groups had seen through enough of its goals to perceive that neither its socialist nor its anarchist incarnation had anything to do with the welfare of workers. One group denounced the International as "the leprosy of Europe," and "the Company of Millionaires on paper."

The utility of anarchism remained apparent to the deep conspirators, however, and over the next several decades the world was treated to its overt works. The noble anarchist Prince Kropotkin surfaced in Russia, wholesale arrests for insurrection were ordered in 1878, and the assassination of Alexander II was successful in 1881 after a series of failed attempts, just as he was about to sign a liberalizing Constitution (pp. 227-8). Assassination attempts were made on King Humbert of Italy, which were finally successful in 1900. Attempts were made on the life of Emperor William I of Germany, but were never successful. The Haymarket Square bombing in Chicago in May, 1886, is still noted worldwide by labor groups on May Day.

President Carnot of France was assassinated in 1894. Empress Elizabeth of Austria was murdered in 1898, King Carlos of Portugal and his Crown Prince in 1908, and King George I of Greece in 1913 (p. 240). Not mentioned by Webster are Presidents Garfield and McKinley of the United States, murdered in 1881 and 1901 respectively.

Perhaps this rash of "anarchic" activity came about as a result of a "re-founding" of the Illuminati sect which Webster describes as follows (p. 231): "What we do know definitely is that the society was re-founded in Dresden in 1880... but it seems that its existence was not discovered until 1899. That it was consciously modeled on its eighteenth-century predecessor is clear from the fact that its chief, one Leopold Engel, was the author of a lengthy panegyric on Weishaupt and his Order, entitled *Geschichte des Illuminaten Ordens* (published in 1906), and in 1903 the original lodge in Ingolstadt was restored." Maybe the conspiracy's Intellectual Party was simply showing off by making these public moves. It seems to us highly unlikely, however, that at the peak of their European accomplishments the conspiracy suffered a lapse of high-level continuity, resolve, or secret leadership. It's just that we cannot today reliably put names on those hidden leaders at the top.

Webster spends a chapter on the movement called "Syndicalism," which is nothing more than a modernized technique of Anarchism. Syndicalism calls for business to be run by worker organizations, and the way to arrive at that state to be the General Strike. The Syndicalist leaders didn't really believe in the workability of their own theory, it being analogous to a ship being navigated by the vote of its crew. It was, however, clearly being sponsored by the same conspiratorial entities extant since Voltaire and Weishaupt. So what was its real utility? Answer: It's no good for *running* a country already State Socialistic, but it might be very useful indeed for trashing a non-socialist country or regime, from whose fragmented pieces a socialist dictatorship might successfully emerge.

Accordingly, general strikes aimed at stopping the functioning of whole countries have been tried a number of times in the past, generally without success. Webster lists (p. 251) a half-dozen of these attempts: "...in Spain in 1874, in Belgium in 1902, in Sweden in 1909, in South Africa in 1911, in France in 1920, and in England in 1926." Thus we may regard Syndicalism, though it may involve rivers of blood and other mayhem, as nothing more than another means to the end of State Socialism. And, as we all know by now, such good ends justify any and all means, however illegal or barbaric.

In 1960 Nesta Webster, still living, updated the 1921 edition of her book, and gave directions to her editor to add newer subject matter which she merely outlined. Thus, the 1971 revision, reprinted in 1994, contains chapters on World War 2, the Chinese Communist Revolution, and the installation of communist regimes throughout Africa. These are interesting and constructive, but we shall confine the last subject of our review to Mrs. Webster's own words on the Bolshevik takeover of Russia, words which she herself slightly modified in 1960 from those appearing in her original 1921 edition.

In approaching her subject, Webster (pp. 274-7) follows the career of Lenin (née Vladimir Ilitch Ulianov). Born in 1870 into the family of a middle-class school official, his outlook on life was shaped by the execution of his elder brother, who had been involved in an assassination attempt on Emperor Alexander III. Lenin chose instead the way of words, and enrolled in Kazan University, obtaining a law degree and a thorough immersion in Marxist theory. In 1897 he was arrested for revolutionary work, and sent for three years to Siberia. Upon his release, he took his socialist endeavors abroad.

In 1898, while Lenin was out of circulation, the Russian Social Democratic Party was formed, not espousing the anarchy of Kropotkin and Bakunin, but rather the State Socialism of Marx, Babeuf, and Robespierre. By 1903, by which time Lenin had again re-surfaced, a meeting of the Party was held in London, where revolutionaries by strange British custom always seem permitted to foregather. At the meeting, the party split in two, the smaller part being the Mensheviks and the larger being the Bolsheviks, the latter being led by Lenin. In 1905, Lenin returned to Russia to take part in the abortive revolution of 1905, and stayed there for two more years strengthening the Bolshevik organization before retiring abroad.

When war broke out in 1914, Lenin offered his services to the German Foreign Office, and he was eventually accepted and assigned the task of demoralizing the French and Russian armies, i.e., aiding the German military. Thus Lenin and a number of other Bolsheviks could properly be thought of, from the outset of the war, as German agents. On March 15, 1917, Czar Nicholas II abdicated (for reasons not discussed); in April, Lenin was on his way in a sealed train from Switzerland to Russia; on May 5, Kerensky became War Minister of the First Provisional Government, and on July 25 the Prime Minister of the Second Provisional Government; in October, 1917, the Bolshevik Revolution put Lenin in power by force of arms, and Lenin's first official act was to dissolve the Duma, the duly elected constituent assembly. Kerensky escaped to Paris, but Nicholas II and his family were imprisoned and then secretly executed by the Bolsheviks on July 16, 1918.

Of critical importance is the matter of how Lenin was gotten to Russia. Much of the answer, says Webster, is contained in *The History of Bolshevism*, written in Russian by General A. E. Spiridovitch, and published in Paris in 1922. Winston Churchill, addressing the House of Commons in November, 1919, described Lenin as heading up in Russia "the leading spirits of a formidable sect, the most formidable sect in the world, of which he was the high priest and chief." Spiridovitch's book, however, reveals the adept of the sect who enlisted Lenin, and who saw to Lenin's transport to Russia. That adept went by the name Parvus, née Israel Lazarevitch Helphand, a Jew from the province of Minsk. Parvus in 1886 joined the German Social Democratic Party, soon became an agent for the Germans, did intelligence work for them, was sent to Constantinople where he laid the foundations of his fortune, and ultimately became absurdly wealthy.

Parvus, says Spiridovitch, was second only to Karl Marx in inspiring Lenin, *with whom Parvus was associated in 1901 in Munich* [our emphasis]. Spiridovitch then quotes from M. A. Landau's book *Lenin*: "It is not Lenin who started this great revolutionary idea, Sovietism, which has nearly conquered the world, it is Parvus – Parvus of the Sultan [Constantinople] and William II [Emperor of Germany, 1888-1918], Parvus the speculator, Parvus who profited by the war, Parvus who created the famous theory that from the Socialist point of view Germany had the right to victory because she possessed the most powerful proletariat and the most widely distributed industry." Webster wraps up:

"What was Parvus? Merely an agent of Imperial Germany? From evidence that cannot be given here he was found to be also an agent of the Illuminati, an active member of a secret society tracing its descent direct from Weishaupt. A fact that lends color to this is that when Parvus suggested to [General] Ludendorff and the German Chancellor, Bethmann-Holweg, that Lenin should be sent back to Russia in the sealed train, it was through Count von Brockdorff-Rantzau, then German Minister in Copenhagen, that the plan was passed on to them. The 'Illuminist' tendencies of this German nobleman became apparent five years later when, after the Germano-Bolshevik Treaty of Rapallo, he was sent to Moscow as German ambassador and endeared himself to the heads of the Soviet Government.

"That Lenin was a paid agent of Germany admits of no doubt whatever, and he himself did not deny it at a meeting of [the Russian Cabinet] in October 1918 when answering this accusation."

Conclusion: The "spontaneous" Russian Revolution was not spontaneous at all, but was planned in great detail for many years by international members of the Great Conspiracy. Then, in an historic blunder of monstrous proportions, it was executed with the financial and logistical support of the leaders of the German military, who were interested only in assuring that Russia's role in the World War was over. The Bolsheviks were the only real "winners" of World War 1, the major losers being the houses of Hohenzollern, Hapsburg, and Romanov, all of which were destroyed.

The Russian Revolution was, in a word, not a stand-alone unique event in history, but a continuation of the conspiratorial revolutionary activity which had dominated European history for nearly 200 years. This conclusion is further supported by examining the nature and the program of the Russian government that emerged. Webster declares (p. 272), "...the Russian Revolution from November 1917 onward was a *direct continuation of the French.* This was admitted by the Bolsheviks themselves, who repeatedly declared that the first French Revolution must be copied in every detail, and who from the outset took Marat and Robespierre and above all Babeuf as their models." A Russian imprisoned by the Bolsheviks wrote to Webster after reading her *French Revolution,* saying, "Your book seems to be the diary of our own revolution, so thoroughly

173

well have our apes learnt their roles.... Everybody in Russia knew by heart that bloody era, though many of the actors hardly knew how to sign their names!"

The system instituted by Lenin was not what the dictionary calls communism, meaning everything being held in common. It was also not Syndicalism, meaning workers running their own industries. Instead, Lenin wrote in May 1918, that Socialism "can only be reached by the development of State Capitalism, the careful organization of finance, control, and discipline amongst the workers." We have been calling their goal State Socialism, but simple slogans are simply incapable of meaningfully describing the substance of the program. The program was in fact that which was envisaged by Babeuf, and thus, in an historical sense, is properly labeled *Babouvisme*, as Webster herself pointed out in her chapter on Babeuf. She describes that program again (p. 280), this time in the words of Bucharin, one of Lenin's lieutenants:

"...In a Communist order all the wealth belongs not to individuals or classes, but to society as a whole.... The work is carried out jointly, according to a pre-arranged labor plan. A central bureau of statistics calculates how much is required to manufacture in a year: such and such a number of boots, trousers, sausages, blacking, wheat, cloth, and so on. It will also calculate that for this purpose such and such a number of men must work on the fields, ...the sausage work, ...the tailoring workshops, etc., and working-hands will be distributed accordingly. The whole of production is conducted on a strictly calculated and adjusted plan, on the basis of an exact estimate of all the machines, apparatus, all raw material, and all the labor power of the community." As Babeuf put it, this was to be "a simple affair of numbering things and people, a simple operation of calculations and combinations."

It may thus be seen, says Webster (pp. 281-4), that Bolshevism and Babouvisme are substantially identical, for the reason that both are founded on the same doctrines – those of Illuminism, to which Webster has presented evidence showing that both Babeuf and Lenin were adherents. We might expect, then, that Bolshevism would be embracing the rest of Weishaupt's program, and that is precisely what is found. Babeuf, Marx, and Lenin are as one in proclaiming what Webster calls "the five abolitions," namely of monarchy and all ordered government, of patriotism toward one's country, of property and inheritance, of all religion, and of marriage and even the concept of family. The collective farms, the government-run industries, the utter suppression of entrepreneurship, the communal education of children, the persecution of religion – all shout out to the world at large that the program designed so many years ago had come into being, and should be taken seriously. Russia had been turned into a gigantic slave state – a plantation – from which there was to be no freedom, no escape, no respite, and no concern for the well-being of its enslaved people. But the long range program encompasses even more. Webster quotes an "important follower of Lenin" as follows: "We have been at work for two years and you see what we have already done, but it will take us twelve years to destroy the civilization of the world."

Webster, not wishing to back away from controversy, notes the appearance in England in 1920 of the famous "Protocols of the Learned Elders of Zion." It was first published in Russia in 1902 by Sergye Nilus, and translated from the Russian by Victor Marsden, the one-time Russian correspondent for the London *Morning Post*. The Protocols purports to be a copy of a series of addresses made by a high-level Zionist to a Zionist assembly, outlining a Zionist conspiratorial plan to take over, by criminal subterfuge and the power of money, the whole of the civilized world. The plan bears a striking resemblance to the Illuminati programs we have discussed, which have been pressed on the world by Weishaupt, Babeuf, Marx, and Lenin.

The Protocols caused a sensation when they first appeared. They enjoyed a certain plausibility because of the predominance of Jews within the Bolshevik movement, which in 1920 was common knowledge. For example, a London Times article on March 29, 1919, stated (p. 285): "Of the twenty or thirty commissaries who provide the central machinery of the Bolshevik movement, not less than 75 percent are Jews.... If Lenin is the brains of the movement, the Jews provide the executive officers. Of the leading commissaries, Trotsky, Zinoviev, Kameneff, Stekloff, Sverdloff, Uritzky, Joffe, Rakovsky, Radek, Menjinsky, Larin, Bronski, Zaalkind, Volodarsky, Petroff, Litvinoff, Smirdovitch, and Vovrowsky are all of the Jewish race, while among the minor Soviet officials the number is legion." Russian Jews had on occasion even boasted of the fact. On April 12, 1919, the Kharkoff newspaper *The Communist* printed Mr. M. Cohan saying, "...without exaggeration, it may be said that the great Russian social revolution was indeed accomplished by the hands of the Jews.... In the committees and in Soviet organizations, as Commissars, the Jews are gallantly leading the masses of the Russian proletariat to victory...."

None of these facts constitute proof, however, of Jewish creation and directorship of the Great Conspiracy. Webster lists (p. 299) some of the cogent counter-arguments. Barruel and Robison, both of whom exhaustively studied the early movement, never mentioned such an influence, even when the possibility was suggested to them by others. Neither Weishaupt, Knigge, or any of the other early leading Illuminati were Jews, nor were the principle revolutionaries of France, nor were the conspirators of

Babeuf. In fact, Jews were specifically excluded from the lodges of the Illuminati (as were Jesuits) by Weishaupt's order. It was not until the mid-19th century that Jews were found taking the lead in the revolutionary movement, particularly in the First International. That leadership had been suggested somewhat earlier by the Jewish Benjamin Disraeli, who in his 1844 novel *Coningsby* had his Jewish hero Sidonia declare, "So you see, my dear Coningsby, that the world is governed by very different personages from what is imagined by those who are not behind the scenes."

A whole cottage industry has arisen seeking to trace the origin of the Protocols, which we can in no way add to. Nor do we wish to, for our ultimate proposed action plan, which we are slowly but surely moving toward, is in no way dependent upon the resolution of the Protocols controversy. There is one thing that we feel very confident about, and don't mind publicly stating: If the highest-most top man, if there is one single man, running the Great Conspiracy today happens to be Jewish, we feel highly confident that he is not running that job *in the name of or for the benefit of* the millions of rank and file Jews living today on this globe. When and if the Great Conspiracy wins their struggle, we believe that those rank and file Jews will find themselves just as fully enslaved as everyone else. Why so many Jews were drawn into the revolutionary movement from the mid-1800's onward is an interesting question, but, from our present point of view, entirely immaterial.

Webster finally leans back in her chair to consider the question, What are the techniques that the Conspiracy has used that have made it so successful in gaining adepts? From her lifetime of study, she boils it down to two labels: *Exploiting Grievances* and *Promising Power*. In the first category is to be found politicians, labor leaders, and recruiters for activist organizations, who promise to raise workers' wages and working conditions, to raise blacks to be economically equal to whites, to raise women to be economically equal to men, to raise homosexuals to be socially equal to heterosexuals, and/or to raise up any and all aggrieved persons or groups to be more nearly equal to their aggrievors. If sufficiently aggrieved, such persons can be aroused and activated such as to make them entirely impervious to reason, and to not see or care that their activator has a hidden purpose, perhaps of getting elected to a position of political authority enabling him to smooth the arrival of the Revolution.

The second category, Promising Power, is the prime motivation for luring entry of future leaders into the secret societies. As Weishaupt planned, members are all to preferentially help each other rather than outsiders whenever in a position to hand out a favor. Members are promised an easy road to wealth, so long as they do as they are told, including keeping the society's secrecy rules. They are led further and further into the realms of illegality, whence they are frozen into continued participation via the forces of blackmail and fear, including the fear of death. If they persist in constructive behavior, the carrot of future rulership of some portion of the Conspiracy will be offered. Since everyone harbors the notion that he is better qualified to rule than anyone else, the offer of power is extremely tempting.

Thus the supply to the Conspiracy of "liberal" writers, clergymen, reporters, politicians, government bureaucrats, teachers, school board members, news commentators, foreign diplomats, etc., etc., is facilitated by turning adepts into the needed arenas of action. How many of such people are currently under the discipline of a controlling entity? No one outside of such an entity can presently know, nor can most of those inside, since they are so well compartmented. These are facts with which any solution to the challenge of the secret societies must ultimately deal.

Webster finally notes her thoughts, and her editor adds his newer contributions, concerning the "watering down" of religion via the "Christian Socialism" of certain prominent Protestant clergy, and similar delusions observable within the Catholic clergy. Her editor adds (p. 306), "With the end of the Second World War there commenced a 'progressive' movement within the Catholic Church itself, and in spite of the many warnings given by the Popes against Freemasonry, a strongly pro-Masonic atmosphere began to make itself felt. Vicomte Leon de Poncins in his work *Freemasonry and the Vatican* says: 'There is at present in Catholic circles a constant, subtle, and determined campaign in favor of Freemasonry. It is directed by the progressive brigade, currently enjoying so great an influence in France, and is assisted by pressures (whether open or secret) on the part of a considerable number of the clergy – pressures also exerted by the Catholic Press, and even by prelates among the French bishops and cardinals.'"

These thoughts of course bring back to mind the Weishaupt-Nubius "Permanent Instruction" discussed by Dillon (p. 140, supra). Instead of looking more deeply into these relatively modern events, however, our purpose is better advanced by following Webster's strong urge to trace the origins of the secret societies. Just three years after the publication of *World Revolution*, she thus produced yet another highly valuable book, which we shall next review.

Chapter 7

"SECRET SOCIETIES AND SUBVERSIVE MOVEMENTS"

(By Nesta. H. Webster, pub. 1924. Pub. 1994 by A&B Publishers Group, 1000 Atlantic Ave., Brooklyn, NY 11238. Available from Omni Publications, PO Box 900566, Palmdale, CA 93590, 805-274-2240, or from Amazon.com, PO Box 81410, Seattle, WA 98108, or www.amazon.com.)

Webster's approach was to do her research and then lay it out to her readers in historically chronological order. We will follow her order from pre-Christian times up through the Knights Templar, after which she jumps to the 18th century, a period which Barruel covers in rather greater detail. But Webster has a number of very important observations to make concerning the early period up to and through the Crusades, which we will find of great value in our effort to identify all the major pieces of the puzzle.

As Webster develops, the structure of the secret societies apparent to us today was not conceived in the "Western Civilization" of Europe, but rather in the ancient countries of the East: Egypt, Babylon, Syria, and Persia. The wealthy rulers of those lands generally declared themselves to be the privileged possessors of the divine truths regarding the past, present, and hereafter, and managed to maintain themselves in power by doling out those truths sparingly to their subjects. The existence of "secret truths" was a concept understood by all.

Schisms were bound to occur, and did, frequently by parties who were, in reality, seeking after political or ecclesiastical power rather than divine or metaphysical truth. It was in such power struggles that secret societies really came into their own. And whether or not today's secret societies still retain a religious component, there can be no doubt that in the historical past, religious differences were the dominant causality. The primary religions affecting our present were those of the Jews, the Christians, and the Muslims, i.e., Judaism, Christianity, and Islam, all of which have undergone schisms of their own. Webster starts by dealing with the oldest of these groups: the Jews.

The religious doctrines of even this oldest group were not all original with them. Monotheism, for example, was apparently a common belief among the inner circle of priests in many ancient countries, specifically including Egypt. Even the belief in a Triune God was said to be held among the privileged few, and Webster (p. 5) quotes a source who claims that priests in such as Egypt, Chaldea [now Iraq], India, and China "kept it a profound secret and imparted it only to a few select among those initiated in the sacred mysteries." While the early existence of this latter belief may lack historically acceptable proof, the existence of monotheism in Egypt prior to the time of Moses is certain.

Moses in turn became learned in the Mysteries of the Egyptians, and drew from them (pp. 6-7) "a part of the oral tradition that was handed down through the leaders of the Israelites." Webster then identifies, from Jewish sources, the several written documents which were ultimately created to record and preserve that oral tradition. There are two primary documents: the Talmud and the Cabala. Each of these is comprised of two parts, the Talmud containing the Mischna and the Gemara, and the Cabala containing the Sepher Yetzirah ("Book of the Creation") and the Sepher-Ha-Zohar ("Book of Light").

The earliest written form of the Talmud appeared in the 2nd or 3rd century A.D., and was called the Mischna. A commentary called the Gemara appeared somewhat later, and the two were combined into what was called the Jerusalem Talmud. It underwent further revisions from the 3rd through the 5th century, producing what is called the Babylonian Talmud, the version in use today. The Talmud relates mainly to rules and regulations concerned with everyday living, such as the making of contracts, the observance of religious proprieties, etc., sometimes in excruciating detail (e.g., whether a louse or a flea may be killed on the Sabbath – the first being allowed, the second being a deadly sin).

The Cabala (sometimes spelled with a *k*, with two *l*'s, and/or with an ending *h*) is quite different. The Hebrew word Cabala signifies "a doctrine orally received," and the two parts of the Cabala are where the theosophical doctrines of the Israelites are to be found. The Sepher Yetzirah, says Webster (p. 7), contains a monologue attributed to Abraham in which, by a process of contemplating all that is around him, "he ultimately arrives at the conclusion of the unity of God." The content of the book is obscure, complex, and almost certainly of extreme antiquity. Its written form may have appeared as early as the 6th century B.C., but surely before the Talmud, which contains references to both the Yetzirah and the Zohar. The Yetzirah is also referred to as the "Book of Abraham" in the Koran, the holy book of Islam, extant in the 7th century A.D.

The Zohar is the part of the Cabala on which Webster fixes her attention. The Talmud relates that the Zohar was reduced to writing in the early Christian era by Rabbi Simon ben Jochai, working from the oral tradition known to him, the only form in which the Zohar then existed. The first written version definitely known to have appeared did so only in the 13th century, having been written by the Spanish Jew Moses de Leon. Some Jewish sources claim that Moses de Leon composed it himself; others claim that he found and reproduced the document of Simon ben Jochai. Webster looks at all the evidence she could uncover, and concludes that Moses de Leon must have worked with documents which greatly preceded the 13th century, and in fact (p. 9), "...the main ideas of the Zohar find confirmation in the Talmud." As the Zohar also deals with the fact of Christianity, at least those parts of it must have been written after the life of Christ. The "early Christian era" of Simon ben Jochai, prior to the completion of the Babylonian Talmud, therefore seems to define a plausible date for the original writing of the material which later appeared in the 13th century Zohar.

That actual content of the Zohar, however, is the real attention-stopper. Webster explains (p. 12): "The modern Jewish Cabala presents a dual aspect: theoretical and practical, the former concerned with theosophical speculations, the latter with magical practices. It would be impossible here to give an [adequate] idea of Cabalistic theosophy with its extraordinary imaginings on the Sephiroths, the attributes and functions of good and bad angels, dissertations on the nature of demons, and minute details on the appearance of God under the name of the Ancient of Ancients, from whose head 400,000 worlds receive the light. 'The length of this face [says the Zohar] from the top of the head is three hundred and seventy times ten thousand worlds....' The description of... this gigantic countenance occupies a large place in the Zoharic treatise Idra Raba."

Webster continues: "According to the Cabala, every letter in the Scriptures contains a mystery to be solved only by the initiated. By means of this system of interpretation, passages of the Old Testament are shown to bear meanings totally unapparent to the ordinary reader. [Webster then gives examples, in which the stories of Noah, Jonah, and Elisha are detailed and travestied, to use Webster's terms.] In the practical Cabala, this method of 'decoding' is reduced to a theurgic or magical system in which the healing of diseases plays an important part, and is effected by means of the mystical arrangement of numbers and letters, by the pronunciation of the Ineffable Name, by the use of amulets and talismans, or by compounds supposed to contain occult properties."

This use of "divine magic" did not originate with the Jews, but "appears to have originated in Chaldea," says Webster, giving the Jewish Encyclopedia as her reference. After its inclusion in the Cabala, it "became the particular practice of Jewish miracle workers." However, there are several other elements of their belief system which were borrowed from earlier cultures.

First, the ancient Egyptians believed themselves to be "the peculiar people specially loved by the gods," clearly an antecedent to the Chosen People theory at the foundation of Cabalistic and Talmudic writings. But those writings went further, claiming for the Jews the *exclusive* enjoyment of divine favor. All non-Jews were destined for Hell, and were even denied human attributes.

Second, other cultures believed in a Man-God Redeemer who would present himself as the teacher and liberator of fallen humans who had lived in an earlier Golden Age free of care and evil. One source is quoted, "[This] tradition of a Man-God... was constantly taught amongst all the enlightened nations of the globe.... The sacred and mythological traditions of earlier times had spread throughout all Asia the belief in a great Mediator who was to come, of a future Savior, King, God, Conqueror, and Legislator who would bring back the Golden Age to earth and deliver men from the empire of evil."

Third, even the conditions surrounding the appearance of the Messiah were similarly proclaimed by Zoroastrians of Persia. Webster's source (Drach) shows that "five hundred years before Christ, Zerdascht, the leader of the

Zoroastrians, predicted the coming of the Messiah, at whose birth a star would appear. He also told his disciples that the Messiah would be born of a Virgin, that they would be the first to hear of Him, and that they should bring Him gifts." Drach avers that the same tradition was taught in the ancient synagogue, and writes, "This oral doctrine, which is the Cabala, had for its object the most sublime truths of the Faith which it brought back incessantly to the promised Redeemer, the foundation of the whole system of the ancient tradition."

Lastly, and perhaps surprisingly, the doctrine of the Trinity was incorporated. Webster's sources state (p. 15): "Whoever has familiarized himself with that which was taught by the ancient doctors of the Synagogue... knows that the Trinity in one God was a truth admitted amongst them from the earliest times." And again: "It is incontestable that the Zohar makes allusions to the beliefs in the Trinity and the Incarnation." And more: "A great part of the explanation given in the writings of the Cabalists resembles in a surprising manner the highest truths of Christianity." The Jewish Encyclopedia notes that what appears to be Christian in the Cabala is actually ancient esoteric doctrine, apparently affirming that "the ancient secret tradition was in harmony with Christian teaching," says Webster.

But by late pre-Christian times, says Webster, "the philosophy of the earlier sages was narrowed down to suit the exclusive system of the Jewish hierarchy, and the ancient hope of a Redeemer who should restore Man to the state of felicity he had lost at the Fall was transformed into the idea of salvation for the Jews alone under the aegis of a triumphant and even avenging Messiah. It is this Messianic dream, perpetuated in the modern Cabala, which nineteen hundred years ago the advent of Christ on earth came to disturb."

SECRECY OR FREEDOM?

Jesus' coming was more of a collision than a disturbance. Lo, after ages of waiting, the Redeemer was here! But, says Webster (p. 17), "it was not to the mighty in Israel, to the High Priests and the Scribes, that His birth was announced, but to humble shepherds watching their flocks by night." The High Priests had not sought 'a light to lighten the Gentiles' but rather the fulfillment of the expected exaltation of the Chosen People. Further, Christ proclaimed his divine message directly to the poor and humble, where it was largely accepted, but it was rejected by the High priests. Christ thereupon regaled the High Priests in such words as: "Woe unto you, Scribes and Pharisees, hypocrites! for ye neither go in yourselves, neither suffer ye them that are entering to go in." Drach interprets these words to mean that the Priests were being accused of concealing from the common people "the traditional explanation of the sacred books by means of which they would have been able to recognize the Messiah in the person of Jesus Christ." The priests battled back, and won the tactical battle by maneuvering Pilate and the people into condemning Jesus to die by crucifixion.

Christianity was thus brought into the world in the midst of strenuous conflict with the priestly leaders of Judaism. Christ, notes Webster, had "put down the mighty from their seats, and exalted them of low degree." He was therefore "doubly hateful to the Jewish hierarchy in that he attacked the privilege of the race to which they belonged by throwing open the door [of salvation] to all mankind, and the privilege of the caste to which they belonged by revealing sacred doctrines to the profane and destroying their claim to exclusive knowledge."

Not too surprisingly, the subsequent priestly writings in the Cabala and the early editions of the Talmud were later found to contain "abominable calumnies on Christ and Christianity." One researcher says that in these writings,

186

"Our Lord and Savior is [described as] 'a fool,' 'the leper,' 'the deceiver of Israel,' etc. Efforts were made to prove that He is the son of Joseph Pandira before his marriage with Mary. His miracles are attributed to sorcery, the secret of which He brought in a slit in His flesh out of Egypt. He is said to have been first stoned and then hanged on the eve of the Passover. His disciples are called heretics and opprobrious names. They are accused of immoral practices, and the New Testament is called a sinful book. The references to these subjects manifest the most bitter aversion and hatred."

Reactions against such calumnies occurred within both Christianity and Judaism. Because of the Christian reaction, attempts were made to "clean up" the Talmud by deleting or softening the most objectionable passages. As a result, only expurgated versions are available in English or French (p. 19), and unlike the sacred books of most other religions, "the book that forms the foundation of modern Judaism is closed to the general public." Within Judaism, many Rabbis and scholars have rejected the written Cabala (p. 9), with one (Theodore Reinach) declaring the Cabala to be "a subtle poison which enters into the veins of Judaism and wholly infests it." Another describes it as "one of the worst aberrations of the human mind." A leading anti-Cabalist (Graetz) leads the faction declaring the Zohar to be the 13th century work of Moses de Leon, apparently in order to support his (Graetz's) claim that the Cabala is at variance with orthodox Judaism, and so the ancient priestly orthodoxy could not have been responsible for writing the Cabala. Other Jewish writers, however, embrace rather than distance themselves from the Cabala. One (Adolphe Franck) describes the Cabala as "the heart and life of Judaism." A (non-Jewish) researcher writes, "The greater number of the most eminent Rabbis of the 17th and 18th centuries believed firmly in the sacredness of the Zohar and the infallibility of its teaching."

At about the time of the birth of Christianity, which may be seen as the greatest of all the schisms of Judaism, there appeared also the first instances of cultish secrecy impacting our "West," and were aimed primarily at the new religion. The first notable instance involves the Essenes, an ascetic Jewish sect extant from the 1st century B.C. to the 2nd century A.D. They owned their worldly goods in common, and thus practiced a peaceful communistic existence, as did later religious orders. They pre-dated Christianity, and had no negative interaction with it. In their theosophy they were Cabalistic, though of an early kind "uncontaminated by the anti-Christian strain introduced into it by the Rabbi's after the death of Christ," says Webster (p. 27). Their significance to our study is that they in fact constituted one of the very earliest of what we have come to call a secret society. I.e., the cult contained four degrees of initiation, and its members were "bound by terrible oaths not to divulge the sacred mysteries confided to them," which were in fact the secret Jewish traditions now known as the Cabala.

The next step upward for secret societies concerned the Gnostics. This was a group which first clearly appeared in the 2nd century A.D., and was "extinct by the sixth century," says our encyclopedia. It's influence went much further, however. Its belief structure linked Christianity with earlier faiths, aimed at creating "a sort of universal religion containing the divine elements of all," says Webster. She notes that the Jewish Cabala was similarly formed from a number of heterogeneous sources, and proceeds with her evidences (pp. 28-29) that Gnosticism was in fact a product of Jewish Cabalism, and that the object was to inject Cabalistic mysticism and magic into Christianity. "Indeed," she says, "the man generally recognized as the founder of

Gnosticism, a Jew commonly known as Simon Magus, was not only a Cabalist mystic but avowedly a magician, who... instituted a priesthood of the Mysteries, and practiced occult arts and exorcisms."

Gnosticism was therefore a perversion of Christianity, the worst elements of which were the profanation of the Christian mysteries leading to the black magic practiced in the Middle Ages, and the actual glorification of evil, practiced by Ophites and Cainites, the incidence of which still plagues our society today. These latter sects, Webster notes, were enemies not only of Christianity, but also of orthodox Judaism, against which their hatred was especially directed. Another Gnostic sect, the Carpocratians, rejected all revealed religion, and essentially *deified humanity* (Webster's term), anticipating the humanist doctrines (e.g., "secular humanism") of the modern secret societies and of today's Socialists.

Various sects of the Gnostics claimed to possess the "true" version of one or another of the Gospels, and set about to pick the various Gospels apart. The Gnostics thus reduced the perversion of Christianity to a system by means of "binding men together into sects, working under the guise of enlightenment, in order to obscure all recognized ideas of morality and religion." One such sect, the Valentinians, professed to hold secret doctrines superior to the writings of the apostles, restricted that knowledge to only the sect's highest elites, communicated by secret symbols and emblems, and adhered to the secret rites and trials of certain predecessor societies. They thus sought a return to the system of exclusive ownership of secret mysteries by ecclesiastical elites, such as was previously enjoyed by the Scribes and Pharisees who were denounced by Christ, that system being the very antithesis of what Christ sought to bring to humanity.

The parallels between the modus operandi of the Gnostics and that of the 18th century Masons and Illuminati could not be more obvious. As we recorded in our first chapter, Barruel noted that Weishaupt had ordered his Scotch Knights to especially study the doctrines of the ancient Gnostics (and also of the Manicheans, our next topic), in their preparation for elevation to the degree of Epopt, or Priest of Illuminism. We can now easily understand why.

We next turn, with Webster, to the Manicheans of Persia. Its founder, Curbicus (or Cubricus, or Corbicius), later taking the name Manes, was born in Babylonia in about 216 A.D., thus giving Manicheanism its start in the 3rd century A.D., a century or so later then Gnosticism. Barruel gives a somewhat fuller description of the life of Manes and the birth of his movement, but Webster adds a number of significant details. Manes' doctrines, she says, were borrowed from a combination of Zoroastrian, Christian, and Gnostic ideas, from which he created and began to teach his own philosophic system.

(Our encyclopedia says that Zoroaster, or Zarathustra, lived in Persia in about 1000 B.C., and created the national religion of Persia, the followers of which are still today known as Parsees. The religion taught the existence of one god who created the world, the existence of heaven and hell, immortality, a day of judgment, the resurrection of the body, and the coming of a Messiah. The supreme being created two entities, Ormuzd and Ahriman, the sources of all good and all evil, respectively. The religion was forcibly replaced by Mohammedanism upon its arrival in the 7th century A.D.)

Webster says that Zoroastrianism became "so perverted and mingled with Cabalistic superstitions" that it was rejected by both Persian priests and our Christian Fathers. But Manes carried the perversion even farther, declaring (p. 33) that "all matter is absolute evil, the principle of evil is eternal, humanity itself is of Satanic origin, and the first human beings, Adam and Eve, are represented as the offspring of devils." Some of these same notions, says Webster, are to be found in the Jewish Cabala, where it is said (p. 34) "that Adam... cohabited with female devils whilst Eve consoled herself with male devils, so that whole races of demons were born into the world."

The Manichean perversions and demonology, whether obtained from Persian Cabalized Zoroastrianism, or directly from Jewish Cabalism, or from both, lived on for many centuries, leading to the placation of the powers of darkness practiced by, among others, the Paulicians of the 7th century and the Bogomils of the 12th century. Manichean doctrines were also adhered to by the Cathari (of the 11th to 13th centuries), and particularly by the Cathari's western branch, called the Albigenses, both of which names were mentioned by Barruel. The lower class of Albigeous initiates, constituting the bulk of the sect, gave themselves up, says Webster (p. 75), "to every vice, to usury, brigandage, and perjury, and whilst describing marriage as prostitution, condoned incest and all forms of license."

The Manichean perversions obviously also made their way into the rites and practices of Freemasonry. Recall that one of the three doctrinal classes into which Barruel divided Masonry was the Cabalistic (the others being the Hermetic and the Eclectic), the Cabalistic being characterized by a belief system involving dual deities of Good and Evil, each accompanied by an army of either good or bad spirits (angels or devils). The Masons also picked up the Manicheans' symbolism of the martyring of Manes, their organizational secrecy, their successive degrees, their acceptance of immoral principles, their goals of "Liberty and Equality," their secret signs and grips, and even their demand for the abolition of *all* laws, i.e., producing anarchy, as has been described by Barruel.

Webster next turns to Islam. That faith was started by the Prophet Mohammed, who lived from 570 A.D. to 632 A.D. Dogmas of the faith, summarized in our trusty encyclopedia, include belief in Allah (the sole creator and Lord of the Universe), belief in his angels (impeccable beings created of light), belief in good and evil genies (created of smokeless fire, but lacking perpetual life), belief in God's prophets and apostles (including Adam, Noah, Abraham, Moses, Jesus, and the greatest of all, Mohammed), and finally belief in the Holy Scriptures revealed to those prophets, the Koran being the most important. Revelations made to Mohammed during his lifetime, coming from the angel Gabriel, the Holy Ghost, and/or Allah himself, were dictated to a scribe, and following Mohammed's death were compiled into the Koran by Abu Bakr, who became in 632 the first orthodox Caliph, the title given to the temporal and spiritual head of Islam.

The religion started by Mohammed dethroned Persian Zoroastrianism in bloody conflict, but was also itself subject to an almost immediate major schism. One faction of Islam (the Sunnis) advocated the "orthodox" faith and manners contained in the "Sunna," which had been written into the Koran by the first Caliphs; the other (the Shiites) supported the blood line of the Prophet. That split still exists today. The latter line was in turn split after several generations, with the "Ismaili" branch of the Shiites captured in about 872 by one Abdullah ibn Maymun. This man, says Webster (p. 37), was "an intriguer of extraordinary subtlety," who altered the branch into one not just unorthodox, but actually subversive of Islam and, in fact, of all religious belief. He had been brought up by his learned and free-thinking father in the bosom of Gnostic Dualism, and like his father became a pure materialist. His pretended

192

adherence to Shiism was merely a ploy to facilitate his rise to the leadership of the sect.

The immense importance of this man, says Webster, lay in the incomparable skill with which he created and used a secret society to attain his ends. His organization was known as the Batinis, having seven degrees of initiates. The methodology he developed was precisely that later used by Weishaupt in organizing the Illuminati. Webster defines that basic system (p. 38) as "the setting in motion of a vast number of people and making them work in a cause unknown to them." She quotes the description of the project given by Reinhart Dozy in his *Spanish Islam* (1913):

"[Maymun sought] to link together into one body the vanquished and the conquerors; to unite in the form of a vast secret society, with many degrees of initiation, freethinkers – who regard religion only as a curb for the people – and bigots of all sects; to make tools of believers in order *to give power* (our emphasis) to skeptics; …to build up a party, numerous, compact, and disciplined, which in due time would give the throne, if not to himself, at least to his descendants. Such was Abdullah ibn Maymun's general aim…. The means which he adopted were devised with diabolical cunning….

"It was not among the Shiites that he sought his true supporters, but among… the Manicheans… and the students of Greek philosophy; on the last alone could he rely; to them alone could he gradually unfold the final mystery, and reveal that Imams [infallible Shiite successors of Mohammed], religions, and morality were nothing but an imposture and an absurdity. The rest of mankind… were incapable of understanding such doctrines. But to gain his end, he by no means disdained their aid; on the contrary, he solicited it, but he took care to initiate devout and lowly souls into only the [lowest] grades of the sect. His missionaries, [whose] first duty was to conceal their true sentiments and adapt themselves to the views of their [listeners], appeared in many guises.... They won over the ignorant vulgar with feats of legerdemain which passed for miracles.... In the presence of the devout, they assumed the mask of virtue and piety. With mystics they were mystical.... By means such as these, the extraordinary result was brought about that a multitude of men of diverse beliefs were all working together for an object known only to a few of them...."

Thus was the "technology" of secret societies greatly advanced. Two successor branches of the Batinis followed almost immediately, the Karmathites (in 892) and the Fatimites (in 909), existing side by side for about 100 years. The Karmathites were so named from an initiate of the Batinis named Karmath, who attracted followers by first inducing them to transfer their moneys to him, then, when much impoverished, to accept the notion of abolishing all private property and establishing a system of all goods and wives to be held in common (i.e., communism and free love), and finally to discard all the restraints of piety and religion, and to revel in the pillaging of the goods and the blood of their adversaries. They "rapidly became a band of brigands," says Webster (p. 39), "massacring all those who opposed them, and spreading terror throughout all the surrounding districts." The plan of Abdullah ibn Maymun of taking over from within without overt violence was thus discarded in favor of a wild lust for power by conquest. The sect came to dominate a large section of Arabia, including the holy city of Mecca, for about a century before it was itself extinguished by the fire and sword of the counterrevolution which their violence inevitably provoked. We would add our note that Robespierre and his cohorts did not learn well from this bit of history, and were, like the Karmathites, physically extinguished, though their ideas, in both cases, lived on.

The Fatimites, who were named after Mohammed's daughter Fatima, established themselves in Egypt, and stayed more in tune with the fundamentals of the Batinis. Six successive Fatimite caliphs of the blood line of Abdullah ibn Maymun led to Caliph Hakim, who in the year 1004 founded the Dar ul Hikmat, or House of Knowledge, known more familiarly as the Grand Lodge of Cairo. Under the direction of Hakim, two more degrees were added to the seven of Abdullah ibn Maymun, the first four being used to lure adepts toward the higher secrets by various religious misrepresentations, and the last five being used to reverse course and to tear down all revealed religion in its entirety. One of Webster's sources, writing in 1887, notes that the society's use of "Insinuating Brothers" for enlisting and initiating adepts was precisely the same as was later used by Weishaupt. Another source (Joseph von Hammer, *The History of the Assassins,* Eng. trans., 1835) speaks as follows of Hakim's secret Fatimite lodge (pp. 42-43):

"To believe nothing and to dare all was, in two words, the sum of this system, which annihilated every principle of religion and morality, and had no other object than to execute ambitious designs with suitable ministers.... [Such a system has] no other aim than *the gratification of an insatiable lust for domination,* instead of seeking the highest of human objects, [and will] precipitate itself into the abyss, and mangling itself, [be] buried amidst the ruins of thrones and altars, the wreck of national happiness, and the universal execration of mankind." The emphasis above is our own, as the attributed motivation is identical to that voiced by a famous socialist author, to whose views on 20th century efforts to dominate the world we devoted a whole chapter of our earlier book (Chapter 6 of *How The World Really Works*).

One successor sect to that of the Fatimites in Cairo was known as the Druses, whose uniqueness involved the worship of its originator, the Caliph Hakim. Remnants of the sect are still found in and about Lebanon, and show a striking resemblance to Freemasonry, particularly in their three common degrees and their use of signs, passwords, and such other devices to assure the secrecy of their grand mysteries.

A second successor sect had a much greater impact on subsequent human history, however. It was the sect known as the Assassins, formed by the Persian Hasan Saba in about 1090 A.D. and remaining politically powerful until about 1250. Hasan Saba was born into high political circles and was well-educated, having Omar Khayyam as a schoolmate. He vacillated between Sunniism and the Shiism of his father, and ended up rejecting both, fleeing his offices and titles, and establishing his own sect on the southern shores of the Caspian Sea. The sect used hashish to ensnare recruits, and came to be called the Hashishiyin, from which the word assassin is derived. Hasan organized the sect in precisely the manner of the secret societies of his Fatimite predecessors, but with the terrible addition of utilizing wholesale assassination to eliminate those who opposed him. Thus, the sect, in conformance with its public image, demanded strict adherence to Islam of its recruits, who were then gradually turned away from all religion and morals to do the secret work of the sect, which was nothing more than attaining the secular ends of its hidden leadership, to gain which any and all means were justified.

As Webster's source Joseph von Hammer put it, "Opinions are powerless, so long as they only confuse the brain without arming the hand.... It is nothing to the ambitious man what [his followers] believe, but it is everything to know how he may turn them for the execution of his projects." Webster herself adds (pp. 45-46) that "it was not mere theory, but the method of enlisting dupes and placing weapons in their hands that brought about the 'Terror' of the

Assassins six centuries before that of their spiritual descendants, the Jacobins of 1793." Lenin put it even more brusquely: "Revolutions are made out of the barrel of a gun," as he proved by his rout of Kerensky in 1917.

As von Hammer describes, a virtual Reign of Terror was brought to an immense region throughout the East. The Assassins "spread themselves in troops over the whole of Asia.... In the annals of the Assassins is found the chronological enumeration of celebrated men of all nations who have fallen the victims of the Ismailis, to the joy of their murderers and the sorrow of the world." However, the indulgence of the leadership in blood lust inevitably recoiled on their own heads, and assassination of its leaders by their own sons became the common method of succession, until the sect was finally wiped out by a Mongol invasion in 1250. Its methodology survived into the modern secret societies, however, showing up, for example, in the indoctrination of Weishaupt's Kadosch adepts, who were taught that assassination is the proper end of Princes and Priests everywhere; its similar promotion by Mazzini, the vigorous Carbonari activist who favored assassinating whomever he considered to be an enemy; and the actual 19th and 20th century usage of assassination, which was to some degree enumerated by Webster in her *World Revolution*, which we reviewed in our previous chapter.

As Webster puts it (p. 48), "The sect of Hasan Saba was the supreme model on which all systems of organized murder working through fanaticism, such as the Carbonari and the Irish Republican Brotherhood, were based; and the signs, the symbols, [and] the initiations of the Grand Lodge of Cairo formed the groundwork for the great secret societies of Europe. [But] how came this system to be transported to the West?" She proceeds to answer her own question by looking to the Crusades and the Knights Templar.

197

The First Crusade started in 1096, six years after the formation of the Assassins, and ended victoriously with the capture of Jerusalem in 1099. Nineteen years later, the Knights Templar was formed, with the purpose of protecting Christian pilgrims visiting Jerusalem. (In Chapter 1 we reviewed Barruel's findings on the history of the Templars, which the reader might review at this point. See p. 26 ff.) Whereas Barruel concluded that the Templar apostasies were derived from the Cathari, Albigenses, Begards, etc., who were generally sprung from Manichean and Gnostic sources, Webster identifies a very important additional path via the Assassins, with whom the Crusaders were in contact during the bulk of the period of the Crusades, and from whom the enthusiasm for political assassination arose. One of her sources (Dr. F. W. Bussell, D.D.) wrote that the Templars indisputably had "long and important dealings [with the Assassins], and were therefore suspected (not unfairly) of imbibing their precepts and following their principles."

The Templars, of course, first encountered the Assassins as enemies, but soon picked up from them not only the organizational precepts of the Eastern secret societies (unknown leaders and goals, and multiple degrees, starting as innocent, moral, and open, and ending as guilty, immoral, and secret), but also, within the secret upper levels, the apostasy and secularism common to the Assassins and their Fatimite predecessors. That secularism, apparent in the Assassins' drive for power and wealth via murder and plunder, may have been the source of the corruption which led the Templars down a similar path toward the renunciation of their vows of poverty, their growth into a rich and powerful body, and their spread by the end of the 12th century over the bulk of Europe. A Masonic writer in a 1780 book put it (pp. 49-50):

"The [Crusades] became for them (the Templars) only the opportunity for booty and aggrandizement. [Their motives became clear] when they were seen to enrich themselves even with the spoils of their confederates, to increase their credit by the extent of the new possessions they had acquired, to carry arrogance to the point of rivaling crowned princes in pomp and grandeur, to refuse their aid against the enemies of the faith, ...and finally to ally themselves with that horrible and sanguinary prince named the Old Man of the Mountain, Prince of the Assassins."

The French King, Philip le Bel, did not envy the Templar wealth, says Webster (p. 60), put did fear the power that such wealth conferred. The Templars "constituted an *imperium in imperio* that threatened not only the royal authority but the whole social system." A 1922 writer described the Templar power as follows: "As the Templars had houses in all countries, they practiced the financial operations of the international banks of our times; they were acquainted with letters of change, [and] orders payable at sight; they instituted dividends and annuities on deposited capital, advanced funds, lent on credit, controlled private accounts, [and] undertook to raise taxes for the lay and ecclesiastical seigneurs." In a word, Philip saw them as a threat to society, as no laws existed to protect individuals from such overweening financial power, other than the existence of the feudal system itself. Thus Philip acted, and the Knights Templar were outlawed and abolished.

Webster then defines a remarkably helpful classification of all these early sects and societies. She says (p. 74) that "from very early times, occult sects had existed for two purposes – esoteric and political." The first group, having secret doctrines privy only to a select few, included such as the Gnostics, the Manicheans, the early Ismailis, the Paulicians, the Bogomils, the Cathari, and the Luciferians. Later, Voltaire's "Philosophers" might be included. The second group, which combined secrecy and occultism with *the political aim of domination*, included the later Ismailis, the Karmathites, the Fatimites, the Assassins, the Templars, the later Freemasons, and, of course, the Illuminati and its progeny, including the Carbonari, the International, the Bolsheviks, and more modern societies yet to be named. This second group of course makes use of the basic common doctrine of the first (the destruction of all religion and religion-based morality) in order to facilitate the corruption of target populations, dissolve their societal foundations, and thereby ease the task of conquest, which is the ultimate goal.

Webster's enumeration of the historical sects, which we have modestly supplemented, has enabled us – at least those of us who have struggled to understand who or what is driving the World Revolution – to begin to grasp a fundamental modus operandi which has been at work over the centuries, and is continuing to this present day. It is *not* that there has existed some single group which has been secretly chiseling away at all the societies of the world for all these past centuries, the identity of which has remained hidden despite our best efforts. To the contrary, the identity of the groups seeking political control and domination via the mechanism of secret societies does *not* appear to have been controlled by any single central intelligence, but has instead been subject to sporadic death and replacement as old conspiracies are obliterated and newer ones are born. A sequence such as Manicheans, Assassins, Templars, and Illuminati does not imply a 1500-year unified plan, but rather the accidental creation of a sequence of individual societies driven by man's fatal flaw: that Power Corrupts (a flaw with which our U.S. Constitution has specifically tried to deal).

On the other hand, it is quite clear that secret society mechanics *have* been developed with some continuity over a period of centuries, always being gradually improved as newer conspiratorial groups have studied the past to learn what has worked best, and then sought to make even further improvements. The methodology of the secret societies for accomplishing desired actions has been studied, honed, and finely tuned, and is operating today as smoothly as a Stradivarius violin. That methodology is crucial to today's conspirators, and will ultimately be the target of our efforts, no matter *who* is pulling the strings at the apex of the Grand Conspiracy.

As we stated at the beginning of this chapter, we will not follow Webster's discourses in the eras following that of the Templars, as the first several chapters of her book contribute the most to our theme. We make one exception, however, for the young Professor Weishaupt, who Webster also believes did not produce his masterpiece out of thin air. Webster says (p. 202) that, while Illuminati initiates are decorated with many of the same titles used in ancient sects, Weishaupt's theories appear to be unrelated to those of the ancients. She continues:

"The more we penetrate into his system, the more apparent it becomes that all the formulas he employs which derive from any religious source – whether Persian, Egyptian, or Christian – merely serve to disguise a purely material purpose, a plan for destroying the existing order of society. Thus all that was really ancient in Illuminism was the destructive spirit which animated it and the method of organization it had imported from the East. Illuminism therefore marks an entirely new departure [i.e., beginning] in the history of European secret societies. Weishaupt himself indicates this as one of the great secrets of the Order. 'Above all,' he writes to Cato (née Zwack), 'guard the origin and the novelty of [our Order] in the most careful way.' He says again, 'The greatest mystery [i.e., secret] must be that the thing is new; the fewer who know this, the better.'"

Weishaupt's strategy, of course, is to convince his adepts that his "mysteries" stem purely from the wisdom of the ancients, and he must never let them suspect that those mysteries may have been born in the busy mind of a young professor. Though Weishaupt does tell his highest level adepts that he invented the whole thing, such a unilateral creation appears to Webster to be impossible, as it does to us (p. 60, supra). She says (p. 203), "It would therefore appear possible that Weishaupt, although undoubtedly a man of immense organizing capacity and endowed with extraordinary subtlety, was not in reality the sole author of Illuminism, but [was] one of a group, which, recognizing his talents and the value of his untiring activity, placed the direction in his hands." She then indulges in a speculative effort to identify such a group. For our purpose, however, those speculations are immaterial, and we therefore next turn to some of the little-known facts about the Protestant Reformation of the 16th century, about two centuries after the Knights Templar was abolished.

Chapter 8

"PHILIP II"

(By William Thomas Walsh, pub. 1937 by Sheed & Ward, Inc., New York. Reprinted 1987 by Tan Books and Publishers, Inc., PO Box 424, Rockford, IL 61105, 800-437-5876, or www.tanbooks.com.)

This is a magnificent 770-page biography which tells the story of 16th-century Europe as seen through the eyes of King Philip II of Spain. The author is a distinguished Catholic writer and historian, the author of some sixteen works between the years 1910 and 1948. It is one of the very few historically reliable books which help to fill in the gaps in our knowledge of true history in the period from the Renaissance to the onset of the House of Hanover in England, i.e., through the 15th, 16th, and 17th centuries. The book is as readable as the best historical novel, though the author's obvious priority is to truthfully portray both the victories and defeats, and the strengths and warts of his principal character. We heartily recommend this book, not just for the material which we will abstract, but for the joy of experiencing the panoramic landscape of the 16th century which Walsh has so expertly painted with his words.

At the time of the birth of Philip II in 1527, Spain had only very recently been freed from nearly 800 years of Moorish conquest and occupation, and her Jewish minority, which had become dominant under the Moors, legally expelled (in 1492), following the similar action in England (in 1290) and France (in 1394). Significant minorities remained, however, of both Moors and "Marrano Jews" (real or pretended converts to Catholicism). Philip's father,

King Charles I of Spain, was also the Holy Roman Emperor Charles V, and was charged with the responsibility of protecting the Catholic Church and the Catholic countries of Europe from the ongoing depredations of its enemies, recently the Moors and the Cathari/Albigenses, etc., but now the Turks and the newly arising Western schismatics: the Lutherans and the Calvinists. Charles's aunt (the sister of his mother Queen Juana) was Catherine of Aragon, the wife and Queen of Henry VIII of England. Juana and Catherine were daughters of the former King Ferdinand and Queen Isabella of Spain. Spanish Catholicism was strong and unified, their armed forces were unmatched in all of Europe, and Columbus' expeditions to the New World, instituted by Ferdinand and Isabella, were promising to pay off in gold and new colonies. Philip II learned at his father's knee of the challenges and responsibilities which would be handed to him upon his father's death, which finally came in 1556.

But Philip's future troubles were brewing even in the year of his birth. Henry VIII had started his reign as a strong Catholic, and a defender of the Pope against the attacks of Luther on Papal authority, attacks which had become highly public at the Diet of Worms, convened by Philip's father in 1521. By 1527, however, King Charles' ambassador to England conveyed (p. 17) "the startling news that Henry, inflamed with lust for Anne Boleyn, and artfully managed by upstarts and sons of usurers, was planning – but secretly, for fear of a popular uprising in her favor – to divorce [Catherine]." King Charles responded, voicing his concurring belief that Henry was being manipulated: "Knowing his great personal virtues, ...we cannot in any manner be persuaded to believe in so strange a determination as this on the part of His Serenity [Henry].... [It] is not to be presumed that His Serenity would consent to have [the Princess Mary] or her mother [Catherine] dishonored.... Nor is it likely that these things originate with His

Serenity, but with persons who bear ill-will towards His Most Serene Highness, the Queen, and Ourselves, and [who] care not what evils and disasters may spring therefrom...." Charles was obviously suspicious of a court conspiracy of some sort.

England, which had been Catholic for 900 years following the arrival of Christian missionaries from Rome in about 600 A.D., was about to undergo a social and political revolution which would affect the whole of Europe. A brief outline of the Anne Boleyn affair is as follows:

Anne was the daughter of Sir Thomas Boleyn, whose father was the Duke of Norfolk. Anne as a young girl attended the Princess Mary, Henry's younger sister, upon her wedding in France to Louis XII of France, just three months before Louis' death in 1515. Anne stayed in France for the next seven years or so as the protégé of Marguerite of Angoulême, the sister of King Francis I of France. She returned to England in perhaps 1522 as a lady in waiting to Queen Catherine. She caught the eye of King Henry, who became hopelessly infatuated. Anne demanded marriage, however, and Henry maneuvered from about 1527 to 1532 to obtain permission from Pope Clement VII to divorce Catherine and marry Anne. The Pope never gave it, but he was, unfortunately, bullied into giving permission to Cranmer, Henry's Archbishop of Canterbury, to issue local church bulls, or edicts.

Anne, a month or two pregnant, secretly married Henry in January, 1533. On the following May 23, Cranmer convened an ecclesiastical "court" in which he found Henry's marriage to Catherine to have been null from the beginning, bastardizing their daughter, the future Queen Mary. On May 28, he held another court and found Henry's recent marriage to the now noticeably pregnant Anne to be entirely lawful. The baby, the future Queen Elizabeth, was born on September 7, 1533. Three years later, in January of

1536, Queen Catherine, who had been banished from the court, died, with some suspecting poison. Then in May of 1536, Anne Boleyn was arrested, imprisoned in the Tower of London, charged with adultery, a treasonous offense, and on May 15 condemned to death, along with four alleged paramours. Her marriage, quickly found by Cranmer to have been unlawful, was annulled on May 17, bastardizing Elizabeth. Anne was executed on May 19. *One day* later, Henry married his next wife, Anne's maid of honor Jane Seymour, for which marriage Cranmer pulled the necessary dispensation out of his hat. Jane gave birth in October of 1537 to Henry's successor, the (legitimate) Edward VI, and then died a few days after the birth.

Some of the more important facts underlying this seemingly tawdry affair are as follows. Anne Boleyn, says Walsh (p. 39), "whose power lay in the mysterious sexual attraction she exerted over Henry, had been educated in the most corrupt and anti-Catholic court in southern Europe, that Navarrese court of Marguerite of Angoulême, sister of Francis I, and author... of works both pious and salacious.... There is no doubt of the laxity of faith and morals in the semi-pagan atmosphere of Marguerite's court, or of the instant appeal that Luther's teaching made to persons already anxious to escape from the reproach of a divine standard with which the Catholic Church persisted in confronting human guilt. Marguerite herself became a Protestant. As early as 1521, her preacher Gerard Roussel... hurried to Germany to see Luther. Long before Englishmen dreamed of a separation of England from the Catholic Church, Anne Boleyn returned to England a secret heretic."

In the English court, "the more sinister Thomas Cromwell," says Walsh, advised Henry to seek opinions from learned Rabbis in Venice, Bologna, Rome and elsewhere justifying on religious grounds his desired divorce from Catherine. Henry surrounded himself with such people in England, who not only helped him make his case to the Pope, but also helped him to pack the Parliament with those who would support his fight against his Catholic opponents. Rather quickly, the underlying issues emerged. The Parliament's historian wrote (p. 37), "Great industry had been used in managing elections for this Parliament, and they were so successful in returning such members as the King wanted, that he was resolved to continue them till they had done his work, both in the affair of the Divorce, and the business of the Reformation." A parliamentary letter pleading the King's case was sent to the Pope, but the Pope demurred. "[His] answer," wrote the historian, "had very little effect on the minds of those who were [already] *resolved to abrogate the Pope's supremacy in England and strip the Church of its overgrown possessions.*" [Our emphasis.]

"There," continued Walsh, "lay the real issue. Secret and powerful forces, which had not yet disclosed their hand, were using the King's weariness of his wife, his infatuation with Anne, and his hope of a male heir as instruments in pursuit of their own ends." Catherine herself said as much in a pleading letter to the Pope: "...my plea is not against [King Henry], but against the inventors and abettors of this cause.... If I could only have [the King for] two months with me, as he used to be, I alone should be powerful enough to make him forget the past; but as they know this to be true, they do not let him live with me. These are my real enemies who wage constant war against me; some of them [in order] that they may rob and plunder as much as they can...."

And what were the long-term goals of these "real enemies?" In a word, to destroy and supplant the two powerful elements of the existing English power structure: the ancient landed nobility with all its traditions, and the

Catholic Church, with its responsibility for preserving the teachings of Christ.

Thomas Cromwell was perhaps the chief resident planner of the underlying scheme. "Cromwell the money-lender," says Walsh (p. 40), "was one of the first of the men of obscure origin who arose to form the new ruling class of England.... Thomas, one of those born usurers who could be so useful to great men, became a confidential agent of Wolsey [the Archbishop of Canterbury preceding Cran-mer]." When Wolsey fell from power, Cromwell formed direct contacts with the King, the Duke of Norfolk, and the Boleyns, enabling him to become "the master of royal policy," in Walsh's words. "Norfolk had him elected to the Parliament of 1529. Cromwell also had international con-tacts, [and] had traveled about the continent.... With no religion but greed for gold and power, he was utterly unscrupulous.... All his life, even after he had grown enor-mously rich on the loot of the monasteries, he added to his wealth by usury. He was the founder of that Cromwell family which for the next century would throw its powerful influence between the English people and the Catholic faith they still loved. *His nephew and the daughter of another usurer from Genoa became the grandparents of Oliver Cromwell* [of 17th century fame]."

The English public first learned of Catherine's de facto removal when Anne appeared on Easter Eve, 1533, wearing regal garments and Catherine's royal jewels. The public was stunned when asked to pray for the health of "Queen Anne," and, says Walsh (p. 42), "...most of the people left the church in disgust before the sermon was over." Henry was secretly excommunicated in July. After the birth of Elizabeth, Catherine and her daughter Mary lived in constant fear of assassination; had Anne's child been a boy, the succession would clearly have gone to him, but lacking that, Mary was still a viable candidate, and a princess whom the people greatly loved. In March, 1534, Pope Clement finally pronounced formally that Henry's marriage to Catherine had been and was valid. The split with the Vatican was now complete, leaving Cromwell free to move on with his agenda. "The English Revolution," says Walsh (p. 44), "so skillfully and gradually promoted by a small minority acting through bribed or cowed politicians, was now entering upon its final and decisive phase."

Using Cranmer, Cromwell sought signatures of all the clergy declaring that the Pope had no more jurisdiction in England than any other foreign bishop. Many signed. A few resisted, including two whole Franciscan monasteries, the members of which were carted off and imprisoned in the Tower. In November, 1534, the "bought and bullied Parliament" passed acts making Henry the head of the English Church, and granting him the "first fruit" payments previously made to the Pope. The physical property of the Church was not yet touched, however. To convince the remaining clergy to conform, the executions of imprisoned clergy began. On May 4, 1535, the Charterhouse monks were publicly drawn and quartered, with Anne Boleyn's father and brother present, accompanied by her grandfather, the Duke of Norfolk, who was one of the judges who had condemned the monks. On June 27, John Fisher, the Bishop of Rochester, was executed, in the face of his having been made a Cardinal by the new Pope Paul III, in the hope of forestalling the execution.

Then on July 6, 1535, came the execution of Sir Thomas More. Both Fisher and More had refused to sign Henry's Oath of Supremacy. Thomas More, however, was exceedingly well known and loved throughout the Christian world, even including the Protestants of Germany. This was the moment when, if Emperor Charles had been able, he would have had the substantially unanimous support of the English people, the Pope, and most of Europe had he mounted an invasion of England and overturned the corrupt regime of Henry, Boleyn, Cromwell, et al, and restored the religion and the peace of mind of the English people. However, Charles V was at that very moment highly unavailable, absorbed as he was in a desperate battle in Tunis defending the interests of the Catholic world against the onslaught of the Turks. The Turks were also hammering Hungary, and aiming at Austria. Simultaneously, Germany was splitting into multiple sects, with the common thread being hatred of the Catholic Church. Cromwell was undoubtedly aware of Charles' urgent burdens, and was thus emboldened to seek the prompt completion of his English Revolution. Following the executions, the great bulk of the English clergy was cowed into submission, agreeing to preach from their pulpits that the King was indeed the new Head of the Church. The consolidation of the conspirators' victory, including the theft of the church properties, was soon to follow.

We now move about 20 years further into Walsh's narrative, where he discusses (pp. 90-95) Philip and his father, Emperor Charles, having to deal with apparently subversive movements in the Netherlands, over which Charles, having inherited that monarchy, was ruling through his sister Mary, who was also the Queen . The movements appeared to favor both the Protestants and the Turks in their opposition to Catholicism. Walsh essays an explanation of the larger historical forces at play, to which we will append an hypothesis of our own.

One of the forces has to do with the conflict between Judaism and Christianity, particularly its embodiment as Catholicism, militant and armed. Christianity was born in bitter enmity with Judaism, as Webster clearly elucidated. The Jews then underwent the Dispersion, during which their cultural center existed in Babylonia until about 1040, says our trusty encyclopedia, when the pressure of fanatic Islamic sects forced it to move. It then lodged in Spain, where it coexisted comfortably with the Moors who had conquered and occupied Spain some 300 years earlier. The Jews in fact culturally dominated both the Moors and the Christians in Spain until, in 1492, the Jews were formally expelled by Ferdinand and Isabella upon the substantial completion of the Spanish military effort to defeat the Moors and reclaim control over the whole of Spain.

As Walsh points out (p. 90), perhaps 160,000 Jews were forced to leave Spain, a small number compared to the number who remained as Marranos, baptized Catholics, retaining their wealth and power. Many of these latter secretly harbored both their Judaism and a reinforced hatred toward the Christian Church. The Spanish action, which produced a new dispersion of Jews throughout Europe, was clearly counterproductive in the long term. The Marranos attached themselves to the various Protestant movements throughout Europe, many in cities of southern France which had been previously "hospitable to the Albigensian heresy, and now nourished [the heresy] of the Huguenots [French Protestants]." Marranos also attached themselves to court entourages throughout Europe, including those in England, in the German court of Philip's cousin Maximilian (a contender for the crown of Holy Roman Emperor), in the decadent French court of Francis I, which was grossly "infected" with Protestantism, and even among the ecclesiastics and tutors within the Spanish court itself.

Walsh then introduces the second of the major historical events bearing on these mid-16th century developments. The expulsion from Spain had first produced an influx of Jews into southern France, northern Italy, Sicily, Greece, Turkey, and southward into Suez and Cairo, these locations being on the long-established route of overland trade to the Indies, along which the Jewish refugees found a means of support by performing trade brokerage services. In 1500, however, along came Vasco da Gama, returning to

Lisbon after having sailed around the Cape of Good Hope, and discovering the sea route from Europe to the Far East. The Atlantic seaports immediately grew in importance relative to the cities along the overland routes, and the Jewish dispersion accordingly shifted northward in Europe to England and the Atlantic coastlines of France and the Netherlands.

The tolerant Charles permitted the Marranos to settle in the Netherlands, where the peace and order he maintained there were ideal for the support of commercial activities. "The Jews availed themselves of the opportunity," says Walsh (pp. 91-92). "In less than a generation they had made Antwerp the center of world trade and finance. There at the convergence of great waterways were dumped for their benefit the goods from the rivers of south and central Germany, ...from the Atlantic and Mediterranean coasts, and from the Indies of both Spain and Portugal. The Jewish merchant who came and went as a 'Lombard,' a 'Genoese,' and an 'Italian,' or more commonly a 'Portuguese,' had found a new earthly paradise. He was not long in rebuilding the Jewish commercial supremacy of the Middle Ages, which had been shattered, or at least greatly restricted, by the rising of the guilds of Christian workmen."

The discovery of the sea route to the Far East was to have an immense impact on the future of Europe. Let us recapitulate and fill in a little more of the history which Walsh has raised, but only lightly developed. Our primary source for the following is the Universal World Reference Encyclopedia, pub. 1946 by The Encyclopedia Library, Inc., New York. We shall refer to it as the UWRE.

Despite the destruction and dispersion of the Jews from Jerusalem in 135 A.D., the Jews retained their cultural cohesion, with their centers of culture existing in Babylon until about 1040, and then in Spain under the Moors until 1492, as discussed above. Even before the 135 dispersion, they maintained commercial colonies and trading posts throughout the Mediterranean world, and following the dispersion extended them as the boundaries of the "known" world expanded to include such as Crimea, Russia, India, and central Asia as far as China. During their "Spanish Epoch," they further distinguished themselves in secular affairs, attaining eminence in science, medicine, and finance. This summarizes the UWRE's description of the "Jewish commercial supremacy of the Middle Ages" to which Walsh referred.

The guild system involved groups of tradesmen who banded together to help define municipal constitutions which would protect their interests. Guilds eventually became so strong that anyone wishing to participate in municipal government was obliged to join a guild. The guilds introduced a democratic element into society, and became protectors of citizens' liberties and the seat of much political power. The system began from ancient roots, attained significant strength only by the mid-12th century, and lasted to about the mid-16th century. Reading between the lines, we may infer that the guilds imposed restrictive laws on Jewish finance and commercialism in order to protect individuals from the excesses of such commercial power, thus constituting the restrictions on the "Jewish commercial supremacy of the Middle Ages" noted by Walsh.

The guild system was considerably stimulated by the Crusades, which ran from 1100 to about 1270. The Crusades required the outfitting and supplying of hundreds of thousands of men with food, armor, ships, etc., and commercial cities sprang up along their routes to supply those needs, along with a more advanced economic organization than had previously existed. The Crusaders brought back to Europe the knowledge of and the desire for the new-found products of the East, such as cotton, silk, glassware, jewelry, spices, and more. The cities and trade routes developed during the Crusades remained afterwards to supply those wants.

But most significantly, our UWRE notes, "The development of banks and banking also received great stimulus from the Crusades. The need for funds was in part supplied by corporations of Italian bankers. As a whole, Italy received the greatest commercial stimulus from the Crusades. Venice and Genoa in particular were great beneficiaries." Recalling Walsh's allusions to "the Jewish merchant who came and went (in Antwerp) as a Lombard, a Genoese, or an Italian," and recalling also Barruel's discovery of the 1460 document (p. 33, supra) pointing to the secret principles of Masonry being "brought into Europe by Venetian merchants coming from the East," we are led to look into the historical development of Venice and Genoa.

Venice was founded in 421 A.D., as a place of refuge from Attila the Hun. In 697 the Venetian system incorporated an elective prince, called a Doge, or Duke. His power was, at first, absolute. Venice's peninsular location was highly defensible, and its secure seaside location attracted commerce with the rest of the Mediterranean, bringing wealth and power to Venice. From the beginning of the 9th century, Venice exercised ever increasing power via her mighty armories and naval armadas. During the 12th and 13th centuries, she was one of the chief launching pads and armorers of armies of Crusaders first heading eastward, and later returning into Europe. Near the end of the 13th century, she equipped and sent Marco Polo off to China, whence he reported back in 1295 on the wonders of Kublai Khan. Venice regarded trade with the East to be her exclusive monopoly, and carried on sporadic warfare with Genoa, who sought a piece of that action. Genoa succumbed in 1396, when she was absorbed by France, losing her existence as a separate state.

In 1310, Venetian political power passed from the Doge, who remained only as a figurehead, to the famous "Council of Ten," which exercised an authority as absolute, arbitrary, and unquestioned as that of the most despotic monarch. The difference was that the Council was able to secretly nominate and select its own members and leaders, and so was not subject to the vagaries of succession via familial lines. (This principle is further explained in Chapter 6 of our *How The World Really Works*, hereinafter "HTWRW," p. 125.) The system remained in place until Venice was overcome by Napoleon in 1797.

But getting back to the Venetian banks. Our UWRE notes, under the subject "Banking," that "Modern banking... is usually dated from the establishment of the great Venetian banks (1400-1600), and it received its greatest stimulus from the influx of gold taken from the Spaniards returning from America in the Elizabethan age." (It doesn't say how the gold was "taken," but Walsh clears that up later in his book.) We note with interest that these banks, the *first* banks of significance in Europe, were formed entirely within the "reign" of the Council of Ten, suggesting that the banks and the Council acted coopera- tively, if not from common leadership. We may therefore conclude that Venetian traders and commercial companies, whether they were actually aware of it or not, were acting in the interests of the Venetian State, its Council of Ten, and its "Great Venetian Banks."

But wait! Just a few paragraphs back, we were quoting Walsh who was referring to the "*Jewish* commercial supremacy of the Middle Ages," for which we found some words of support in our UWRE. So we perforce must ask, Which is it? Jewish or Venetian? Or, possibly, is it both? The events of recorded history do not appear to us to evidence any organized conflict between Venice and commercial Jewry. To the contrary, it would seem that the

Jewish commercial and money-lending activities, visible for example to Emperor Charles V, were more likely to be the activities of *agents* of those selfsame Great Venetian Banks, the prime source of bulk Middle Ages capital. This thought is a portion of the hypothesis to which we earlier referred, but there is more to be added to it.

In 1492, Columbus discovered the Western Hemisphere (though he didn't then know it), and Vasco da Gama in 1500 found an ocean route to the Far East. The seaports of western Europe were poised to dominate this trade, at the expense of Venice. As our UWRE puts it, "[T]he commerce of Venice was destroyed by the discovery of the route to India by the Cape.... From this time the prestige of Venice declined, and her power gradually sank as a state." Venice's decline was further hastened by Turkish conquests in the latter half of the 15th century of Constantinople and nearby lands on the Balkan peninsula on which Venice depended for its Middle East commerce, specifically including Greece and Albania. Venice ultimately succumbed to Napoleon in 1797.

The Venetian bankers and Council, in 1500 at the height of their powers, must have been able to clearly see the handwriting on the wall as to the future of Venice. But did that necessarily have to mean the decline and end of their own power and influence? Might it not be possible for them to secretly pick up and move their operational headquarters and their banking establishments from Venice to some other location closer to the new center of commercial activity? Were not the European monarchs already deeply in debt to them? Is it not possible, and will not history confirm it to be a fact, that that is exactly what they attempted to do? All that would be necessary would be to burrow from within the governments and societies of the target countries, perhaps using the techniques developed by the Middle East's plethora of secret societies, until those target countries could be overtly taken over, permitting the final financial and power consolidation to be undertaken more openly.

(One final observation intrudes. Our UWRE says that in 1516, Venice established laws declaring boundaries for Jewish ghettos, and such laws spread elsewhere. We might speculate as to why the Council of Ten did this, even as we acknowledge that speculations do not history make. As a minimum, and whether the Council was composed of Jews, Gentiles, or both, the Council felt that the segregation, or apartheidization, of the Jewish population was a good thing. No conclusion beyond that is possible without additional hard facts.)

Our working hypothesis is now complete, and we shall continue to test it as additional pertinent facts are encountered. But for now, we shall return to Walsh. With the sea route to the Far East opened, he says, great quantities of goods from India accumulated in Lisbon, and in response a powerful syndicate was formed in Lisbon between "the great Marrano mercantile and banking house of Francisco and Diogo Mendes" and their partners, "chiefly the Italian Affaitati," who participated in distributing the goods throughout Europe (p. 92). The syndicate was highly successful, and successors of Diogo spread the business into Antwerp, and before 1525 into England. Henry VIII, with Thomas Cromwell at his elbow, intervened to protect Diogo when he was arrested in 1532 for Judaism.

The business came to be known first as the Spice Trust of Antwerp and Lisbon; then, as its banking and money-lending practices expanded into a de facto international bank, it became known as the House of Mendes, or by the shorthand sobriquet Nasi. Diogo's wife Gracia, an inveterate anti-Catholic, had earlier fled to Antwerp with her daughter Reyna and nephew Joseph Miques. Joseph, "a man of uncommon charm and adroitness," soon had many of the young noblemen of the Netherlands in his debt. Even the Emperor owed him a large sum for a few years. The Emperor's sister Mary, Queen of Hungary and regent over the Netherlands, gave Joseph her protection. Joseph married Reyna, and began calling himself Joseph Nasi, signifying his deep commitment to the goals of the Trust. He built an elaborate network of spies, "from England to Constantinople," to serve Trust objectives. In time, he and his associates acquired so much power for themselves and the Spice Trust that Walsh considered them to be the financial equivalent of the Rothschilds of the 18th-century and beyond.

By 1540, Charles finally became aware (p. 94) "that the Marranos he had allowed to settle in Antwerp were proselytizing against the Christian religion," and ordered the arrest of such persons. In 1542, the Bohemian Diet banished Jews from Bohemia, charging them with supplying Christian military information to the Turks. In 1545, Charles, "informed that Marranos from Spain were secretly shipping arms and munitions to the Turks, for use against Christendom and the Empire," ordered the arrest of suspected merchants in Germany, Italy, and elsewhere within the Empire. In 1549, he expelled the Marranos from Antwerp, though many remained as "Catholics," and others migrated to England as "Protestants."

Philip, observing the above at his advanced age of twenty-one, began developing his own world-view. In this, the world was divided into two parts: Christendom, of which Spain was the chief defender, and the kingdom of the antichrist, consisting of "a tacit federation of Jews, Marranos, Mohammedans, the various squabbling sects of Protestants, and the lukewarm or fatuously blind or hypocritical Catholics boring from within to the advantage of the enemy without." He put his cousin Maximilian, the future Holy Roman Emperor, into the latter camp. Today, about 450 years later, we are still trying to divine exactly what the whole truth was about How The World Really Worked at that moment in history. There is nothing in Walsh's description of Philip's world view that would yet invalidate our own hypothesis, however.

We move forward a few more years to 1552, "the most calamitous year of [Charles V's] life," says Walsh (p. 118). He has been in northern Europe attempting to stay the advance of the Protestant sects among the German and other nobility. His hitherto "Catholic" colleagues have awaited their chance, and have now, openly or secretly, joined the Protestant forces and turned against him. He barely escapes with his life, and, old and defeated, seeks money to pay his troops, pay his other debts, and try to avoid utter ruin. Philip is regent, and effective monarch back in Spain, and has the chore of finding gold to pay the monstrous and ceaseless costs of Charles' wars – wars aimed at preserving the Holy Roman Church for the whole of Europe. Walsh writes (p. 120):

"Ruling the richest country in Europe, with the gold from the Indies pouring into Seville, he [Philip] found himself almost bankrupt. The wars of Charles had drained the [Spanish] peninsula and nearly ruined the Empire and the Spanish crown." Philip protested to his father, and received a reply, stating, "We did everything that was in Our power to avoid this present war ... but the King of France and the German rebels forced Our hand.... We have been forced to take up a further sum at exchange [i.e., borrow at interest] in Flanders, assigning [repayment to merchants] in Spain.... We beg you affectionately... to see that the merchants are paid... for which purpose the gold and silver from Peru must serve."

Walsh comments, "Dutiful Philip obeyed as usual, and commandeered the gold arriving at Seville, most of it consigned to private individuals. The worst of it was that...

after he had begun his rule by aiding his father to perpetuate that vicious system by which his country was to be systematically drained of its new wealth, for the enrichment in the end of international bankers," after all this, Charles was again beaten in the field, to the delight of his opponents. Thus began the process of the "taking" of gold from the Spaniards returning from America, to which we referred above. This principle of using wars to accomplish wealth transfers has remained operative up to and through the 20th century, as is repeatedly detailed in our HTWRW.

Philip and his father see a way out, and grasp at a straw. Mary Tudor has just attained the throne in England, while retaining the Catholic religion instilled in her by her mother Catherine, the first wife of Henry VIII. Mary is looking for a husband, and Philip's first wife recently died in childbirth. Philip sees English help in defending Catholicism, and Mary sees aid from Philip in promoting it in England. In July of 1554 they are married, but the conditions attached to the union were written to assure that the new king would not have sufficient power to force the restitution of the Church's looted properties. Only the Pope had seen the dangerous unexpected consequence, but his advice was ignored. Walsh writes (p. 125), "Pope Julius III saw plainly enough that, so long as the church property stolen by Henry VIII remained in the hands of the new upstart nobility, it would be used by [those] beneficiaries to prevent any real Catholic restoration.... The lands of the church must therefore be given back to her."

Charles, however, feared starting a new Protestant rebellion, and Philip dutifully went along. The stolen church properties did therefore remain in the hands of those Protestant *nouveaux riches*, including such as William Cecil, who first appeared as advisor to Henry's successor Edward VI; John Russell, whose great English House of Russell was founded on a healthy share of Catholic Church loot; and Sir

Thomas Gresham, "a sly, plausible fellow," says Walsh, "of a family of usurers, who made himself indispensable to Henry VIII as an agent in Antwerp, where he was always able to obtain a loan when it was needed." Sir Gresham, famous for his "law" stating that bad money will always drive out good, was the money-changer who personally saw that the gold and other treasure that Philip brought along with him to England was safely stowed in the Tower of London, where it remained in his charge.

Mary made a mild attempt late in 1555, with Philip gone to the Netherlands attending his dying father, to get Parliament to restore to the Church its stolen properties (p. 165). She desisted, however, upon observing the solid and well-organized opposition from the Parliamentary leaders, the very people who would suffer the loss of their ill-gotten gains. Sir William Cecil led that opposition, he who, an open Protestant under Henry and Edward, had become an enthusiastic Catholic upon Mary's accession (p. 145), and who would re-embrace Protestantism in concert with the soon-to-be Queen Elizabeth. The Pope had correctly foreseen the future, and no effective Catholic counterrevolution came to be mounted in England. Mary died childless in November of 1558, dashing the last hopes of Charles, Philip, and the Pope for that counterrevolution.

Charles abdicated in late 1555, making Philip the King of Spain, of the Netherlands, and, in name at least, of England. Charles' brother Ferdinand, already King of Bohemia, became Holy Roman Emperor. Present at the abdication ceremony was one William I of Orange, a prince of Nassau, the name of a European royal family which had ruled chiefly in Germany and the Netherlands from as early as the 10th century. William, the progenitor of William III of the Glorious Revolution of 1688, was a protégé of Charles, though he was mistrusted by Charles' sister, Queen Mary of Hungary, because of his fluctuations between

Protestantism and Catholicism. Though warned concerning William's insincerity, Charles stayed his course, as he had concerning the non-restitution of the Catholic Church's English properties. Philip thus "inherited" William I of Orange upon Charles' abdication, who then retired to a Spanish monastery until his death in September of 1558. The death of Mary Tudor two months later dissolved Philip's kingship over England, but Philip, then at age 29, was finally free to become his own man.

Walsh, looking at Philip's status at the beginning of his kingship in 1556, unburdens himself (pp. 170-172) of his own view of the forces influencing the major actors playing out the European drama. Philip, says Walsh, "began to rule under a crushing burden of debt." He had a large income, amounting to some 5 million ducats (Venetian gold pieces) a year, but that was about the amount that he was in debt to the usurers who had been financing Charles' wars. "He commonly paid 14 to 20 percent for long-term loans, and much higher rates for temporary accommodation." He hated usury, which the Church regarded as the vilest of sins, but, as he was unable to raise by taxation the amounts he "needed" for the wars into which he was "forced," he and other Catholic rulers became addicted to usury, and therefore protected the money-lenders on whom they depended.

Though not yet fully visible, Walsh believes that continued reliance upon indebtedness to external suppliers of gold *at interest* was gradually destroying the institution of the monarchy, which was step by step being overcome by "a revolutionary rival whose soldiers were gold coins and whose ministers were promissory notes.... It did not occur to the kings that if the money-lenders ever got power enough [and got out] from under the public spirited repression of the Church, they would destroy their [royal] masters." We do, of course, fully concur with this view, and find it still applicable to today's governments, no matter what the form.

Walsh continues: "As the moral influence of the Church was weakened, ...usury began to accumulate wealth and to organize its influence." Early on, it supported Protestantism, until successful Protestants gratefully supported and indulged in money-lending themselves, whence a future writer would "chronicle the capitulation of the new Protestant England to 'usury, a trade brought in by the Jews, but now perfectly practiced almost by every Christian, and so commonly that he is [taken] but for a fool that doth lend his money for nothing.'" Later, usury would support political liberalization, or democratization, producing democratic parliaments anxious to keep taxes low for their constituents. Royal revenues thus lagged behind total money growth, which accumulated in private hands faster than in those of the kings. Going to private individuals for loans, monarchs were forced to pay usury. Since the Catholic Church opposed usury as a matter of principle, usurers treated the Catholic Church as an enemy, and supported instead "the multiplication of sects, factions, and opinions [which] would in time throw all power into their hands."

Philip only very late began to divine something of this picture. He had spent the several years from 1556 through 1558 fighting with France over various pieces of European real estate, especially in Italy. Toward the end of 1558, Charles, just before he died (pp. 201-202), "sent Philip word that he should make peace as soon as possible, and devote his energies to the defense of Christianity against heresy." A similar appeal came from Pope Paul IV, who saw Protestantism making great strides while the Catholic powers were squabbling amongst themselves. Finally, says Walsh, "[Philip] sees the folly of a perpetual war with France. He sees much, but not enough." What he did not see was the importance of influencing his dying wife, Queen

Mary Tudor, to throw her succession to the Catholic (and French) Queen Mary Stuart of Scotland rather than to Elizabeth, because of what he knew of Elizabeth's character and her past. Not being able to stomach the idea of doing something which might result in an increase in French power, he finally wrote to both Mary and the Pope encouraging their support of Elizabeth, in the hope that his gut feeling about her pretended adherence to Catholicism was wrong.

His gut feeling was right, however, and English Protestantism became consolidated under Elizabeth. At the funeral of Charles V late in 1558, many eulogies were spoken of him. "Hardly anyone," says Walsh (p. 207), "except Pope Paul IV and a few other discerning religious, said the one truly important thing about the reign of Charles, which gives it its peculiar significance in history: under him Christendom was divided into hostile camps, and the heresy to which Charles had given political freedom would envelop and poison the whole world.... Charles saw [this] danger only in his last days. One of his bitterest reflections on his bed of pain was that he had not had Luther put to death when the monk was in his power at the Diet of Worms some thirty-seven years before. Now it was too late."

Writing these words in 1937, Walsh is understandably pessimistic, and in the present year 2000, we are even closer to the brink. Yet we still have good reason to look with some hope to the future, as we shall shortly develop.

Elizabeth did not keep Philip guessing very long. Her first official act after Mary's death was to appoint William Cecil secretary of her Privy Council. His program had been readied in advance, indicating a secret prior understanding between Elizabeth and Cecil. Her hard-core Catholic councilors were dropped, and the incoming Parliament was properly packed with Protestants, both with as little public notice as possible, so as not to alarm (or awaken) the overwhelmingly Catholic English people. Cecil, the real leader, had at that moment neither an army, equipment, munition factories, or public opinion on his side, but, says Walsh (p. 212), he did have "the advantage of working in the dark, [and] a complete organization of his own ready to take over gradually the functions of government."

The ruling cabal was drawn from a group of Cambridge habitués whom we shall briefly identify for future reference. They began with Thomas Cromwell, previously mentioned as chief aide to Henry VIII in managing his divorce from Catherine and his marriage to Anne Boleyn. Cromwell became chancellor at Cambridge. Out of Cambridge came also Thomas Cranmer, whom Henry had made Archbishop of Canterbury to assist in the same project. Cecil had himself been a classical scholar at Cambridge, and now brought in numbers of others of his and Cromwell's Cambridge friends to help. Walsh declares, "It is interesting to notice how many of the men through whom [Cecil] ruled England for a long generation were from Cambridge, and how closely the group was united by intermarriage and by the economic bond of the church loot." A partial list includes Francis Russell, Thomas Sackville (the first cousin of Anne Boleyn), and Thomas Gresham, previously noted as Henry VIII's financial fixer and Antwerp agent.

Gresham's father, Sir Richard Gresham, "was a merchant," says Walsh (p. 214), "knighted for raising money for Henry VIII, and enriched by the spoils of the Church." His son Thomas, after a stint at Cambridge, followed his father's path, and in 1543, "joined the *Mercer's Company*, a secret society which had more lords and knights in it than mercers (Queen Elizabeth herself was a free sister of the organization), and later the *Merchants Adventurers*, also a secret society, whose members virtually monopolized the commerce of the country, and had a huge trade with the

Levant.... [Even after Thomas was himself knighted,] he continued as goldsmith, money-lender, smuggler, and general financial factotum and thimble-rigger for Cecil."

The italicized references above are the first which Walsh makes to formal secret societies involved in the 16th-century conflict, but they won't be the last. Walsh then asks: how did it all happen that there were so many dedicated men all appearing at the same time and place to help out in an undercover takeover of England? He doesn't unambiguously answer his question, but we, with the advantages of the researches of Barruel, Dillon, and Webster at our fingertips, can probably visualize a plausible answer with little difficulty.

On the Continent, there were two other historically notable conspirators making common cause with Cecil's group, and against whom Philip spent several decades of conflict. The first was the aforementioned William I of Orange, protégé of Charles V, and therefore a candidate for governor of the Netherlands, replacing his aunt, Queen Mary of Hungary, who was retiring. Philip, having been warned against William by Mary and others in his own entourage, appointed instead his half-sister Margaret, the illegitimate daughter of a Flemish lady and his father Charles. Philip gained a governor he could fully trust, but also turned William I of Orange into his lifelong enemy (p. 230).

The second Continental conspirator of great note was Admiral Gaspard Coligny. This gentleman was born of a father known as General Gaspard Coligny and mother Louise de Montmorency. The latter was herself raised in the same corrupt and heretical court as was Anne Boleyn, that of Marguerite of Angoulême, the Queen of Navarre. The heresy was propagated through these several generations to three of the four sons of Louise and General Coligny, but Gaspard the younger, says Walsh (p. 285), "was the most impressive member of the family, with a regal presence, a persuasive personality, and a genius for intrigue and organization, second only, perhaps, to that of Cecil."

The anti-Catholic works of these conspirators were focused in France, with their support coming primarily from the Calvinists, rather than the more Germanic Lutherans. Members of the French anti-Catholic movement were give the nickname Huguenots. The movement was never a large mass movement among ordinary French people, but rather consisted of a tiny minority, perhaps one-thirtieth of the French people by 1569, led primarily by the noble families of the southern provinces (p. 283). The movement nevertheless got very bloody, and was to involve a total of eight wars during the following century and a quarter.

The movement got underway (p. 280) with a conspiratorial effort hatched in Geneva in August of 1559, just a month or so after the death of King Henry II of France (in a jousting accident), and the accession of the first of the three sons of Henry II and his Queen, Catherine de' Medici. One day after the accident, Throckmorton, Cecil's ambassador to France, wrote Cecil that the moment was favorable for those wishing to get revenge on France. The monarchy, now formally in "the weak and inexperienced hands of young Francis II and his wife Mary Stuart," who was the same Mary Queen of Scots later beheaded by Queen Elizabeth, was actually being run by the Queen-Mother Catherine de' Medici, who, though a dominant personality, cared more for her family's position than she did for the welfare of France or the Catholic Church.

The conspiracy sought to raise troops, march on the court of Francis II, kill Francis and his chief advisors (the Duke Francis of Guise and his brother the Cardinal of Lorraine), expel Francis' mother, and make sure her younger sons and daughters were raised as good Protestants. The plot raised thousands of men who were ready to march by February of 1560, but it was then discovered, and the young monarchs were hustled to safety by Duke Francis to the well-fortified castle of Amboise. The suspected conspirators, which included Admiral Coligny, his brother Odet (Cardinal Chatillon), and Cecil's ambassador Throckmorton, were brought to the castle and accused. Throckmorton denied the charge, skillfully covering up the traces of his involvement. Various others who were more physically involved were found, however, and confessed and were executed. The affair became known as the Tumult of Amboise, and marked the beginning of the Huguenot wars.

The war started in earnest about a year later. The Coligny brothers and other Huguenots persuaded the Queen-Mother to invite leading Calvinist preachers to come to a public meeting with important Catholics to seek a compromise. The meeting occurred, the Calvinists presented their religious position, and the Catholics theirs. Thereupon, the Huguenot propaganda machine went to work, declaring to the public that they had "won a victory," and felt justified in pressing their case forward. Walsh writes (p. 289):

"During the weeks following the Colloquy, the storm of hate, which had so long been gathering, burst in all its fury. Almost simultaneously, as if by a concerted signal, well-organized bands of Calvinists fell upon the Catholic churches, convents, schools, and libraries. At Montpelier they sacked all the sixty churches and convents, and put one hundred-fifty priests and monks to the sword. At Nîmes they.... At Montauban they.... At Castres.... Within a year the Calvinists, according to one of their own estimates, murdered 4000 priests, monks, and nuns, sacked 20,000 churches, and destroyed 2000 monasteries with their priceless libraries and works of art.... Sacred vessels from the churches were melted into money to pay German mercenaries, who were urged to be ruthless. Coligny took an active part in many of the atrocities.... Hundreds of cities and villages were burned. Lyons and its prosperous commerce were ruined.

"Although these atrocities were perpetrated by a small minority in an overwhelmingly Catholic country, all the forces of the national and local governments seemed paralyzed and impotent for the moment. The Huguenots had a majority in the States-General and friends in the Parliament of Paris. There seemed to be men everywhere in important positions to protect them and to sidetrack any attempt to punish them."

Does all this seem the work of Christians, albeit non-Catholic, seeking freedom to express their Christian beliefs? Or does it more closely presage the methods and tactics of the Jacobins who would appear on the world stage during the French Revolution and the Napoleonic Wars?

In September of 1562, Coligny and his brother Cardinal Chatillon negotiated the Treaty of Hampton Court with Elizabeth and Cecil, whereby, for payment of 100,000 gold crowns, the Colignys gave England the port of Havre on the English Channel, which Cecil immediately garrisoned, following which the adjacent cities of Rouen and Dieppe were similarly garrisoned. (In the several prior years, Sir Thomas Gresham had organized and protected an arms smuggling operation from Antwerp to London to help arm Cecil; that trade could now proceed openly via Havre.) The English were now actively taking part in the French War. Troops were similarly on the way from German Protestant groups. The Duke Francis bravely and successfully responded, but was cut down by the poisoned bullet of an assassin, who confessed having been hired by Admiral Coligny. The Duke's brother was momentarily away in Italy, leaving France without competent military leadership. The Queen-Mother capitulated, signing the Treaty of Amboise in March, 1563, giving the Huguenots amnesty and freedom of worship. That was fine with them, but was not, of course, the whole of what they really wanted, and the conflict merely underwent one of its many pauses.

It had by this time become thoroughly understood in Spain, says Walsh (p. 301), "that the various enemies of the Catholic Church and Catholic culture, whatever their differences in creed, dogma, race, or nationality, were united in action by some extraordinary principle of cohesion and cooperation. It was almost as if there existed, in opposition to the [Roman Church], an actual organization throughout the world – at any rate throughout Europe – of an invisible kingdom of opposition. It had all the characteristics of some of those widespread secret societies of the Middle Ages, but on a larger scale." And, of course, newly-operative secret societies actually *did* exist, and the power-seeking cabal visibly headed by Cromwell, Cecil, Coligny, et al, were making full use of them, as Walsh presently details.

We should keep in mind at this point our operative premise, or hypothesis, that at the real core of the conspiracy are the owners of the accumulated wealth of centuries of uninhibited commercialism, heretofore resident in Venice and environs, and now in the process of moving to the Atlantic coasts of Europe, the better to acquire and maintain the worldwide political and commercial dominance which they covet. Secret societies to them are nothing more than tools, a means which they, and others before them, have found useful in attaining and maintaining political power. It is not that they are presently laying waste to Europe because they are members of a secret society which has long had such a goal in mind; it is rather that, having recently settled on such an expansion of their goals, they are utilizing secret societies as one of the means of attaining them. If preexisting societies can be used, use them; if new ones would be helpful, create them.

Sir Thomas Sackville, mentioned above as one of Cecil's cabal, was, says Walsh (p. 303), from 1561 at least, the Grand Master of the Grand Masonic Lodge at York. Queen Elizabeth, always fearful of plots against her life, "hearing that the Masons had certain secrets that could not be revealed to her, sent an armed force to break up [the annual Grand Lodge meeting] at York on December 27, 1561." But Sackville managed to included a number of Freemasons in that force, who returned "a very honorable report to the Queen," such that she never further attempted to dislodge or disturb them. "This Masonic [account] adds," says Walsh, "that when Sackville resigned his office in 1567... the Grand Lodge was divided into two. Francis Russell, second Earl of Bedford, was chosen head of the northern Lodge, and our financier Sir Thomas Gresham, who had come home in great haste when the Netherlands became too hot for him, was Grand Master in the South." Both of these men were listed above as members of Cecil's cabal. Also as noted earlier, Queen Elizabeth herself had joined the secret society known as the Mercer's Company, possibly to try to keep track of what these secret entities were up to.

Walsh points out that most modern encyclopedias date the present form of Freemasonry from the early 18th century, at which time (i.e., 1717) it was changed from "an operative body into one partly speculative." However, says Walsh, "The evidence of its existence before the 18th century is overwhelming." The Edinburgh Lodge has minutes back to 1599, which is back into the lifetime of Queen Elizabeth. "If the order at that time was 'purely operative' and not speculative," he asks, "what were men like Sackville and Gresham doing in it?"

Walsh next goes to the Charter of Cologne, which we discussed in our review of Dillon's book, and which documents an international Masonic meeting in Cologne in 1535. Walsh adds a good deal more, first by identifying one of the signatures on that document as "Colligni," and matching that signature, not to Admiral Gaspard Coligny, but more likely, based on compatible employment and dates of birth, etc., to Gaspard's older brother Odet, the Cardinal Chatillon. Further, he buttresses the authenticity of the document by pointing out that the record of the Cologne Convention was introduced and discussed at the Masonic Convention in Basle in 1563, at which the Cologne record was accepted as authentic, and the signers verified as being Masons in good standing. Odet, born in 1517, was just eighteen in 1535, but it should be pointed out that he was made a Cardinal at age sixteen, upon which he went to Rome and voted in a papal election. At age 17 he was made the Archbishop of Toulouse, and in the following year, 1535, he was given the bishopric of Beauvais. In the several preceding years, he had traveled widely with "his heretical mother," as Walsh describes Louise de Montmorency, whom we have also mentioned above. He therefore appears to have been sufficiently mature to have attended the Cologne Convention.

Walsh sought to find a connection between Cecil and Masonry, but got no further than matching certain heraldic symbols on the Cecil coat of arms with corresponding Masonic symbols, not terribly conclusive. Be that as it may, the men through whom Thomas Cromwell and William Cecil did their work, such as the Colignys, Francis Russell, Thomas Sackville, and Thomas Gresham, not only did have better-documented connections, but so did many of their progeny. "The descendants of most of these Protestant chiefs," says Walsh (p. 315), "are found within a generation or two to be leaders of Masonry. For example... we find [William I of Orange] in one of his marriages becoming son-in-law to Admiral Coligny, and his direct descendants are high officials of Freemasonry when concealment is no longer necessary. Before the end of a century, his great-grandson, William III, will be joining the Freemasons at a time when, with their connivance, he is being placed on the throne of England to replace the legitimate Catholic monarch, James II; and the expenses of the expedition will be paid by a Jewish banker of Amsterdam, Isaac Suaso, who in return for his two million *gulden* will be made Baron de Gras...."

Walsh notes next the existence of a different and apparently entirely separate secret society discovered in Spain under the name Alumbrados, translated as Illuminates. "They," he says (p. 316), "were engaged in a wholesale campaign of defamation against the clergy and the Church, of seduction of rich widows, the compromising of young girls in nocturnal orgies, assassination, and all manner of subversive activity." Arrests were made, and the sect scattered, generally northward, with the Illuminati name, at least, appearing two centuries later in France and Germany, as discussed by Barruel.

Two other names are worthy of mention. The first is Francis Bacon, later named Lord Verulam. His father Nicholas Bacon, brother-in-law of William Cecil, was one of Cecil's gofers who managed to enrich himself with the spoils of the English Catholic Church. Francis wrote an allegorical treatise called *The New Atlantis*, which Catholic readers have interpreted (p. 319) as a hidden outline of the work of Masonry completed to that moment via the use of "innocent novices, the elaborate spy system, the use of great wealth to gain power under cover of philanthropic and scientific purposes, the oath of secrecy..., the essentially anti-Christian tendency..., the far-flung system of intrigue and espionage, even a hint of world-domination...." Conspirators of this type don't seem able to keep their mouths shut. Similar writings have come from the pens of Benjamin Disraeli (*Coningsby*), Col. Edward Mandell House (*Philip Dru, Administrator*), and even Professor Carroll Quigley

(*Tragedy and Hope*), the latter of which we reviewed in our HTWRW.

Walsh's last name of note is John Emmanuel Tremelius. This gentleman, shortly before the year-long Huguenot-led blood bath which started in late 1561, communicated to Elizabeth's ambassador Throckmorton that he, Tremelius, was traveling about Europe, seeking to form a Confederation of Protestant Princes, and wished to ask the blessing of Elizabeth in this endeavor, as well as for "letters of credence" from the Queen to facilitate his entree. This activity then occupied him for some years. Philip found out about his role only by 1568, and upon inquiring was told by his London ambassador that Tremelius was "a heretic... and in the pay of the Queen." Walsh comments (p.323), "The report was not quite accurate, for it made Tremelius an Oxford man. Cecil, who was better informed, left a record at the same time which corrects the Spanish account." Tremelius had not lectured at Oxford, but at Cambridge, where he was a friend of Cranmer, Anne Boleyn's chaplain. He was thus an early participant in the Cromwell-Cecil shadow government-in-training at Cambridge.

Walsh quotes the historian Prescott on the effectiveness of the cabal: "The Protestants of that time constituted a sort of federated republic, or rather a great secret association, extending through the different parts of Europe, but so closely linked together that a blow struck in one quarter instantly vibrated to every other." So even historians who were blind to the depth of the involvement of "secret associations" were nevertheless impressed by the wide scope and efficiency of their labors.

There is much more of interest in this book, but we must regretfully leave it. Elizabeth stayed in power and, by a few years, outlived Philip, who died in 1598. His major regret on his death bed was that he had not seen the truth about Elizabeth much earlier, when he might have easily squelched the secret English palace coup, and saved England for Catholicism. The center of gravity of European commercialism was now slowly but surely shifting to England. Sir Francis Drake, Elizabeth's hired pirate, was busy accelerating the "taking of gold from Spaniards returning from America" by conventional piracy. In 1588 Philip finally assembled his famous Spanish Armada in an attempt to invade England and set matters straight, but he was defeated by the weather in the English Channel, and thus failed to reverse the course of history.

Our next chapter features an author who bypasses our tentative hypotheses, and dives right in, calling spades by their true name.

Chapter 9

"AGAINST OLIGARCHY"

(Essays and speeches by Webster G. Tarpley, 1970-1996. Available on the Internet at www.tarpley.net/aobook.htm. Not available in book form.)

Perusing Mr. Tarpley's web site quickly gives one an appreciation of the vast energy and erudition that went into his work of uncovering and then publicizing the history and works, up to the present time, of those who would rule us. We have undertaken to review those parts of his Internet-published works which bear most directly on our own theme.

His work entitled *Against Oligarchy* consists of seven parts, parts one and two being labeled "Venice" and "The British" respectively. "Venice" contains seven "chapters," five of which we shall reference; "The British" contains nine, of which we shall reference four. The total of nine chapters which we shall reference are listed below, with Tarpley's chapter titles preceded by a shorthand reference label which we shall use. (For example, "V5" refers to Tarpley's chapter 5 within his part one, "Venice.")

V1   The Venetian Conspiracy (1981)
V2   The Role of the Venetian Oligarchy in Reformation, Counter-Reformation, Enlightenment, and the Thirty Years' War (1992)
V4   How the Dead Souls of Venice Corrupted Science (1994)
V5   Venice's War against Western Civilization (1995)

V6 The War of the League of Cambrai, Paolo Sarpi and
John Locke (1996)

B1 How the Venetian System Was Transplanted Into
England (1996)

B3 The British Empire Bid for Undisputed World Domination, 1815-1870 (1992)

B4 Lord Palmerston's Multicultural Human Zoo (1994)

B5 King Edward VII of Great Britain: Evil Demiurge of
the Triple Entente and World War 1 (1995)

Tarpley starts right in with some history of old
Venice. It was formed during the 4th and 5th centuries by
Roman aristocrats seeking a refuge from the Huns. Somewhat earlier, the Roman Emperor Constantine the Great
rebuilt the ancient city of Byzantium, and in 330 A. D.
renamed it Constantinople (now Istanbul), and made it his
new capital city. In 395 the Byzantine, or Eastern, branch
of the Roman Empire split from the Western, and shortly
thereafter, in 476, Rome and the Western Empire fell. The
Eastern Empire survived much longer, however, until
Constantinople was overrun in 1453 by the Ottoman Turks.

The Byzantines for a time occupied portions of Italy
south of Venice until around the 8th century, shortly after
Venice elected its first doge (or duke) in 697. The early
Venetians developed and maintained a relationship with
these Eastern Romans, which in fact developed into an
alliance with the Byzantine Emperor Justinian in Constantinople. It was then reinforced in later years (V1, p. 3) "by
intermarriage of doges and other leading Venetian oligarchs
with the nobility of Byzantium." The Byzantine Empire of
course looked toward Asia and Africa, an outlook which
Venice copied. In Tarpley's words, "Venice looks East,
toward the Levant, Asia Minor, central Asia, and the Far
East, towards its allies among the Asian and especially

Chinese oligarchies which were its partners in trade and war."

Up until 1382, says Tarpley, the dogeship was monopolized by the LONGHI, the oldest families, many of whose names go back to the 4th century. After 1382, a set of CURTI, newcomer families, came into ascendancy. Old or new, the families grew rich via the East-West trade which flowed through Venice. Venetian production was nearly non-existent (except for ships), but they led the Mediterranean world in warehousing and transshipping strategic commodities from around the world, and grew rich by becoming the world's greatest middle-men, or traders. They built their own merchant galleys in the world's largest shipyard, and protected their fleets with state-regulated convoys. This led, by natural extension, to the highly profitable supplementary activities of state-sanctioned piracy and buccaneering. Similarly, wars were looked on as "eagerly sought-after opportunities to loot the enemy's shipping with clouds of corsairs."

But beyond trade monopolization, and even its attendant extension into piracy, the deeper reality was, says Tarpley, that "the primary basis for Venetian opulence was slavery," which was practiced as a matter of course against all the nearby indigenous peoples, including Saracens, Turks, Mongols, various Christians, including Italians, Greeks, Germans, and Russians, and, a little later, black Africans. The Venetians bought slaves for working their overseas empire (islands such as Crete, Cyprus, and Corfu), and for resale to others as galley slaves, disposable army troops, and harems for the entire Ottoman empire, from the Balkans around to Morocco.

Remarkably, they managed to keep their system going for a whole millennium without significant interruption. How did they do it? The key was in the way the authority of the state was organized. First, the system was precisely oligarchic. In early times, those able to be assessed a large sum were permitted in; thereafter, noble status was strictly limited to those presently noble plus their male descendants. The interests of all individual oligarchs were subordinated to the well-being of the oligarchy as a whole. A ubiquitous spy system made it impossible to generate secret opposition cliques. Official terror was rife, resulting in the simple disappearance, or the appearance floating in a canal, of persons felt to be making unoligarchic waves, including the doge himself. The common people had nothing whatever to do with the government, which was a closed system of interest only to the included noble families.

All included nobles voted, by an arcane and tortuous process, for the doge, who was elected for life. Also elected, but always for short terms, were ambassadors, war and naval ministers, state prosecutors, six advisors for the doge, and other officials. Vote-buying, graft, and other forms of corruption were rife, with the result that the topmost elite of ten to fifteen wealthy and powerful families remained in iron control, and always able to select future leaders from among their own group. By 1310, the famous Council of Ten was established, which Tarpley describes (V1, p.6) as "the coordinating body for foreign and domestic political intelligence operations." It met in secret with the doge and his six advisors, and had the power of life and death over "any person inside Venetian jurisdiction, or abroad." The Venetian people were subjected to an "intricate system of local control... supplemented by an unending parade of festivals, spectacles, and carnivals," requiring little in the way of local police power.

The continuity of the oligarchy, says Tarpley (V5, p.2), is defined by the continuity of the family fortunes (called fondos), not by the continuity of blood lines. The largest fondo was an endowment fund of the Basilica of St. Mark. This fund absorbed the fortunes of nobles who died without heirs. The fund was managed by a state commission created for that purpose, and was "closely associated with the Venetian state treasury," as Tarpley puts it. Around this central fondo were arrayed the individual fortunes of the great families, some of whose names were Mocenigo, Cornaro, Dandolo, Contarini, Morosini, Zorzi, and Tron. These wealthiest of the wealthy Venetians later transferred their holdings into northern Europe, creating in the process the Bank of Amsterdam and the Bank of England, which were the major European banks of the 17th and 18th centuries, respectively.

The loyalties of the Venetians were discovered by Western Europe fairly early (V5, p. 3). Charlemagne recognized in about 800 A. D. that Venice was his enemy, was not loyal to or a part of the West, and was instead an integral part of the Byzantine Empire, under the protection of the Emperor Nicephorus. Charlemagne's son King Pepin of Italy tried to conquer the Venetians in their watery redoubt, but was unsuccessful. Surviving that crisis, Venice developed, over the next several centuries, into "the second capital of the Byzantine Empire," via its policies of usury, slavery, and dynastic intermarriage within Byzantium. By 1082, it had acquired tax-free trading rights throughout the Byzantine Empire.

Then in 1202, it accomplished one of its greatest coups (V1, pp. 11-12). The Fourth Crusade was on. A French army was being outfitted in Venice, and, to pay for the equipage, was induced by the Venetians to sack and pillage on the way to Jerusalem. They did so, besieging Constantinople itself, and finally breaking through its walls. Then, "in an orgy of violence and destruction," they sacked it, loaded up their booty, and returned to Europe. Venice installed a puppet regime, and took possession of the Byzantine naval bases throughout the Mediterranean. Loot poured into both Venice and Europe. In addition, Venice also collected a bribe from the sultan of Egypt, who had paid the Venetians "to keep the Crusaders out of Palestine in the first place." Venice thus managed to strengthen and enrich itself by playing off the Crusaders against the Byzantines, betraying both of them while elevating Venice and its oligarchy to the sole leadership of what they intended to be a new Roman Empire with its center at Venice (V5, p. 4).

A little later in the same century, the nephew and other relatives of Ghengis Khan, after advancing into Iran, were found moving through Russia and the Ukraine and, by 1241, into Poland and Hungary. By 1258 they had moved their southern front forward to Baghdad, and destroyed it. Why were the Mongols so effective? Tarpley quotes one historian as follows (V1, p. 12):

"The Mongols did not sweep in wildly and suddenly, like reckless barbarians. No indeed, they advanced according to careful plan. At every stage, the Mongol generals informed themselves ahead of time about the state of [the] European courts, and learned what feuds and disorders would be advantageous to their conquests. This valuable knowledge they obtained from Venetian merchants, men like Marco Polo's father. It was not without reason that Polo himself was made welcome at the court of Kublai, and became for a time administrator of the Great Khan."

Such merchants, of course, would be agents of the Venetian intelligence apparatus, seeking to implement the foreign policy initiatives of the Venetian state. Marco Polo himself set out toward China only by 1271, though his father or other relatives may have had earlier contact. Tarpley asserts that the Venetian family from which Marco Polo came "was responsible for directing the destruction of Ghengis Khan against Europe. The omnipresent Venetian intelligence was also a factor in the Mongol destruction of the Arab cultural center of Baghdad in 1258."

But why? Tarpley asserts (V5, p. 4) that it had to do with the Venetian effort to establish their new empire. "During the 1200's, the Venetians, now at the apex of their military and naval power, set out to create a new Roman Empire with its center at Venice. They expanded into the Greek Islands, the Black Sea, and the Italian mainland. They helped to defeat the Hohenstaufen rulers of Germany and Italy [the Ghibellines]. Venetian intelligence assisted Ghengis Khan as he attacked and wiped out powers that had resisted Venice." (Including the Assassins? Cf. p. 197.)

The 1300's were dominated by the Black Plague, which in mid-century wiped out about a quarter of the European population, and the Hundred Years' War, which ran from 1339 to 1453. The war was a running battle between England and France, involving the French effort to evict England from holdings which it claimed on the European continent. With the exception of the city of Calais, which Philip II of Spain had to deal with later, the English were finally evicted, with the glorious assistance of St. Joan of Arc. This war was urged onto Edward III of England by his friend and ally, the Venetians, who no doubt found the war both profitable and a useful mechanism for keeping France and England occupied while Venice was consolidating its power in Italy.

While the war was still being waged, the phenomenon of the Renaissance was born. With broad strokes, Tarpley pictures its significance as follows (V6, pp. 1-2): Before around 1400, human societies were generally composed of two-class systems: ruling elites and the masses. The latter made up 95 percent of the population, and were poor, illiterate, land-laboring peasants, serfs, or slaves, whose lives were nasty, brutish, and short. In medieval Europe, the ruling 5 percent were feudal aristocrats who were generally ignorant, brutal, and crude, excluding the case of the Venetians, who had inherited the refined methods of Byzantium, Babylon, and Rome. The breakup of this pattern began in the 1300's with Dante and Petrarch, leading to the Italian Renaissance of the 1400's, culminating in the Council of Florence in 1439, led by Cosimo de' Medici of Florence. The essence of the change was the recognition that every human being is made in the image of God, each possessing dignity to be respected and the right to seek his own destiny. In consequence there occurred an explosion of human creativity in the fields of art, science, and societal organization. Men had to be given room to breathe freely, rather than live the lives forced on them by despots. The first modern nation-state was created by Louis XI (1461-1483), financed by taxation of a middle class engaged in manufacture and commerce, and dispensing with the feudal aristocracy.

The Venetians were not pleased (V1, pp. 14-18). In 1423, Doge Tommaso Mocenigo urged the oligarchy toward an expansionist policy which would bring to them the gold of and the power over all of Christendom. Accordingly, during the first half of the 15th century, they extended their hegemony up the Po River to within a few miles of Milan. Milan was defended by Francesco Sforza, installed with the help of Cosimo de' Medici, binding Milan and Florence into an alliance. The Peace of Lodi in 1453 stopped the Venetian expansion, and brought peace to northern Italy for the next forty years.

In the meantime, the Ottoman Turks, who had been crushed by the Mongols in 1402, were recovering, and had made their first unsuccessful try at besieging and conquering Constantinople, now back in the hands of the Byzantine Paleologue dynasty. The Byzantines were supported by the Pope, the Medici, and others participating in the 1439 Council of Florence, all of whom were seeking to reunite the Greek and Roman branches of the Catholic Church. Sforza, de' Medici, and the Pope all sought to enlist the aid of the nominally Christian Venetians in the fight against the Turks, but got nowhere. Sforza wrote that the Venetians were "obstinate and hardened, always [seeking] to fulfill the appetite of their souls to conquer Italy and then beyond, ...thinking to compare themselves to the Romans when their power was at its apex."

So Venice deserted the Christian cause, and supported the Turks, bringing about, in the process, the end of the Byzantine Empire. Tarpley writes that during the early 15th century, "the Turks possessed a combined warehouse-residence-safe house in Venice, the Fondaco dei Turchi, which facilitated dealings between the doge and the sultan. Spurred on by Venetian financing and Venetian-procured artillery, the Sultan Mohammed the Conqueror laid siege to Constantinople and captured it in 1453." These actions elicited words from the French ambassador to the Holy Roman Emperor describing the Venetians as "traders in human blood, traitors to the Christian faith, who have tacitly divided up the world with the Turks, and who are planning... to reduce Europe to a province and to keep it subjugated to their armies." Pope Pius II chimed in, "[The Venetians] are hypocrites. They wish to appear as Christians before the world but in reality they never think of God and, except for the state, which they regard as a deity, they hold nothing sacred, nothing holy. To a Venetian, that is just which is for the good of the state; that is pious which increases the empire.... They are allowed to do anything that will bring them to supreme power. All law and right may be violated for the sake of power." It would seem that, back in the mid-1400's, there were already plenty of people who well understood How The World Really Worked.

Shortly after the death in 1483 of Louis XI, the Venetians conned his less-brilliant offspring, Charles VIII, into invading Italy and conquering the Kingdom of Naples which he coveted. Charles did so in 1494, in the process unseating the Medici regime in Florence, and installing oligarchic enemies who immediately sought to crush the Florentine Renaissance. Six years later, another blow from the next French king, Louis XII, overthrew the remaining Renaissance figures in Milan, completing the loss of all three cities of Florence, Naples, and Milan to the Renaissance. However, these Venetian initiatives produced a counter-thrust: the famous War of the League of Cambrai.

Recognizing the mischief already accomplished by the Venetians, and the greater amount intended, the European powers met in Cambrai, France, late in 1508, and organized what amounted to a "World War" against Venice. The League included Pope Julius II, the Holy Roman Emperor Maximilian I of Germany, King Louis XII of France, the Queen of Spain, the King of Hungary, the King of Cyprus, and the Dukes of Florence, Milan, and a handful of others. The announced purpose of the alliance was to carve up the Venetian "empire" and distribute it to the League participants (primarily France and Germany), expunging the historical entity which was Venice.

Tarpley relates how they nearly succeeded (V6, pp. 3-4). On May 14, 1509, a French army of 20,000 men clashed with and demolished an equal-sized army of Venetian mercenaries outside of Milan, close to which the Venetians had advanced in the mid-1400's. In a single day, the remaining Venetian forces were driven all the way back to the Venetian lagoons. There they held out, but they had lost their entire land empire. Further, a few months earlier, news had arrived of the defeat by the Portuguese navy of an Egyptian fleet engaged in Far Eastern trade, portending the end of the Venetian monopoly of the spice trade, via either the overland route or Vasco da Gama's newly-found ocean route around Africa. Venice was forced to reexamine its fundamental options.

In the short term, they needed some friends who could provide some help. They found a very important one: Cardinal Wolsey in England. Wolsey, then 38 years old, was running foreign affairs for Henry VIII, the brand new King of England, then 19 years old. Tarpley says, "Advised by Cardinal Wolsey and the Cecils, Henry VIII urged Pope Julius to betray the League of Cambrai, and ally with Venice." [William Cecil, so important during Elizabeth's reign, was not born until 1520, but his father was a bureaucrat in Henry VIII's regime. Wolsey, however, had been around Europe, had noticed and hired Thomas Cromwell to assist him in planning his great College of Christ Church at Oxford, and had been chaplain to both the Archbishop of Canterbury and to Henry VII. His early biography, including any connections he might have had to Venice, or to Pope Julius II, or to Freemasonry would certainly make interesting reading. But see p. 309, below.]

Julius II, Pope since 1503, was a professional soldier from Genoa named Giuliano della Rovere, the same man who, in 1494, was advisor to the French army of Charles VIII which crossed the Alps, invaded Italy, and brought about the fall of Florence and Naples. Though Julius took the side of the League when it was first formed, his commitment rapidly evaporated when confronted with a bribe he couldn't refuse. The bribe, says Tarpley (V1, p. 20), was "mediated [between the Pope and] the Venetians by Agostino Chigi, the Siena Black Guelph banker from whose financial empire the infamous Siena Group of today derives. He proposed that the Venetians stop buying alum (needed in textile and glass manufacture) from the Turks, but contract for a large shipment at higher prices from the alum mines at Tolfa in the Papal States – mines for which he, Chigi, was acting as agent [to the benefit of Julius]. To sweeten the pot, Chigi offered the Venetians tens of thousands of ducats in much-needed loans [to hire more Swiss mercenaries]." A loan from Henry VIII (i.e., from Wolsey) had previously been offered to Venice, along with a friendship treaty.

Venice gratefully accepted all the above, and was back in business, and Julius, with his pieces of silver in hand, had by February of 1510 switched sides. As a cover, he organized the battle cry, "Italy and Freedom," and spread the pretense that the war was to "unify Italy," and to "kick out the barbarians," meaning the French and Germans. Tarpley continues (V6, p. 4), "In the summer of 1510 the French and Imperial forces reached the lagoons a second time, but their flank was attacked by Julius, and Venice was preserved. Julius II [and, we would say, Cardinal Wolsey] must bear the historical responsibility for permitting the survival of Venice and thus of oligarchy into the modern world." The war see-sawed onward, with the French, the Spanish, and the Germans all changing sides at least once, until it came to a non-conclusive end in 1517, with Venice still intact.

A couple of issues might be clarified before we move on. Agostino Chigi was more than just a Siena banker. A brief search around the Internet reveals that Agostino was the first of the Chigi clan to gain eminence, but hardly the last. He was the personal banker of Pope Julius II and also of his successor, Pope Leo X. The clan acted as bankers to the Church for over three centuries, with at least one becoming a pope himself (Alexander VII in 1655), and with many acquiring the status of princes of the empire, or otherwise being in the service of the papacy.

Tarpley also notes (V2, p. 3) that while Venice was courting imminent disaster, they permitted the creation of what he calls "the Jewish community of Venice," a status apparently more liberal than the ghetto status required of Jews living on the terra firma, i.e., outside the lagoons. But we noted earlier that our UWRE recorded the creation of Venetian ghettos in 1516, following which the institution

247

spread elsewhere. It might appear that when the military pressure subsided, and when money was not so urgent a problem, the treatment given Venetian Jews went back to its prior "normal" state. We are still missing definitive facts which might substantiate such speculations.

The Venetian oligarchs thus survived their short-term League of Cambrai crisis, but observed that they had still lost their Far Eastern trading dominance, and to survive in the long term, they needed a viable long-term plan. In 1992, Tarpley wrote (V2, p. 3) that, after the Cambrai affair, the Venetian patricians "realized that the lagoon city could now be crushed like an egg-shell, and was not a suitable base for world domination. As after 1200 there had been talk of moving the capital, perhaps to Constantinople, so now plans began to hatch that would facilitate a metastasis of the Venetian cancer towards the Atlantic world. To make matters worse, the Portuguese access to India had undercut the Venetian spice monopoly through the Levant; there was talk of building a Suez canal, but this was abandoned. Venice had always thrived through divide and conquer. If Europe could unite against Venice, what could Venice do to divide and rend Europe so thoroughly that it would tear itself to pieces for more than a century?"

In a 1996 article (B1, p. 4), Tarpley declares that the oligarchy settled on a plan of "transferring its family fortunes (fondos), philosophical outlook, and political methods into such states as England, France, and the Netherlands. Soon the Venetians decided that England (and Scotland) was the most suitable site for the New Venice, the future center of a new, world-wide Roman Empire based on maritime supremacy. Success of this policy required oligarchical domination and the degradation of the [English] political system.... The overall Venetian policy was to foment wars of religion between the Lutherans, Calvinists, and Anglicans on the one hand, and the Jesuit-dominated

Catholic Counter-Reformation of the Council of Trent on the other. The Venetians had spawned both sides of this conflict, and exercised profound influence over them."

He identifies in a 1995 paper one of the main actors who was to manage the upcoming conflict (V5, p. 5): "One result of the Cambrai crisis was the decision of Venetian intelligence to create the Protestant reformation. The goal was to divide Europe for one or two centuries in religious wars that would prevent any combination like the League of Cambrai from ever again being assembled against Venice. The leading figure of the Protestant reformation, the first Protestant in modern Europe, was Gasparo Contarini."

Tarpley spends a great deal of time and words on Contarini and his works. First, the Contarini name is among the LONGHI, i.e., is one of the oldest names in the Venetian oligarchy, having produced seven doges. Gasparo served Venice as ambassador to Emperor Charles V, and ambassador to the Vatican. He also entertained Pope Julius' banker Chigi during the negotiation of Venice's bribe to the Pope (V2, p. 3). In 1527, as the dominant political figure of the Venetian oligarchy, he sent his uncle, Francesco Zorzi (also of an old oligarchical family), to England to advise Henry VIII concerning the Boleyn affair, where Zorzi played on Henry's passions and simultaneously founded (B1, p. 4) "the powerful Rosicrucian, Hermetic, Cabalistic, and Freemasonic tradition in the Tudor court." Contarini, while in the Pope's College of Cardinals, took Ignatius of Loyola under his wing as protégé, appointed Ignatius his personal confessor and spiritual advisor, and personally interceded with the Pope to ensure the founding of the Society of Jesus as a new church order (V1, p. 22). Its functions would be to manage Catholic education, and enforce the reforms of the Council of Trent.

But perhaps most important, and to ensure that both the Protestants and the Catholics would be well-armed for a good long war, Contarini also became the hidden planner of the Protestant Reformation. Tarpley continues on with the citation noted above (V5, p. 5): "Contarini was a pupil of the Padua Aristotelian Pietro Pomponazzi, who denied the immortality of the human soul. Contarini pioneered the Protestant doctrine of salvation by faith alone, with no regard for good works of charity. Contarini organized a group of Italian Protestants called gli spirituali, including oligarchs like Vittoria Colonna and Giulia Gonzaga. Contarini's networks encouraged and protected Martin Luther and later John Calvin of Geneva." Thus, as the conflict advanced, Contarini's networks among the Venetian oligarchy split into two branches: a pro-Protestant party called the Giovani, supportive of Lutherans, Calvinists, and Anglicans, and a pro-Catholic party called the Vecchi, supportive of the Vatican and the Hapsburg dominions in the Empire. Tarpley goes into a fascinating amount of detail (V2, pp. 3-13) about how this complex matter was managed during the first half of the 16th century. Contarini died in 1542, having served the oligarchy long and well.

After 1582, the oligarchy came to be controlled by the Giovani. Venice was then in serious decline, exacerbated by the monetary starvation of the Venetian state by the repayment of its public debt to its oligarchic lenders, leading to the flight of such capital out of Venice. "One destination," says Tarpley (V2, p. 14), "was certainly the Amsterdam bank, which was founded at about this time." Spain also was exhausted from her warfare, and toward the end of the 16th century was seeking peace with France, England, the Dutch, and even the Ottoman Turks. The Venetians were alarmed (V2, pp. 16-17), seeing the possibility that Spain might then opt to turn on Venice. The religious wars would simply have to be restarted, and occupy all of Europe for another century or so until Venice's move to England could be completed and consolidated.

The war which was created was called by historians the Thirty Years' War. The leading Venetian who manipulated the European powers into fighting each other was this time a Servite monk named Paolo Sarpi, a member of the Venetian Giovani faction. Our trusty UWRE doesn't mention Sarpi in its coverage of the Thirty Years' War, and doesn't mention the Thirty Years' War in its coverage of Sarpi. Tarpley does, however, go into lots of that detail (V2, pp. 14-22), suggesting where other historians might look to find the buried motivations behind one of the more senseless events in our Western history. Sarpi got the Venetian-desired war started, which lasted from 1618 to 1648, and shortly thereafter died (in 1623), his main contribution to Venetian welfare accomplished. The war wiped out about half of the population of Germany and one third of the population of Europe during its 30-year span, and in the long term settled virtually nothing.

We turn our attention now to Tarpley's account of the preparation of England as the site of the New Venice. As Walsh previously described, Queen Elizabeth, under the influence first of William Cecil, and then later of his son Robert Cecil, consolidated the separation of England from the Roman church, as desired by Venice. "The Cecils," says Tarpley (B1, p. 5), "were notorious assets of Venice; their ancestral home at Hatfield House was festooned with Lions of St. Mark." The Cecils advised and helped Elizabeth to build the English navy and merchant marine into institutions befitting a major world power, and to otherwise build England into a more credible challenger of Spain.

When Elizabeth died, Robert Cecil orchestrated the accession of the Scottish Stuart king as King James I of England. Cecil for a time was his key advisor, later being replaced by Francis Bacon, mentioned earlier by Walsh as the writer of *The New Atlantis*. James, a pederast and open homosexual, was also an enthusiastic advocate of the divine right of kings, which attracted Paolo Sarpi to him since it challenged the rights of the Pope, but it also made James difficult to control. Bacon could not get James to support Sarpi's Thirty Years' War, and James' son, King Charles I, was equally disappointing, actually helping the French to defeat the Venetian-supported Huguenots.

The main problem with divine rights was that they couldn't produce tax revenue in England, since Parliamentary approval was needed for taxation, and for a monarch to request Parliamentary approval would be acknowledging a monarchial status somewhat less than divine. The Stuarts therefore tried, unsuccessfully, to rule autocratically, without convoking Parliament, but succeeded only in creating a vast antagonism between the two branches of government. The Venetians wanted no part of the divine right folderol. What they were used to, and wanted for England, was a weak Doge managed by a strong consortium of rich nobles who would run the country for the maintenance of the power and profit of the consortium. The Stuarts therefore had to go, as did the very concept of a strong monarchy.

The English Civil War between the Parliament and the monarchy began in 1641, when King Charles tried to arrest parliamentary leaders with whom he was struggling, but was forced to flee London when he found that local support favored those leaders. The opposing factions were both Protestant: the Anglican royalist cavaliers vs. the Parliamentary Puritan Roundheads. The latter group was in turn divided into a Scottish-Calvinist "Presbyterian" faction, which sought to negotiate with Charles, and Oliver Cromwell's Independent, or "Congregationalist" faction, which sought to defeat and execute the king, and then abolish the monarchy and the House of Lords. "Oliver Cromwell," says Tarpley (B1, p. 7), "was a Venetian agent," and was a direct descendent of the sister of Thomas Cromwell, the controller of Henry VIII. Marriage ties existed between the Cromwell family and Venetian financial circles, as Tarpley briefly describes.

By 1646, the Royalist forces were defeated. Charles I was soon captured, tried for treason, and executed in January of 1649. The Presbyterian faction of Parliament was expelled by Cromwell, leaving only a "Rump Parliament" to work out a system of governance with Cromwell. Several efforts were made to create a Doge-Council system, all unsuccessful, up to the time of Cromwell's death in 1658. His final effort at governing amounted to a military dictatorship, an effort described by our sometimes trusty UWRE as being one in which "he was obliged to maintain his power, as he had acquired it, against his better will, by a severity often amounting to tyranny."

Now without a strong leader, the Parliament and the army, after two more years of chaos, restored the monarchy, and in 1660 recalled Charles II, the son of the executed Charles I, to the throne. Though Cromwell had failed to produce a permanent Doge system, he had brought about some significant changes. The British navy was vastly strengthened, and its permanent presence in the Mediterranean established. He had made war on Spain, acquiring Jamaica (the center of the New World slave trade), Nova Scotia, and other New World properties. Portugal's status had become that of an English satellite. He had reduced Scotland to English rule, but with formal union still about fifty years distant. He had also instituted the systematic starvation of Ireland, eventually killing about one third of the Irish population. As Tarpley describes it (B1, p. 10), these actions "laid the basis for the myth of a 'British' people as a label imposed on Irish, Scottish, Welsh, and English victims of an oligarchy not of Englishmen, but of Venetians and their tools."

The Stuart kings Charles II and his brother and successor James II were tolerated only for a short time.

Charles accepted a subsidy from Louis XIV of France in order to have resources with which to circumvent the programs and policies of the "Venetian" Parliament, which wanted instead to diminish the growing power of France, Spain having already been disposed of. In addition, Charles announced as he was dying that he was a Roman Catholic, further violating Venetian doctrine. His brother James then likewise proclaimed his Catholicity, and accepted the continued support of Louis XIV. He further began appointing Catholics into his military officer corps, which was the last straw. Tarpley says (B1, p. 11), "The Anglo-Venetians decided that they were fed up with the now-Catholic pro-French and wholly useless Stuart dynasty. Representatives of some of the leading oligarchical families [secretly] signed an invitation to the Dutch [William III] of Orange [p. 232, supra], and his Queen Mary, a daughter of James II." William invaded, James' army deserted him, James fled to France, William ascended the throne of England, and the "Glorious Revolution of 1688" became history.

It was actually the Anglo-Venetians who were the victors. The oligarchy's powers and privileges were now written into law. Parliament became supreme over both the monarch and the state church. Ministers could be removed from office by a majority of Parliament. Raising taxes, raising armies, and suspending laws were sole prerogatives of Parliament. The price at which a seat could be bought was determined by how much graft it could raise. In 1694, the Bank of England was formed, the stockholders of which are unknown to the public to this day, though we can now make some pretty good guesses. Immediately thereafter, the English national debt was born, and the pattern of central bank operations established, a pattern copied by the Federal Reserve System under which the American public labors today. We have reviewed in our own HTWRW an excellent book by G. Edward Griffin – *The Creature From*

254

Jekyll Island – detailing how this oligarchic money machine operates to enrich its creators.

Thus, it took nearly 200 years, but the Venetians finally conquered England, without the English or practically anyone else even knowing it. As Tarpley puts it (B1, p. 12), "When George I ascended the throne in 1714, he knew he was a Doge, the [first among equals] of an oligarchy. The regime that took shape in England after 1688 was the most perfect copy of the Venetian oligarchy that was ever produced." Further (B4, p. 10), the British oligarchs did at that time even "call themselves the Venetian Party. The future Prime Minister Benjamin Disraeli [would] write in his novel *Coningsby* that the Whig aristocrats of 1688 wanted 'to establish in England a high aristocratic republic on the model of [Venice], making the kings into doges, and with a Venetian constitution.'" It is that same oligarchy which continues to trouble the whole world today.

But even before King George I came along, the British Venetians set off on their path of empire, starting with the War of the Spanish Succession, 1701-1713. William III was still king when the war started, but died in 1702 from a fall off his horse. His successor was Queen Anne, the sister of his deceased wife Mary. Both Mary and Anne were daughters of the former King James II. Queen Anne, says our UWRE, was a weak monarch, influenced first by the Duke of Marlborough, the Lord John Churchill, a supporter of King William III, and ancestor of the 20th century's Winston Churchill. As a result of the War of Spanish Succession, in which Churchill was a successful general, the British acquired Gibraltar from Spain, plus Newfoundland, Hudson Bay, and other Canadian property from France. The British were now supreme on the oceans, and had won, says Tarpley (B4, p. 11), "the monopoly on slave commerce with Spanish America. The British [thus] became the biggest slave merchants in the world. The wealth of Bristol and Liverpool would be built on slaves." Scotland also was formally annexed into "Great Britain" during the reign of Queen Anne.

British dominance was further solidified by the conflict from 1756 to 1763 known as the Seven Years' War. The prime result of this war was that the French were virtually expelled from both Canada and India, with their territories in those countries, specifically including Quebec City, going to the British. French power was momentarily reduced to a nullity. Both of these 18th century wars between England and France were known in American history as the French and Indian Wars, with the Indians generally being used by the French to prosecute a sort of guerrilla war against the English colonists. More realistically, the Indians were pawns, and the colonies were prizes, in the big-power struggles centered in Europe between England and France.

Besides working on increasing the physical strength of their English base, and decreasing that of their European opponents, the Venetians also undertook, at the beginning of the 18th century, the destruction from within of the established French society. Their on-site agent was a Venetian nobleman named Antonio Conti (1677-1749). Tarpley says of him (V5, p. 8), "Conti went to London where he became a friend of Sir Isaac Newton. Conti directed... the creation of a pro-Newton party of French Anglophiles... who came to [be] known as the French Enlightenment. Conti's agents in this effort included Montesquieu and Voltaire." Tarpley fills in more of the picture in another article (V4, p. 11): "Montesquieu, before Voltaire, Rousseau, and the Encyclopedia, was the first important figure of the French Enlightenment – more respectable than Voltaire and Rousseau – and the leading theoretician of political institutions. Conti met Montesquieu at the Hotel de Rohan, and at another salon, the Club de l'Entresol. Later, when Conti had returned to Venice, Montesquieu came to visit him there, staying a month. MONTESQUIEU WAS AN AGENT FOR CONTI."

Tarpley continues, "Montesquieu's major work is The Spirit of the Laws, published in 1748. This is a work of decidedly Venetian flavor, with republic, monarchy, and despotism as the three forms of government, and a separation of powers doctrine. Montesquieu appears to have taken many of his ideas from Conti... [and] raises the theme of Anglophilia, praising Britain's allegedly constitutional monarchy as the ideal form. With this, the pro-British bent of Conti's Enlightenment philosophes is established."

Tarpley lists his source material linking Conti to Voltaire and Montesquieu at V4, pp. 14-15. His work thus completes the circle by connecting Venice to the personages of Voltaire and Montesquieu, who were extensively covered by the researches of Barruel (p. 84, supra), and named as laying the foundations of the French Revolution, though Barruel was unable to identify from whom those inclinations were acquired.

We jump ahead now, past the French Revolution and its Napoleonic postlude, which we have extensively covered, to the era of Lord Palmerston, about which Tarpley has a great deal to say. But before getting to his main themes, he mentions briefly Palmerston's involvement with the Opium Wars against China. We would note, however, the extreme importance of this issue, which became a thrust of British foreign policy at about the time that the British Venetians were spreading their wings shortly after the Glorious Revolution. The (private) British East India Company (BEIC) opened an office in Canton in 1715, and began opium operations in China. In 1757, during the Seven Years' War, the British conquered Bengal (now Bangladesh), and turned it into a British colony, the main product of which then became opium, produced by and for the BEIC.

SECRECY OR FREEDOM?

In 1783, the British Prime Minister Lord Shelburne, who had just negotiated the peace treaty with the American colonies, completed an effective coup in England, having bought the necessary seats in Parliament, and then united the government and the BEIC into a single entity, with England providing military support for the BEIC's operations, and then sharing in its profits. By 1840, Lord Palmerston, then Prime Minister, ordered up the first Opium War to enhance those profits, and by 1859, again as Prime Minister, prosecuted also the Second Opium War. The British use and ongoing control of the opium trade as a means of financing their governmental operations is spelled out in great detail in "Dope, Inc.," by the editors of the Executive Intelligence Review, which we have in turn reviewed in our own HTWRW.

Tarpley's sketch of Palmerston is drawn via biographical looks at three of his conspiratorial subordinates, or agents, whom Tarpley stylizes as "stooges." While Palmerston can himself manage the Foreign Office and the domestic bureaucracy, he found these agents to be needed for hands-on work in the field.

The first of the agents is Giuseppe Mazzini. He is philosophically wedded to the belief that man lives only for the benefit and promotion of his own independent national grouping, which should be run by a centralized dictatorship. He curiously omits naming Ireland as a group deserving such independence, and likewise supports one and only one monarchy, namely Queen Victoria's, since, he says, that monarchy has especially deep roots among the people. In the conspiratorial world, he started as a Carbonari, then in 1831 created his own secret society, Young Italy. That arena of effort was found to be his forte, and the creation of such organizations engaged his efforts for the next forty years.

Thus, in the 1830's, in addition to Young Italy, Mazzini created, says Tarpley, (B4, p. 6), "Young Poland, [and then] Young Germany, featuring Arnold Ruge, who had published some material by an obscure German 'red republican' named Karl Marx.... In 1834 Mazzini founded 'Young Europe,' with Italian, Swiss, German, and Polish components [aimed at Metternich]. By 1835, there was also a Young Switzerland. In that same year Mazzini launched Young France.... There was also Young Corsica, which was the Mafia." By the end of the century, says Tarpley, these entities had been joined by Young Argentina, Bosnia, India, Russia, Armenia, Egypt, the Czechs, and "similar groupings in Romania, Hungary, Bulgaria, and Greece." There was also Young America, "a Masonic group in the United States gearing up to support the pro-slavery Franklin Pierce for President in 1852.... And yes, there is also a Palmerston-Mazzini group for Jews, some-times called Young Israel, and sometimes called B'nai B'rith." (Tarpley notes later in his article, however (B4, p. 13), that instead of being a group "for Jews," B'nai B'rith was created as "an abject tool of British Intelligence, run and directed to serve the interests of British imperial policy, and not the interests of Jews, nor even of B'nai B'rith members."

There is a pattern to all this, orchestrated by Palmerston. The primary power centers left to be attacked by the British Venetians were, first, "Prince Metternich's Austrian Empire, a very strong land power," then Imperial Russia, the Kingdom of Prussia, the Ottoman Empire, and of course the United States. Prussia and the Turks would be put off till later, but would presently be used to at least weaken Russia and to destroy Metternich. A plan was also launched to split up the United States and retake the weakened pieces one by one.

The one prime result of the "European Revolution of 1848" was the replacement of King Louis Philippe by Emperor Napoleon III, the latter by coup in 1852 (p. 162, supra). Napoleon III, the "second stooge" of Palmerston (more about that in a moment), brought with him a large French land army, suitable for fighting in the upcoming Crimean War. Then on February 21, 1854, says Tarpley (B4, p. 14), on the eve of that war, an interesting group was assembled in the London home of the U.S. consul to Britain, George Sanders. The group consisted of:

George Sanders - leader of Young America, and President Pierce's British consul

Giuseppe Mazzini - Young Italy, and Palmerston representative

Felice Orsini - a Mazzini lieutenant

Giuseppe Garibaldi - Young Italy, and 1848-49 militarist for Mazzini

Louis Kossuth - Young Hungary

Arnold Ruge - Young Germany

Ledru-Rollin - Young France

Stanley Worcell - Young Poland

Aleksandr Herzen - Young Russia, and agent of Baron James Rothschild of Paris

James Buchanan - next President of U.S., 1856-1860

Unnamed - representative of London investment firm of George Peabody

The plan was to attack and weaken Russia using forces from France, England, Turkey, and hopefully the United States. Despite efforts to involve the U.S., it stayed out, and emerged, says Tarpley, "as the only power friendly to Russia during the Crimean conflict." This played a crucial role in Lincoln's effort to preserve the union during the upcoming Civil War, as we will discuss in our next chapter. (George Peabody, the precursor of J. P. Morgan & Co., "became wildly successful as the London agent for the

Union government during the Civil War." - HTWRW, p. 113.) The Crimean War did otherwise attain the conspiracy's goals, separating Russia from Austria, the latter then being attacked first by France, and then by Germany, finishing her off as a strong, independent European power. Germany then turned on and defeated France, dethroning Napoleon III and establishing the weak Third French Republic, as previously described (p. 145, supra). The British Venetians then had only Russia, Germany, and the United States to worry about, but World War 1 was only about 45 years away.

Returning for a moment to Napoleon III (B4, p. 9), he nicely defined the role of a "throwaway stooge." He started as a secret society Carbonaro close to Mazzini, and later showed up in the British Museum in close touch with Lord Palmerston. He was sent to Paris upon the Revolution of 1848, where he used his name to gain the presidency of the Second French Republic. In 1852 came the coup which made him Emperor. He continued doing the work of Palmerston, such as building the Suez Canal which the British soon controlled, and installing the Austrian Hapsburg Maximilian as the French Emperor of Mexico, in support of the Confederacy during the American Civil War. In 1870 Napoleon III was turned out of office by the army of Bismarck, whose monarch, King William of Prussia, was thereupon elevated to Emperor William I of all Germany. In the course of this turmoil, the Pope was divested of his properties and the bulk of his temporal authority, which was the first and primary goal of the Italian Carbonari (p. 138, supra).

The last of Tarpley's "Three Stooges" is the aristocratic Scot, David Urquhart (B4, pp. 8-9). This gentleman was secretary of the British embassy in Constantinople in 1835, was entranced by Turkish culture, and became an ardent lifelong enemy of the Russian court. He was a member of Parliament from 1847-1852, vigorously opposing Palmerston, whom he accused of being a Romanov agent. Palmerston found such crazy accusations helpful, since they tended to obscure his own real anti-tsarist policies.

From the late 1830's, Urquhart had taken up the cause of the English "Chartists," a working-class movement aimed at raising the economic and political status of the working man. To this end, he controlled a weekly paper called *The Free Press* which he used to teach workers what he called dialectics. One of Urquhart's writers for his paper was none other than Karl Marx, who in 1849 had permanently moved to England, where so many earlier revolutionaries had found refuge. Marx now began work on his magnum opus, *Das Kapital*, the first volume of which was published in 1867. Tarpley says that Marx was "a professed admirer of Urquhart – acknowledging his influence more than that of any other living person." Further, he says that it was Urquhart who prescribed the plan for *Das Kapital*, and that Urquhart was, in reality, "the founder of modern communism!"

Does it make sense? Whatever the true relationship between Urquhart and Palmerston, the system of communism codified by Marx in Palmerston's England was later used to conquer Russia (WW1), to destroy Germany (WW1 and WW2), and to greatly weaken the United States (WW2 and the Cold, Korean, and Vietnamese Wars). Perhaps it's just a coincidence that these three impacted countries were exactly the last major powers still standing in the way of the British Venetians at the end of the Franco-Prussian War in 1870. Or is it more likely that those Venetians, back in the 1840's, were even then diligently planning the future?

Tarpley then moves to the preparations for World War 1. As noted above, the strong powers remaining to be reduced were Germany, Russia, and the United States. Secondarily, the Ottoman Turks were still in there. The plan that was ultimately developed was to surround Germany with an alliance of countries, specifically including Russia, strong enough to defeat Germany, and in the process perhaps bring down Russia as well. However, during the reign of Emperor William I, the highly astute Otto von Bismarck was in charge of foreign affairs, and Germany managed to avoid traps leading to unwanted conflicts. Bismarck sought and obtained a working alliance with Russia, exactly because he knew that the strength of that combination could not be successfully challenged, and so would not be. Our UWRE notes that by 1887 he had alliances made with Austria, Italy, Rumania, and Russia. He had also tried for an alliance with Great Britain, but had failed. William I died in 1888, however, and his successor, William II, disagreed with Bismarck's policies and forced him to resign. Bismarck's astute plan for keeping the peace came under attack and began to crumble.

The actor holding the center of the world's stage for the next 20 years or so, the man most singly responsible for bringing on World War 1, was, says Tarpley (B5, pp. 1-21), King Edward VII of England, secretly representing, of course, the British Venetians.

Edward VII was born in 1841, the eldest son of Queen Victoria and her cousin and husband Prince Albert of Saxe-Coburg-Gotha. He was for sixty years the Prince of Wales and heir to the British throne. His father Prince Albert died in 1861, whereupon his mother the Queen went into "deep mourning," says Tarpley (B5, p. 3), retreating to her Scottish castle in Balmoral, and living the life of an occultist, which included the pretense that her husband Albert was still alive. Tarpley includes many more details, very interesting, but thematically irrelevant.

What was relevant was that Prince Edward thereafter became engrossed with the affairs of state, and spent the following forty years before Victoria's death in 1901 in preparing himself to rule, and rule he did, personally, with his own highly trained hands. In 1863 he became a member of the Queen's Privy Council, took his seat in the House of Lords, and married the Princess Alexandra of Denmark. They had six children, whom he married off among the European royalty as advantageously as possible. His second son succeeded him as King George V. On a personal level, Edward was a legendary hedonist and sex maniac, whose countless mistresses were of both high and low estate, including even, says Tarpley (B5, p. 4), "some of the can-can dancers painted by Toulouse-Lautrec."

Edward's first son, "Prince Eddie," was the prime suspect of being the legendary Jack the Ripper. Freemasonic intrigue, and an official cover-up were both apparent. An eminent British surgeon who claimed knowledge of the Ripper's identity died mysteriously, upon which his family burnt all his papers. Sir Charles Warren, the chief of the London police, and Master of a new Freemasonic lodge in London, was accused of suppressing evidence and intimidating witnesses, and resigned, says Tarpley (B5, p. 6), "among a public outcry about Masonic conspiracy." His Scottish rite lodge "had been founded in 1884 with a warrant from the Grand Master of British freemasonry, [who just] happened to be Edward VII." That position of course gave Edward unequaled access to both the official and the secret centers of power in Europe and throughout the whole world.

Becoming king in 1901, Edward lived only until 1910, but he managed by that time to have built such a sturdy wall of alliances around Germany that he and his Venetian cohorts and dupes were confident that Germany would be defeated when war broke out, and they worked specifically toward that goal. How had the alliances been built? That is precisely the theme of Tarpley's "B5" paper, and he goes into a great amount of detail. We'll try to provide a convincing summary of this "blacked-out" segment of Western history which Tarpley has illuminated for us.

Edward's central modus operandi was to get the people he wanted into the positions he wanted, and then work his will with them by manipulating their weaknesses. Tarpley quotes the former French foreign minister Emile Flourens (B5, p. 11), who wrote in 1906 that Edward's triumphs were attributable to his "profound knowledge of the human heart and the sagacity with which he could sort out the vices and weaknesses of individuals and peoples, and make these into the worst and most destructive weapons against them." Edward's primary goals were to get rid of the Bismarckian influence in Germany, and wean Russia away from Germany and toward France and England, thereby isolating Germany from any strong supportive power..

That first step became possible with the death of the 90-year old Emperor William I of Germany. The new Emperor William II, better known in popular history as Kaiser Wilhelm, was a nephew of Edward VII, and highly manipulable. In addition, says Tarpley (B5, p. 11), "Edward made a detailed study of [the Kaiser's] psychological profile, which he knew to be pervaded by feelings of inferiority and incurable Anglophilia.... Wilhelm felt inferior to British royalty. Wilhelm's greatest secret desire was for acceptance by the British royals." With this as his background mindset, the young and unstable Kaiser, chasing his elusive fantasy of friendship with and acceptance by the masterful British elites, dismissed Bismarck in 1890, and permitted Germany's "Reinsurance Treaty" with Russia to lapse (B3, p. 10), in effect inviting the French to tender an alliance offer to Russia, which was in fact accepted in 1894. Edward and his minions continued to reinforce the Kaiser's fantasy right up to the very start of WW1, but without ever concretizing the fantasy with such a thing as a written treaty. The Kaiser bought the policy of forever chasing after rapprochement with London, and let slip the very real protection available to Germany by retaining and strengthening her previous alliance with Russia.

During the course of his reign, Edward managed to make alliances with a long string of countries that would later oppose Germany in WW1, including France and Russia (the two most important ones), Italy, Japan, Norway, Denmark, Spain, and Portugal. We'll briefly summarize Tarpley's account of the first four.

At the turn of the century, Japan and Russia were at loggerheads over Asian spheres of influence (B5, p. 14), and in 1901, Japan, seeking an ally, sent its prime minister to London. Edward wined, dined, and "socially lionized and decorated" him. Within a month, an Anglo-Japanese treaty was signed, stating that if Japan and Russia went to war, Britain would remain "benevolently neutral," that is, would not join the war, but would prevent other powers from coming to the aid of Russia. Japan did start that war in 1904, and as a result Russia lost the bulk of its navy, and in the following two years also underwent the trauma of their 1905 Revolution, which Tarpley states that Edward helped to instigate. Japan later honored her treaty with Britain, and in 1914 declared war on Germany.

Next came France (B5, p. 15). Edward offered France Britain's interest in Morocco in exchange for giving Britain a free hand in Egypt. The deal was unequal, since both Germany and Spain had competing claims on Morocco. But early in 1903 Edward visited Paris, turned on his charm, gave speeches in French about his affection for all things French, accepted the plaudits of the French press, and reveled in the public mania surrounding him. The deal therefore got signed in 1904, with the help not only of Edward's personal demagoguery, but also of Edward's secret network of Anglophiles in France, including Clemenceau and the French Foreign Minister Delcasse. As Edward expected, Germany protested the French appearance in Morocco, French hatred of Germany was rekindled, and the confrontation escalated to threats of war. By 1905, with France's ally Russia weakened by its own war, France was driven further into the arms of Edward, whose alliance could offer some meaningful security. The real war did not happen then, but joint Anglo-French war planning was actually started, and one of Edward's two critical alliances was now safely in place.

Not the last, but of critical importance, was the alliance with Russia (B5, p. 17). The key Russian in Edward's network was the Russian Foreign Minister Izvolski, to whom Edward broached the idea of an Anglo-Russian pact in April of 1904, immediately after the Anglo-French pact went into effect. The Russian pact was signed in 1907, defining British-Russian spheres of influence in Iran, Afghanistan, and Tibet, and expressing no British objection to Russian expansion into the Balkans, an approach which would obviously lead to confrontation with Austria and Germany. How far Russia had come from its Bismarckian alliance with Germany! In 1908, Edward sailed to Reval (now Tallinn, Estonia) to meet his nephew, Tsar Nicholas II, and advised him to build up his army facing Germany. When the war came, Russia would suffer nine million casualties, the highest of any of the WW1 belligerents, and would subsequently be enslaved by the Venetian-engendered Bolsheviks.

Finally (B5, pp. 17-18), Edward went to Naples in April, 1909 to have a chat with King Victor Emmanuel III of Italy, accompanied by Edward's agent, the Italian Foreign Minister Tittoni. At their meeting, Edward offered a toast to an "alliance" between Britain and Italy, an alliance for which history can find no written documentation. However, when the war started, Italy reneged on her "Triple Alliance

Treaty" with Germany and Austria, and nine months later declared war on them instead. One might take this as an indication that at least a verbal Anglo-Italian agreement had been reached.

Thus, in a 20-year period, Edward VII had done an outstanding job of converting Germany's circle of support into a circle of enemies, though few outside of the circle's core organizers could have been aware of its full extent or its volatility.

The mechanics for getting the war started in 1914 (B5, pp. 6-8) heavily involved Sir Edward (not Albert) Grey, the British Foreign Minister from 1905 to 1916, also godson of Edward VII, and a key member of his entourage. Edward VII had died in 1910, but of course the British Venetian Oligarchy (let's name it the BVO) and its program lived on. Their strategy for starting the war was to convince the Germans that the British would never go to war against them, while at the same time convincing the Russians that the British would honor their Triple Entente commitment to go to war in support of Russian aggression. The strategy up through mid-1914 had been very successful, with the British ambassador to Germany declaring at that time that Anglo-German relations were "more friendly and cordial than they had been in years."

The fuse was lit on June 28, 1914 with the assassination in Sarajevo of Archduke Franz Ferdinand, the heir to the Austrian throne. The hottest heads in Serbia and Austria were shortly at each other's throats, backed by those in Russia and Germany who wanted and incited them on toward war. There were cooler heads, of course, in both Germany and Russia who wished to discipline the unruly kids and not let the fuss escalate to an unlimited war. Sir Earl Grey, the perceived friend of both sides, stepped in to mediate. He could, says Tarpley, have done one of two things to prevent the holocaust. He could have warned

Germany that in a general war Britain would fight alongside the French and Russians, whereupon the Kaiser would be strongly motivated to tell Austria to go take a cold shower and cool off. Or Sir Grey could have told the French and Russians that, despite the Triple Entente agreement, he had no intention of getting embroiled in a Balkan squabble, a stance which would have frightened the French and urgently motivated the Tsar to apply a large paddle to the backsides of those Russian and Serbian brats who were screaming for war.

Sir Grey, however, did neither. Instead, he dropped hints in Paris that England would support France and Russia, and saw that they were passed on to Czar Nicholas II, via Russian Foreign Minister Sazonov, "a British agent," says Tarpley. The path toward Russian aggression was thereby encouraged rather than discouraged. Simultaneously, Grey continued with the pretense of mediating the conflict, efforts which never seemed to bear any fruit, but which reinforced the impression among the Germans and Austrians that England really did want to keep the peace, and would not go to war over the Balkans. The Kaiser felt that, lacking their British ally, the French and Russians would likewise refrain, and so felt no great urgency about forcing the Austrian war hawks to back down.

On July 26, 1914, King George V told the Kaiser's brother in England that Britain had "no quarrel with anyone, and I hope we shall remain neutral." Two days later, Austria declared war on Serbia, and one day later, on July 29, the British fleet was put on a full war footing. Then, to the astonishment of the Kaiser, Russia mobilized in support of Serbia, and on July 31 Germany sent Russia an ultimatum demanding cessation of mobilization. Upon receiving no response, on August 1 Germany declared war on Russia. Germany then asked France her intentions, and upon receiving an unsatisfactory response, declared war on her on

August 3. On August 2 Sir Grey dropped his mask as mediator, and late on August 4 Britain declared war on Germany.

It was only then, early in August of 1914, that the Kaiser realized that he had been had. Tarpley quotes the Kaiser, as recorded by a later researcher, as saying: "England, Russia, and France have agreed among themselves... to take the Austro-Serbian conflict for an excuse for waging a war of extermination against us.... That is the real naked situation slowly and cleverly set going by Edward VII and... finally brought to a conclusion by George V.... So the famous encirclement of Germany has finally become a fact, despite every effort of our politicians and diplomats to prevent it. The net has been suddenly thrown over our head, and England sneeringly reaps the most brilliant success of her persistently prosecuted purely anti-German world policy.... A great achievement, which arouses the admiration even of him who is to be destroyed as its result. Edward VII is stronger after his death than am I who am still alive!"

In similar vein, the German military writer Reinhold Wagner wrote, shortly after the war began, the following admirably concise indictment of the dead King Edward: "The greatest criminal against humankind which the twentieth century has seen so far was King Edward VII of England. For he was the one, HE was the one, who has instigated the world war of today."

As we all know, the war brought the Hohenzollern, Hapsburg, Romanov, and Ottoman dynasties to an end. Germany was laid low, and crushed under the overwhelming weight of the Versailles Treaty, which brought on the subsequent disasters of Hitler, World War 2, etc. Russia, which the BVO's used as a pawn to help bring on WW1, suffered even more under the BVO's Bolshevik regime, which, unlike the German Weimar Republic, treated their own people as slaves and prisoners to be utilized. Tarpley had noted that after the Franco-Prussian War of 1870, the British Venetians had only Russia, Germany, and the United States to worry about. At the end of World War 1, that list had been reduced to just Germany and the United States, with Germany having been dealt a near-fatal blow. But World War 2 was coming up, which would substantially finish the job on Germany, after which serious work could get started on the United States. A good deal of the groundwork had already been laid, as we will show in our next chapter.

Chapter 10

"TREASON IN AMERICA"

(By Anton Chaitkin, pub. 1985 by Executive Intelligence Review, PO Box 17390, Washington, DC 20041. Available from Ben Franklin Booksellers, PO Box 1707, Leesburg, VA 20177, tel. 800-453-4108.)

The thrust of Chaitkin's book is to identify the existence of two opposing movements which largely controlled the ebb and flow of the American nation during the 19th century. The first was an American nationalist group, which included such as Benjamin Franklin, George Washington, Alexander Hamilton, John Quincy Adams, Henry Clay, Abraham Lincoln, and Lincoln's economic advisor Henry Carey. The opposing group, in the service of the British "Venetians" so expertly uncovered by Webster Tarpley, included families having last names such as Lowell, Russell, Cushing, Perkins, Higginson, Prevost, Gallatin, Burr, and Astor. The former group favored individual liberty protected by the Constitution; the latter group was wedded to oligarchism. The issue in contention was nothing less than which of the two groups should control the new American nation. Chaitkin's theme is that, though the British lost the American Revolutionary War, they have never given up trying to weaken, split up, or otherwise emasculate the U.S., in order to further their secret goal of recovering "their colony." And as Tarpley has pointed out, by the middle of the 20th century, with the bulk of Europe subdued, the British oligarchs saw the United States as the only serious impediment remaining to their domination of the entire world.

Chaitkin builds his story largely from family documents, which he finds more reliable and revealing than the more formal historical works financed by the oligarchs themselves and their institutions. Chaitkin's book, thoroughly referenced and indexed, starts with Aaron Burr.

Burr's maternal grandfather was the Yale-bred Calvinist Jonathan Edwards. Burr's father, Aaron Burr, Sr., attracted to Edwards' religious views, met and married Edwards' daughter Esther, who in 1756 bore Aaron, Jr. In 1757, Aaron, Sr., then the President of the College of New Jersey (now Princeton), died, and the presidency devolved upon Jonathan Edwards, who shortly after also died, as did his daughter Esther. Aaron, Jr. was thus orphaned in his infancy, and was taken and raised by family friends – the merchant Shippens of Philadelphia – and later by an uncle, who saw to his proper attendance at Princeton, from 1769 to 1772. One of his classmates there was James Madison, whose sympathies during those times of turmoil were Americanist. Burr, however, was attracted to the Royalist side, and opposing the Americanists in debate, caught the attention of James Mark Prevost, then (p. 7) "the highest-ranking British military officer in New Jersey."

It was the Prevost family that was to provide Burr with a family and an identity. Burr thus entered the big time, for, says Chaitkin (p. 7), "The Prevost family in Geneva were hereditary members of [Geneva's] ruling Council of 200." Burr would some years later (1782) marry Col. Prevost's widow Theodosia, and so bind himself into the Prevost family. That family was itself intermarried with the Swiss and English Mallet family, making Burr (p. 17) "a husband, step father [of Theodosia's children], cousin, and uncle of Mallet-Prevosts in many very important places." James Mark Prevost and his two brothers had all left Geneva in the 1750's to join the British military, had served with them during the French and Indian War, and continued

273

to serve them during the American Revolution. Burr was obviously aware of whom and what he was allying himself with.

Nevertheless, in 1775, with a public burst of patriotism, Burr applied to General Washington for a commission in the American army. Washington smelled a rat, and turned him down. Burr got around him, however, by following a military expedition under Colonel Benedict Arnold who was on his way north to meet an American force under General Richard Montgomery, with the objective of converging upon and conquering the British in Quebec. Arnold accepted Burr's offer to help, and sent him as a messenger through British territory to Montgomery, who, observing Burr's messengerial success, conferred a captaincy upon him, and charged him with the task of spying and scouting behind enemy lines. Burr did so spy, and apparently otherwise interact with the British military, and when the secret attack on Quebec took place, the Americans were ambushed and slaughtered almost to a man, *excluding*, however, Aaron Burr himself. Canada thus remained English, as it does to this day. Burr returned to Washington's New York headquarters in the spring of 1776, and was given a temporary job as Washington's secretary, but within a few days was again dismissed by Washington. Something still didn't smell right.

The other Revolutionary War event touching Burr was the Benedict Arnold treason. Briefly, the treason was hatched between Peggy Shippen, who was Aaron Burr's step-sister, and her boy-friend, Major John André, the adjutant general of the British army. Burr was at the same time sparking Theodosia Prevost at the New Jersey home of her husband James Mark Prevost, who was off fighting Americans in the southern colonies. In September of 1778, Burr, still in the army, was transferred to West Point, where he was able to learn what he needed of its defenses. In

January of 1779, he returned to the New York area, and Arnold was named commandant. A few months later, Peggy Shippen *married* Benedict Arnold, and went off to join him at West Point. Thereupon, says Chaitkin (p. 14), "the first letters negotiating Arnold's treason, conduited through his wife [Burr's step-sister], went between Arnold and Major André [Peggy's old boy-friend]."

The conspiracy fortunately collapsed, with Major André being captured with the West Point plans secreted in his American clothing. He was hanged as a spy. Arnold escaped to the British lines, and finished the war in their military service. Benedict Arnold's accomplice Joshua Hett Smith was captured, and confessed, but he later escaped custody, made his way to London, and retired "in the comfort and grace of his nephew's family, the *Mallets*." Peggy talked her way out of a treason indictment, and Burr also squeaked by, resigning from the army and returning to a study of the law, though he was to be found in that study in the home of one Thomas Smith, the brother of the convicted Joshua Hett Smith. Even given all these connections, there was insufficient evidence to convict Burr, and he escaped indictment. Aaron Burr's executor, Mathew Davis, wrote in the 1836 edition of Burr's *Memoirs* that Peggy Shippen admitted to Mrs. Prevost in 1780, with Aaron Burr present, that she had persuaded Arnold to surrender West Point to the British. Two years later, Aaron Burr married the widowed Theodosia Prevost.

Back in 1778, when Burr was visiting Mrs. Theodosia Prevost, she introduced him, says Chaitkin (p. 13), "to the works and the world of Jeremy Bentham and Voltaire," the same Voltaire about whom we have extensively quoted Barruel. Mrs. Prevost perhaps obtained her enthusiasm for Voltaire from her husband's brother General Augustine Prevost, the commander of the British forces in the southern colonies, and, says Chaitkin, an acquaintance of Voltaire since at least 1767.

The British surrendered at Yorktown in 1781, and the peace treaty was signed in 1783. In that same year, William Petty, the Earl of Shelburne, Prime Minister from 1782, completed his coup in London, taking the reins of power for the managers of the merged English government and the British East India Company, as previously noted by Tarpley (p. 258, supra). Lord Shelburne was in fact the "manager" of the campaign then being run by the oligarchs against the American colonists. Burr was but one operative in the campaign, and Albert Gallatin, our next point of focus, another. Chaitkin summarizes his theme (p. 4):

"The campaign [to reconquer the U.S.A. for the oligar- chy] was directed by William Petty, Earl of Shelburne, whose new British Secret Intelligence Service repre- sented an alliance of 'noble' families of Switzerland, Scotland, and England. The eyes and arms of this appa- ratus were provided by the British East India Company. Company Chairman George Baring's family, along with the Hopes, were the Anglo-Dutch financial power. Shelburne and Baring used the Company to employ a legion of 'theorists,' including Adam Smith, Jeremy Bentham, and Thomas Malthus. They controlled an elite army of spies and assassins, based primarily in Geneva. We will present here the simple, direct evidence that Burr and Gallatin were not Americans, but British agents based in this Genevan assassin-nobility."

So now to Mr. Gallatin. His family held a seat on Geneva's Council of 200, alongside their cousins in the Mallet-Prevost and Necker families. (The latter family supplied the Genevan banker Jacques Necker to Louis XVI as his Minister of Finance, in which position he managed the last steps of the French financial chaos leading to the storming of the Bastille.) The Gallatins were neighbors of

Voltaire, whom Albert Gallatin, born in 1761, looked upon as a father-figure, and whose philosophy left a deep impression on him. A second formative friendship was with Etienne Dumont, a University of Geneva classmate who left Switzerland to tutor the sons of Lord Shelburne, and to act as translator and agent of Jeremy Bentham.

Albert Gallatin arrived in America just as the war was ending, and upon the British surrender at Yorktown went to Boston to become an instructor at Harvard, as was arranged for him by his family. He moved westward into Pennsylvania in 1786, onto 60,000 acres of land, becoming instantly a political power in the backwoods area. He opposed ratification of the Constitution, but then got himself elected to the Pennsylvania legislature, which met in Philadelphia adjacent to the federal Congress. By 1792 he had become highly active working on committees, writing bills and reports, and otherwise becoming recognized.

Aaron Burr during this same post-war period undertook a law career in New York State, one of his more famous clients being John Jacob Astor, a BEIC associate who arrived in America after the war, made a substantial fortune by the acquisition and sale of fur pelts to his BEIC contacts, and later became the first of a few "American" merchants to acquire entry rights into BEIC ports, and to make therefrom a fortune selling opium to the Chinese.

Burr parlayed his success at courtroom law into appointments as State Attorney General, then Land Commissioner, and then U.S. Senator from New York. He made use of these positions to aid three additional important clients: the McComb Group, which acquired 3.3 million acres of northeastern New York south of the St. Lawrence River; the Holland Land Company, partly owned by Albert Gallatin, which acquired 1.5 million acres in western New York and 3.5 million acres in Pennsylvania; and Captain Charles Williamson, "the most intimate friend and confidential agent of [Scotland's political boss Henry] Dundas and of Prime Minister William Pitt," Williamson representing the English Pulteney Associates. Burr also became agent for Dundas, who, as British secretary of state in 1787, wrote a master plan for extending the opium trade into China, and later personally supervised the BEIC's worldwide opium traffic. Burr, in short, was aiding the British opium trade and their acquisition of control over vast tracts of land within the new American republic.

Both Burr and Gallatin continued to increase their political power from 1792 to 1800, with Burr, in particular, becoming the corrupt political boss of New York, defining the pattern for the Tammany Hall operations of the future. He organized the Manhattan Company with the charter to supply fresh water to New York City, but with the small print permitting it to use surplus funds for any other legal purpose. Lots of dollars were invested, and used to start up the Manhattan Bank (later to become the Chase-Manhattan Bank), but no water was ever delivered, though Burr's campaign accounts flourished. Burr lost his state legislature seat upon the public outrage which followed. He remained strong enough as political boss, however, to see that he obtained the vice-presidential nomination of the Democratic-Republican Party, particularly with the help of Albert Gallatin, who had by then attained the party's leadership in the U.S. House of Representatives. Burr missed being elected President only by the strenuous efforts of Alexander Hamilton who furiously lobbied House members to support Jefferson rather than Burr. Our debt to Hamilton is immense.

Chaitkin suggests (p. 49) that Jefferson and Madison, the party leaders, could not have known the nature of the tie between Burr and Gallatin, i.e., as actual old-world cousins, secretly in the service of hidden superiors across the ocean. Thus, upon being sworn in as President, Jefferson isolated Burr within his administration, whereas he appointed Gallatin his Secretary of the Treasury. Both Gallatin and Burr were just getting started, however, in their efforts to wreck the new American republic.

An early effort (p. 59) appeared in a plan formally submitted in 1800 by "British intelligence officer James Workman" to the British Minister of War Henry Dundas, the object of which was to attack the Spanish holdings in America, especially Louisiana and Florida, by injecting, with the aid of the British fleet, some thousands of guerrilla warriors, perhaps Irishmen, into those territories, gain control by the British, attempt to gain the support of U.S. factions in that enterprise, and then seek consolidation of all English-speaking Americans under British leadership, throughout not only the western hemisphere, but ultimately the entire world. [The plan was much more completely elucidated a century later by John Ruskin, Cecil Rhodes, et. al., as we discussed in our HTWRW, though the notion obviously originated much earlier.]

President John Adams' ambassador to England sniffed out the existence of the same plan in 1798, which Adams angrily rejected. Following Jefferson's inauguration, however, Workman was sent to the U.S. to seek to get the plan implemented under the more amenable administration of Thomas Jefferson. The original alliance of families that had supported the Revolution had collapsed, and the Federalists were outnumbered by the pro-British New Englanders, the anti-industrial southerners, and the Gallatin machine in Pennsylvania. Jefferson was barely in control, and unaware of the real forces he was up against.

With Burr sidelined within Jefferson's administration, the pro-British New England families planned to give him a seat of power as Governor of New York. Hamilton again raised a furor of opposition, and Burr was again defeated. Burr saw that Hamilton had to go, challenged him to a duel, and in July of 1804 killed him. Duel or not, an intentional homicide was against the law, but before the coroner could return his findings, Burr, with the help of $41,783 from John Jacob Astor, fled from New York and New Jersey, both of which states shortly indicted him for murder. In New York, his political cohorts soon managed to reduce the charge to a misdemeanor, and Burr, though roundly hated by the public, retained his post as Vice President, as well as his sub rosa clout.

He then proceeded to help implement the Workman Plan. Chaitkin identifies some of his co-conspirators. There was Robert Livingston and his younger brother Edward. They were of the Scottish Livingstones whose history antedated Henry VIII. Robert, the first of the family in America, established a large estate north of Albany on the Hudson River. Among his other activities, he obtained a commission from the English government for his protégé, Captain William Kidd. Lord Shelburne, after his coup uniting the BEIC and the English government, was encouraging the Scots to return to the English fold, and of course rewarding those who cooperated, such as the Livingstones. Then there was Burr's physician William Eustis, who would later become Secretary of War during the War of 1812. There was also Colonel Charles Williamson, the British military intelligence officer and New York State legislator mentioned above, whom Burr, as his lawyer, had helped to acquire vast tracts of land in upper New York. Williamson visited London in 1803, from which he returned in early 1804, with the new English ambassador Anthony Merry, plus plans from England for furthering English goals. Merry's correspondence with his home office was uncovered much later, outlining Burr's request that he be given a role in aiding England's cause in America. Lastly, there was General James Wilkinson, the highest-ranking Army officer following the death of Alexander Hamilton. Wilkinson and

Burr became acquainted when both were under Benedict Arnold's command at the time of the disastrous Quebec massacre. Wilkinson had later become the chief aide and secretary to General Horatio Gates, whom those opposing Washington during the Revolution were seeking to install in Washington's place.

Napoleon had thrown a monkey wrench into the British plans by his acquisition in 1803 of the Louisiana Territory from the Spanish, and his sale of it to the U.S. This meant that the British would have to fight directly against the U.S. for it, rather than against the Spanish. They nevertheless proceeded with their plan. The various conspirators took their places in the Louisiana environs. James Workman got himself appointed judge of New Orleans County; General Wilkinson was made governor of the Upper Louisiana Territory; John Jacob Astor financed the removal of Edward Livingston to Louisiana. Livingston and Judge Workman joined in creating an organization called the Mexican Association, in the cause of which quasi-military action was to be taken by Irish immigrants upriver northward from New Orleans, aided by a British naval force from the Bahamas to be assembled on Lake Ponchartrain. They were to be met by a band of American mercenaries assembled by Aaron Burr, with the help, among others, of none other than the future President Andrew Jackson in assembling the boats for transporting Burr's "army" down the Ohio River toward the Mississippi and New Orleans. A western buffer state under British protection would thereby be created, as the Workman plan had visualized.

The plot was discovered, however, by at least one Joseph Daveiss, the district attorney for Kentucky, who outlined the plot in a letter to President Jefferson in January of 1806. Shortly thereafter General Wilkinson turned against Burr, perhaps to save himself, says Chaitkin. The general declared martial law in New Orleans and arrested

Burr and several co-conspirators. They were then released by "Judge" Workman, who attacked Wilkinson as a liar. But Burr and the others were rearrested and sent in chains to Washington for trial. (One of those arrested was a Dr. Justus Bollman, accused of helping Burr obtain European arms and financing. He had previously been similarly employed by the daughter of Jacques Necker during the Jacobin assault on France.)

Burr and the other main conspirators managed to obtain acquittals, because of the limited facts that could be marshaled at the time of the trial (e.g., Ambassador Merry's letter was unavailable). Andrew Jackson was not himself charged, having claimed to have previously "warned" of Burr's plan, though he nevertheless denounced Jefferson for "oppressing" Burr. The plot was broken up, however, and Burr emerged more hated than ever by the American public. Disguising himself, he made his way to New York, where he sold all his properties to John Jacob Astor for thousands in cash, with which he fled the country in June of 1808 on a ship to Nova Scotia. He eventually arrived back in England, where he was received to the plaudits of the elite families running that country – the Mallet-Prevosts, Barings, Jardines, Hopes, Ogilvies, etc. – along with their various operatives and paid theorists.

One additional circumstance concerning this episode should be well noted: the secret world of Masonry was raising its ugly head. "In 1783," says Chaitkin (p. 67), "the leader of the Masonic organization of the British army in New York was Grand Master William Walter, who was soon to [flee to] Nova Scotia. Walter arranged that the leadership of this Masonic organization – now no longer to be officially associated with the British army – would be put in the hands of Robert Livingston," who was duly installed as Grand Master of the Grand Lodge of New York on February 4, 1784. John Jacob Astor served as treasurer of the lodge from 1798 to 1800, and Edward Livingston, Robert's younger brother, and Burr's designee as New York district attorney, served as Deputy Grand Master from 1801 to 1803. Edward had also been installed as Grand Master of the Louisiana Masonic Lodge upon his arrival there, and was in sufficient control of the legal community there to have the conspiracy charges lodged against himself dropped. The anti-patriotic Masons had landed in the U.S., and were only just now beginning to make their institutionalized immorality felt.

Though Britain was clearly identified as the power behind Burr's secession plot, Gallatin emerged substantially untarnished, and was retained as Secretary of the Treasury by President Madison. Further, Burr's personal physician, William Eustis, was appointed Secretary of War. Madison started his administration a virtual prisoner of his major advisors, who were, of course, still conniving secretly with the pro-British New Englanders. Gallatin continued the program of starving the infant American Navy in the name of debt reduction as the first national priority. Britain, the ruler of the seas, felt no compunction toward stopping American vessels and impressing American seamen into the English navy. The Americans protested ineffectually, and Jefferson and Gallatin, in 1807, weakly responded by prohibiting American vessels to sail anywhere that they might get captured. The policy continued under Madison, until a more pro-American movement emerged in the U.S. Congress, under the leadership of Henry Clay of Kentucky. Congress wanted to rebuild the military; Gallatin refused; Congress told Madison to dump Gallatin or they would seek a new President in 1812; Madison relented, and the U.S. declared war in June of 1812.

The War of 1812 started off very badly, since no military secrets were secure with William Eustis as Secretary of War. Further, a Canadian invasion was attempted under the leadership of Burr's co-conspirator General James Wilkinson, still amazingly in the army. The invasion predictably failed. British war bonds were actually being peddled to American citizens, paid in gold smuggled generally from Boston to Canada. With the U.S. Treasury bare, and Gallatin under pressure to stop the financial sabotage and raise some money to help prosecute the war, he turned to borrowing money from the banker Stephen Girard of Philadelphia, whose Chinese drug-running activities the state of Pennsylvania was attempting to rein in, and from Burr's financial angel John Jacob Astor, also up to his eyeballs in the BEIC drug traffic to China.

After suffering the burning of the Capitol, the White House, and other government buildings in Washington, the war was finally turned around, largely due to the outstanding efforts of the tiny U.S. Navy, and the support of a growing American Nationalist movement, led by Henry Clay, Mathew Carey, and John Quincy Adams. The war was halted in 1814, but both Burr and Gallatin lived on. Burr had returned to the U.S. at the start of the war, and in the post-war period proposed the presidential candidacy of Andrew Jackson. Jackson succeeded John Quincy Adams, and was guided into the White House by another old conspirator, Edward Livingston, whom Jackson made his Secretary of State. Just prior to the appointment, Livingston was installed as the Grand High Priest of Masonry, evoking from John Quincy Adams, says Chaitkin (p. 89), "his famous *Letters on the Subject of Masonry*, in which he demonstrated the incompatibility of the Masonic oaths of secrecy with the public trusts and the public office which Livingston held." Barruel had expressed the identical views, as we have reviewed in our first chapter (p. 22, supra). Andrew Jackson, though clothing himself in the garb of an American nationalist, was the first of many succeeding

American presidents to indulge in the moral failing of our subtitle: *Political Dissimulation.*

Chaitkin's next major theme involves the planning of the American Civil War. The on-site planners in America consisted, he says (p. 95), of "the Essex Junto... working in close collaboration with agents of the British Secret Intelligence Service (SIS) working out of Boston." The Essex Junto was so-named because most of its members were born in Essex County, Massachusetts, bordering Boston to the north. Its members included Massachusetts Senator George Cabot, Judge John Lowell and his son John, Jr., Timothy Pickering (Sec. of State under John Adams), merchant Stephen Higginson, and Aaron Burr's brother-in-law Judge Tapping Reeve.

The correspondence of these conspirators, some of it published many years later (in the 1870's), provided damning proof of their intention to instigate a North-South split of the American union. For example, Pickering writes to Cabot on Jan. 29, 1804, "I do not believe in the practicability of a long-continued union. A Northern confederacy would unite congenial characters,... while the Southern States... might be left 'to manage their affairs in their own way.' ...But when and how is a separation to be effected? [The effort] must begin in Massachusetts. [But] who can be consulted, and who will take the lead?" Tapping Reeve similarly writes, "Many of our friends... believe that we must separate, and that this is the most favorable moment. The difficulty is, How is this to be accomplished?"

Cabot responds to Pickering on Feb. 14, 1804, which we paraphrase (or decode) as follows: "I understand your frustrations with the present American system. But mere separation now is no answer, as our frustrations are with the system of democracy, rather than our preferred oligarchism, with no relief visible via a popularly-elected government. Separation followed by the desired change requires the existence of a painfully-felt popular struggle distinctly attributable to the wrong-doing of the Southern slave-holder society. We may then utilize the great suffering that such a prolonged struggle might produce by assuring relief upon dissolution, and then, in the chaos of dissolution, establishing the desired forms of the new governments." Higginson similarly responds to Pickering on March 17, 1804: "We must wait the effects of still greater outrage and insult from those in power before we prepare for the only measure which can save the New England States from the snares of [the Virginia republicans]...."

President Madison, in his 1813 inaugural speech, and with the War of 1812 in full swing, alluded to the support being given the British by the Essex group. His accusation was confirmed by their plans to call a convention in Hartford, says Chaitkin, to "crystallize forceful anti-government acts on a region-wide or 'sectional' basis." The convention occurred late in 1814, but suffered a deflationary pinprick by the publication, shortly before the convention, of a book called *The Olive Branch*, written by Mathew Carey, a longtime collaborator of Benjamin Franklin, and later, as Chaitkin notes, "a leading figure of the U.S. secret intelligence service, as well as the leading U.S. economist of the post-1815 period." The book named the names and identified the treasons of the Boston crowd. Not yet in full control of the American media, the Essex conventioneers were consequently discredited, and publicly regarded as treasonous. They had suffered a setback, but continued, in their dark corners, to plan for the future toward which they were so fiercely driven.

Chaitkin includes in a footnote (p. 105) an excerpt of an 1815 letter from Thomas Jefferson to the Marquis de Lafayette, in which he declares that it was the British, and not indigenous Frenchmen, who ran the Jacobin machine during the French Revolution, and that it was the same

British who were running the Boston insurrectionists during the War of 1812. "The foreigner [i.e., the British] gained time to anarchise by gold the government he could not overthrow by arms,... and to turn the machine of Jacobinism from the change [of government] to the destruction of order; and in the end, the limited monarchy [that the republicans] had secured was exchanged for the unprincipled and bloody tyranny of Robespierre.... The British had hoped for more in their Hartford Convention. Their fears of republican France being done away, they are directed to republican America, and they are playing the same game for disorganization here that they played in your country. The Marats, the Dantons, the Robespierres of Massachusetts are in the same pay, under the same orders, and making the same efforts to anarchise us, that their prototypes in France did there."

Jefferson clearly was no slouch, and had learned a great deal from the time he first took office. It is a pity that the historians of the last two centuries have not seen fit even to report the views he ultimately acquired. This would have made it much easier for us to learn from true history, and not be destined to repeat, out of ignorance, the mistakes of our ancestors. But, I suppose, those historians did not perceive that to be their task.

Chaitkin sets the stage for his excursion into Civil War planning by relating the essential backgrounds of the leading Essex Junto families, starting with the Lowells, the Cabots, and the Higginsons. Such families constituted the "Boston Brahmins," the region's financial elite, the "very old money," the heart of the Eastern Establishment. Two facts, he says (p. 109), account for their leadership in bringing on the Civil War. First, they never adhered to the cause of the 1776 Revolution, but rather were the partners and agents of the British loyalists expelled from the U.S. toward the end of the war. Second, they attained their vast wealth and position not by their skill in advancing production to the benefit of the colonial population, but rather from extra-legal manipulations initiated by the British, primarily the BEIC, including piracy, the African slave trade, and most importantly the opium traffic to the Far East. They thus conceived their economic well-being to be tied to that of the British.

(The British economic system was in turn exemplified by the slogan "Free Trade," a system created by the British to facilitate the plunder of its "trading partners," including its own colonies. Adam Smith was the theoretician hired by Lord Shelburne to create a plausible intellectual cover for the system, and The Wealth of Nations was thus duly produced – a plagiarism, says Chaitkin (p. 117), of A. Turgot's *Reflections*, but satisfying Lord Shelburne's instructions back in 1763. The elimination of tariffs protecting local manufactures was and remains an essential element of the British "free trade" system, better described as mercantile despotism. It was over this system that Alexander Hamilton and Albert Gallatin so fiercely collided.)

Chaitkin then plunges into a description of the Perkins family, which supplied a good deal of the leadership of the Essex Junto during the early 1800's. The family was led by Thomas H. Perkins, who built his leadership position within the Junto by seeing to the marriages of his several brothers and sisters to members of the Higginson, Cabot, Cushing, Sturgis, and Forbes families. The Higginsons were in turn intermarried with the Lowell and Cabot families.

The business activity around which the Perkins leadership developed started with the chattel slavery of the South, producing cheap cotton for the mills of England to turn into textiles, which were dumped in India and paid for with opium, which was sold to China (by force), with Chinese silks and spices returned for sale in Europe, the proceeds of which purchased more cotton and African slaves.

288

Thomas Perkins and his brother James until 1792 ran the J. and T.H. Perkins Company, the main commodity of which was African slaves sold into the West Indies. The letter book of his predecessor company, Perkins, Burling & Co., contained correspondence with clients named Cabot and Forbes, as well as some 147 letters concerning delivery of slaves to various other slave dealers.

After 1792, the trading path changed, because another family member, George Perkins, was set up as a "British Empire merchant" in Smyrna, Turkey. He established a source of Turkish opium, which Thomas in turn picked up and delivered directly to China, bypassing the BEIC operation in India. The activity was not contended by the British, but was, in fact, entirely consistent with the plans laid by Lord Shelburne and put into practice by British Secretary of State Henry Dundas. Both Turkish and Indian opium came to be utilized, depending upon relative cost and quality.

The opium syndicate centered around Perkins made millions of dollars for the various families comprising the syndicate. The operations of the syndicate were financed by the Baring Brothers Bank of Britain, the bank of the BEIC, whose chairman in later years became Russell Sturgis, the grandson of Russell Sturgis, Sr., to whom Thomas Perkins had earlier married off his sister Elizabeth. Perkins' sister Margaret was married to Ralph Forbes, whose sons Robert and John took turns running foreign policy affairs for the Chinese Emperor. They became vastly wealthy, and Ralph's grandson William Forbes became President of American Bell Telephone Co. following the Perkins' purchase of Alexander Graham Bell's work. Thomas Perkins' daughter Eliza married Samuel Cabot, via which a vast Cabot fortune was assembled in America. Another of Perkins' sisters married Robert Cushing, whose son John Perkins Cushing emigrated and lived in China for 30 years, became enormously wealthy, and returned to live like an oriental potentate in Watertown, Mass.

Several other names should be mentioned emerging from the Essex County stew. The first is that of George Peabody, who moved from Boston to found a gigantic banking firm in England, hiring and bringing over from Essex County Junius and J. P. Morgan, all of whom would have a big role to play in the money issues surrounding the Civil War. Next we should mention Harvard College, which came entirely under the control of the Essex Junto after the Revolution, and was used for the Junto's purposes. Harvard was a private corporation, having a board which nominated its own successors (as in old Venice!). Judge John Lowell was elected to the board, and Lowells and Cabots have served thereon ever since. Harvard's President from 1810 to 1828 was John Kirkland, who ultimately married into the Cabot family.

During Kirkland's presidency, he took under his wing one Caleb Cushing, cousin of the aforementioned potentate John Perkins Cushing. Kirkland, recognizing ambition when he saw it, schooled Caleb in the Essex tradition, and then set him to work writing editorials for the Junto's organ, the *Newburyport Herald*. Also employed at the newspaper, as a typesetter, was one William Lloyd Garrison, with whom a strange relationship developed. Cushing, a creature of the slave-trading, opium-dealing, British backed secessionists of the Essex Junto, carefully and persistently schooled Garrison on the evils of slavery, until Garrison, who had previously given the institution of slavery no notice, came to believe that it was the ultimate evil, and that violent means, if necessary, were certainly justified to see it overthrown. At this point were the seeds of the Civil War surely being planted. Garrison, says Chaitkin (p. 140), "became *the leader of the most extreme and provocative elements of Abolitionism*, while Caleb

Cushing became *the main pro-slavery spokesman and strategist in the North.*"

John "The Rebel" Lowell, son of Judge John Lowell, also recognizing the energy and ambition of Caleb Cushing, granted him access to his family's legal papers and other documents, and passed to him money and the cooperation of the entire Lowell circle. Caleb would become the weapon brought to bear on the South, while Garrison would concentrate his poisoned words on the North. Between these two pincers, the Essex Junto sought to squeeze the life out of the new American republic.

One of the main tools to be used to extend the conspiracy into the South, and build what would soon be called the Southern Confederacy, was Scottish Rite Freemasonry. Chaitkin alleges (p. 142) that Benjamin Franklin, seeking European support in the upcoming Revolution against Lord Shelburne's Britain, had become Grand Master of a form of freemasonry in France which was allied with Franklin's own Free and Accepted Masons in the U.S.A. Aiding him in this endeavor was the Marquis de Lafayette. Opposing him was a contending French form centered about the Nine Sisters Scottish Rite Lodge in Paris, under the Duke of Orleans as Grand Master. This lodge was the tool of Jesuit, Swiss-banking, and British intelligence forces supporting the French revolutionists and opposing Franklin and the French moderate republicans. Chaitkin then undertakes a sweeping summary of European history, covering the material discussed by Tarpley in our previous chapter, to identify in its proper context the world outlook and goals of those who created and were utilizing the capabilities of Scottish Rite Masonry.

Chaitkin's summary of the preceding millennium is brilliant, and defies summarization by us. We urge you instead to get this book, and absorb it for yourselves. We will pick out only one or two points. First, Chaitkin makes no bones about where stands the Society of Jesus. "Venice," he says (pp. 147-148), "which had just created the Protestant Reformation, organized the Counter-Reformation, too. The Venetian house of Contarini detained Ignatius Loyola, and obliged him to head up a new worldwide secret intelligence service to serve the Venetian interests: the Jesuits." We flinched when such a matter was suggested by Tarpley (p. 249, supra), since Barruel had convincingly defended the Jesuits from such charges. However, we recall that Weishaupt admired the top-down organizational control structure of the Jesuits, and used it to model the structure of his Illuminati. With such a structure, control at the top could set major portions of the Society to the task of creating and running legitimate Catholic schools, convents, etc., while simultaneously having other elements within the Society performing subversive education of individual targets, such as perhaps Voltaire and Weishaupt, as we with some trepidation suggested much earlier (p. 41, supra). The compartmentalized structure of the Society would certainly enable such subversive activities to be kept secret. Must we suppose that Contarini had some other purpose in mind for this "military" structure?

A second point concerns the origin of Scottish Rite Masonry itself. This stemmed from the "Genoese Nobility" of Scotland, perhaps created in part by the lending of Genoese money to English nobility to enable them to purchase from Henry VIII properties he had stolen from the Catholic Church. When the Stuart James VI of Scotland ascended the English throne as James I, advised by Robert Cecil and then Francis Bacon, "The Venetian-Genoese Levant Company took over the commerce of Britain," says Chaitkin (p. 149), and was reconsolidated after the "Glorious Revolution" as the Bank of England. During the Stuart's mid-century exile, the Stuarts used the secret society of Rosicrucians in their attempt to regain power. That cult, created by the Jesuits, had the Jesuit Robert Fludd as its chief spokesman. When the Stuarts regained power, the cult was reorganized with an above-ground component – the London Royal Society – directed by, says Chaitkin, "a crypto-Jesuit, Sir William Petty, the grandfather of the Second Earl of Shelburne" of American Revolution fame. An underground component was also recodified under Petty's direction, with the help of his protégé Elias Ashmole, who was employed to stitch together the Rosicrucianism of Robert Fludd with the old Templar cults of Scotland (emplaced by the 14th-century Genoese mercenary Robert Bruce, who conquered Scotland with a force of Templars fleeing Philip le Bel). The result was the Scottish Rite of speculative freemasonry, which Barruel, Weishaupt, and others perforce had to deal with. From the Glorious Revolution onward, the Scottish Rite has been in the service of the Swiss and British oligarchy – an oligarchy which seeks to rule a world empire via a secret syndicate of wealthy families, hating as their primary enemy the Christianity of St. Augustine and its worldly expression given by the Florentine Golden Renaissance, which proclaimed the inherent worth of every individual, each created in the image of God.

Chaitkin then proceeds to identify the founders of Scottish Rite Freemasonry in the U.S. He is led first to brand as hoaxes promoted by the Scottish Rite itself the many "exposés" as to its conspiratorial Jewish origin. Such disinformation, which Chaitkin calls "lying garbage," serves only to obscure the society's true origins, and to discourage legitimate research to uncover those origins. Chaitkin lists the most significant of the Scottish Rite's American founders, as identified by the Rite's own historians, to be Augustine Prevost, John Mitchell, Count Alexandre de Grasse, Frederick Dalcho, James Moultrie, and John James Joseph Gourgas. Thumbnail sketches of these men follow.

Major General Augustine Prevost led the British forces in South Carolina during the Revolution, and was widely hated. His brother, Col. James Prevost, recruited the largest group of Crown Loyalists used by the British during the war. When he died, his widow married Aaron Burr, as we described earlier. Before the war, Augustine Prevost was the Grand Steward of the Scottish Rite's Lodge of Perfection set up in Albany, New York in 1768. He had two sons – George, who, as Governor General of Canada and Commander of the British Army in North America, invaded the U.S. during the War of 1812; and Augustine, Jr., a major in the British army, who, as a Deputy Inspector of the Lodge of Perfection in Philadelphia, and with his uncle Aaron Burr as his lawyer and advisor, appointed in 1790 one Pierre Duplessis as a Deputy Inspector General, who in turn established in 1790 a Knights Templar organization in Newburyport, Mass. The commander of that organization became Richard Spofford, the father of Caleb Cushing's private secretary.

John Mitchell was officially named as a founder of the Scottish Rite in Charleston, South Carolina in 1801. As Army Quartermaster in Philadelphia during the war, he had been suspected of involvement with Benedict Arnold's treason, but was acquitted by the Continental Congress. The state of Pennsylvania, run by Albert Gallatin, sequestered his records, and they remain sealed to this day.

Count de Grasse, after helping found the Charleston lodge, left America to set up Scottish Rite Supreme Councils in France, Milan, Spain, and Belgium. Following Napoleon's defeat by the British in 1815, de Grasse became the Scottish Rite Supreme Commander in France, from which vantage point he helped coordinate the creation of the insurrectionary machine in South Carolina.

Frederick Dalcho, an English medical doctor, came to the U.S. after the war, helped found the Charleston lodge, tried his hand at pro-British writing, became a deacon of the Episcopal Church, and soon emerged as the leader of Charleston's Episcopal community. He played a "spiritual" role in the "Nullification Crisis" soon to hit the South.

James Moultrie, though his Uncle William fought against Augustine Prevost and was later governor of South Carolina, was born instead to William's brother John, who was the British Lieutenant Governor of Florida, and who helped General Prevost launch his attack from Florida into Georgia and South Carolina. James returned to England after the war, was properly educated in medicine at Edinburgh University, and returned to America, this time to Charleston, where he had actually been born. He helped found the Charleston lodge, gained power through social contacts, and became the head of the South Carolina Medical Society in 1804. (His son, James Jr., also went to Edinburgh, and became president of the American Medical Association in 1851.) By the 1820's, however, James Sr. had become the Grand Secretary General of the Scottish Rite, and its effective chief throughout the South.

John Gourgas' family had emigrated from Geneva to France, and then during the French Revolution to England. The family of John Gourgas' mother held a seat on the Geneva Council of 200. In England, John was a merchant on the Royal exchange, and coming to the U.S. in 1803, plunged right in by taking control of the New York Scottish Rite organization. By 1813, he worked out a national territorial arrangement with the Southern Supreme Council, and remained in control of the Scottish Rite's Northern Jurisdiction until his death at the end of the Civil War. Gourgas' nephew Francis Gourgas became a Massachusetts State Senator, and was an intimate of Caleb Cushing.

We are thus left in no doubt whatever about the origins and the centers of control of Scottish Rite Freemasonry in the U.S. It was fathered by British and Swiss "Venetian" oligarchs whose goal was to regain control of their lost colony. The Scottish lodges were violently opposed to the Americanist lodges of Franklin and Washington, which later patriotic Americans sometimes joined, as did Henry Clay. The public reputation of all of Masonry was blackened when, in 1826, a Mason named William Morgan threatened to publish Masonic secrets he had learned, whereupon he was kidnapped and murdered, to "shut him up" the public believed. The incident produced a (temporary) anti-Masonic furor, which was skillfully used against presidential contender Henry Clay in 1832, resulting in President Jackson's narrow reelection victory. The American-tradition Masons were never again a threat to Scottish hegemony over American masonry.

Chaitkin then proceeds with his unique view of the history of our nation from the end of the War of 1812 through the Civil War. Again, we will try to touch only on the highlights.

Alexander Hamilton's "American System" reigned during the presidencies of James Monroe and John Quincy Adams. The Second Bank of the U.S. was chartered, charged with making loans for infrastructure and manufacturing development, with Greek scholar Nicholas Biddle named its president. The Monroe Doctrine was proclaimed. A protective tariff was passed, encouraging the development of new American industries. A vast program of canal and road-building was undertaken, and the first railroad chartered. The country enjoyed one of its greatest periods of productive growth. It was this growth, to be carried into the South, which was intended to be the force which would enable slavery in the United States to be ended – superseded by the economic forces of freedom.

The conspirators tried again. In 1820 they appointed Dr. Thomas Cooper, an English chemistry teacher, to the presidency of South Carolina College, then being used as a sort of Berkeley to raise up a new generation of revolutionists. Cooper had distinguished himself in the service of the British in France during the French Revolution. In 1827 he took to the podium declaring that the new tariffs constituted an attack of the North on the South, and declared that the South might better separate from the Union than enforce the tariffs. President Adams was appalled, and he vigorously responded, but was himself replaced by Andrew Jackson in 1828. By 1830, another conspirator, James Hamilton, became Governor of South Carolina, and began arming for war against the U.S. In 1831 a Free Trade Convention was held in Philadelphia, two of its principals being John Jacob Astor and Albert Gallatin, its purpose being to bring pressure on Congress. Then in 1832, the South Carolina legislature held a convention which declared that U.S. laws on tariffs were null and void, and heavy penalties would be imposed on citizens trying to obey them. The U.S. Congress finally knuckled under and in 1833 rescinded the tariffs. In 1832 Jackson had vetoed the extension of the 2nd U.S. Bank's charter, a veto which the Congress failed to override. The British banks, now in control of capital, including the bank of George Peabody (p. 319), withdrew worldwide credit, and in 1837, under the new President Martin Van Buren, a protégé of Aaron Burr (p. 89), the economy collapsed. The British banks were there, ready and waiting, prepared to buy up the distressed American properties at bargain prices.

Responding to the economic devastation, the public threw out the Free Traders in 1840 and elected the Whig William Henry Harrison as President, supported by a Whig Congress. A month after taking office, Harrison abruptly died, of a variously diagnosed acute internal distress. His was only the first of such abrupt deaths of nationalist presidents that our country would suffer. His successor, John

Tyler of Virginia, turned out to be one of the many political dissimulators under whom we have labored. Upon taking office, Tyler repudiated the entire Whig program, and vetoed the newly passed bill for restoring the Bank of the U.S. His entire cabinet resigned in protest and disgust, except for his Secretary of State Daniel Webster, who had been, and would remain for the rest of his life, "pathetically in debt" to Caleb Cushing (p. 183).

Cushing himself had similarly presented himself as an American System Whig, and had defeated John Quincy Adams in seeking the chairmanship of the House Foreign Relations Committee. Upon Tyler's ascension, Cushing revealed his true colors, and supported Tyler and the anti-Unionists during the balance of his public career. Now despised by the Whig Congress, Cushing failed three times to obtain Senate approval as Tyler's Secretary of the Treasury, but the Senate did finally approve his appointment as First Minister to China, perhaps because he would then be leaving the country. In this position, however, he pressed a military threat upon China, and obtained the same type of conditions that Lord Palmerston's envoy had gained from the Chinese emperor after the First Opium War. The American treaty included exempting Americans in China from the jurisdiction of Chinese laws, thus immunizing Cushing's drug-trafficking friends. To the everlasting shame of the United States, this sudden sortie into the realm of Imperialism was approved by the Senate in December, 1844, after the Whig Congress saw that their 1844 candidate for President, Henry Clay, had lost, and non-interventionist support could not be expected from the incoming winner, James Polk.

Under Polk, the events surrounding the Mexican War unfolded. Texas had declared its independence from Mexico in 1835, and won independence in 1836 by virtue of Sam Houston's defeat of the Mexican army under Santa

Anna. Under President Sam Houston, Texas sought U.S. statehood, though Mexico, desiring the recovery of Texas, declared that such acquisition would mean war. Clay and Adams favored the acquisition, but not at the cost of a war with Mexico, which would be a repudiation of the Monroe Doctrine. The British favored such a repudiation, however, since it would destroy the ability of the U.S. to lead an alliance of Western Hemisphere free republics, and thus leave the European nations free to rampage as they wished through Central and South America.

Clay's pro-acquisition position was distorted into a pro-slavery position in Pennsylvania and New York (by the usual pro-British cabal), and enough Whig votes were lost to an anti-slavery third party (financed by a pro-Mazzini millionaire named Gerrit Smith, a long-time partner of John Jacob Astor) that Clay lost by a handful of votes. The demoralized Congress thereupon passed a resolution annexing Texas, along with the China Treaty discussed above. In the following year, Polk sent John Slidell, a protégé of Aaron Burr, to Mexico as a "peace commissioner," aping Cushing's trip to China. The Mexicans refused to receive him, Slidell called for the troops, and Polk sent them into Mexico. The war was over by 1847, but the Monroe Doctrine was shattered, and no attempt to repair it would be made until the presidency of Abraham Lincoln.

During the course of the Polk presidency, the Young America movement entered the country's consciousness. It was introduced by one Edwin DeLeon in an 1845 speech to the students of South Carolina College. His father was a close friend of Thomas Cooper, the first American of the period to propose that the South secede. Edwin would later become a lead Confederate propagandist, and close advisor to President Jefferson Davis. During the course of his Young America speech, DeLeon had occasion to praise not only Thomas Cooper, but also Rousseau, the French Ency-

299

clopedists, Thomas Malthus, and Jeremy Bentham. "There is a Young Germany, a Young France, and a Young England," DeLeon said. "Why not a Young America?" His speech exhorted the younger generation in his audience to prepare the way for the conflict which would "extend the area of freedom," by which he was clearly referring both to conquering the Western Hemisphere and also aiding the revolutionary Giuseppe Mazzini in his efforts to overthrow Europe's governments.

Miraculously, it would seem, the Young America movement exhibited a diversity of philosophic goals, simultaneously promoting the expansion of Southern slavery and the expansion of Northern abolitionism. The leader of the latter branch was none other than William Lloyd Garrison. Their commonality of purpose, of course, lay in their mutual desire to split and destroy the Union. Garrison later (1872) wrote an introduction to Mazzini's autobiography, in which he related how, after their first meeting in 1846 in London, he was drawn to Mazzini's brilliance, modesty, and urbanity, and how "...we cherished the same hostility to every form of tyranny, and had many experiences in common." All this adulation about a man who was at one time refused membership in the Alta Vendita because of his bloodthirsty attachment to assassination as a normal modus operandi (p. 142, supra).

In 1848, the Whig candidate, General Zachary Taylor, won the presidency. He was a "war hero," having just led the Americans to a quick victory in the Mexican War. He was a Southerner and a slave-holder, but nevertheless sought to preserve the Union and the Constitution. He opposed the interventionist doctrines of Young America, and said so. He asked for bills to protect manufacturing, transport, and commerce. But a new opponent arose, by the name of John Quitman.

Quitman was a New Yorker moved to Mississippi, where he was authorized by the Scottish Rite Supreme Council of Charleston to found a Scottish Rite organization in Mississippi. He later also brought the South Carolina "Nullification Movement" into his new home state. He was a brigadier-general of volunteers during the Mexican War, and a close friend of Caleb Cushing. Returning home from the war, says Chaitkin (p. 209), "...he presented a plan to President Polk for the permanent subjugation and annexation of Mexico." The plan was ignored by Taylor when he came into office, but Quitman had yet other fish to fry. In 1848 he was elected to the Scottish Rite Supreme Council for the Southern Jurisdiction as Sovereign Grand Inspector General, and in January of 1850 was elected Governor of Mississippi. He was also at that time, says Chaitkin, arranging and financing another of Young America's adventures: the invasion of Cuba!

At this last, President Taylor acted, and a New Orleans grand jury indicted Quitman for financing a military invasion of Cuba in violation of U.S. laws protecting its peace and neutrality. Quitman defied Taylor, sending him a telegram saying he was going to lead an anti-federal army of Texans to retake lands in New Mexico which they claimed as their own. Taylor responded that he would be glad to hang any such persons found in rebellion against the Union, including Quitman. The following day, July 4, 1850, Zachary Taylor fell ill and died of some violent, but inconclusively diagnosed, "stomach distress."

The remainder of Taylor's term fell, in Chaitkin's words, to his "weak Vice President Millard Fillmore," during whose presidency Henry Clay, a Unionist to the end, managed to push through Congress the measures which became the 1850 Compromise. The compromise rejected the extremist positions of both the Garrisons and the Quitmans, and settled the slavery issue for the new southwestern states that were created upon the settlement of the Mexican War. Then in 1852 Clay also died, and, says Chaitkin, "...the Whig Party died with him."

Early in 1852, Jefferson Davis and John Quitman, the latter still under indictment for the Cuba conspiracy, met Caleb Cushing in Boston to plot how they were going to get their candidate, General Franklin Pierce, nominated for President by the Democratic Convention. They defined the factions that would back one Mexican War general, then another, then another, never letting any one quite attain the required two-thirds majority. When the delegates became exhausted, Pierce would be nominated as a compromise candidate, and the factions would then pile on, creating a bandwagon for him. That's what happened, on the forty-ninth ballot. The pick of the Essex Junto and the Scottish Rite was ultimately elected President, the moribund Whigs having been split by Daniel Webster's opposition to their nationalist candidate General Winfield Scott, and having been further opposed by, in Chaitkin's words (p. 216), "the pro-slavery lords of Boston and New York, specifically including the Astors, Vanderbilts, and Roosevelts...."

Pierce, having pledged no sectional bias, picked Caleb Cushing as Attorney General, Jefferson Davis as Secretary of War, James Buchanan (his successor as President) as Ambassador to England, Edwin DeLeon (the father of the Young America movement) as U.S. Consul in Egypt, August Belmont (the official U.S. agent of the British Rothschild bankers) as Ambassador to Holland, etc. With this not-so-secret seditious administration in place, plans went forward for fracturing the Union.

The secessionary soldiers were put in place by J.J.J. Gourgas, the Swiss master of the Northern Jurisdiction of the Scottish Rite, who delegated the field work to Killian Henry Van Rensselaer, an elder of the feudal Dutch family in New York responsible for founding the famous Rensselaer Polytechnic Institute of Troy, N.Y. Van Rensselaer, who had been "knighted" by the British army in 1830, was named Deputy to the Rite's Northern Supreme Council in 1851 for the states of Pennsylvania and Ohio. In 1853 he established his headquarters in Cincinnati, where, coincidentally, a secret organization called the Knights of the Golden Circle cropped up in 1854. One of its members, who talked after being imprisoned during the Civil War, related how the Knights grew into the military organization of the Confederacy, without which the Civil War could never have been fought. The Knights sent recruiters from Cincinnati into the Southern states, and created by 1861 an army of at least 65,000 armed and drilled recruits in the deep South and in the vicinity of Washington, DC.

On the political side, the Pierce administration forced through Congress an act which enabled slavery to be established via local option by the new western states, creating a race to dominance within each such state, financed by the usual Eastern millionaires. Bloodbaths did ensue, such as Chaitkin details for Kansas and Missouri. Pierce was dumped by the disgusted public in 1856, but was replaced by the equally bad James Buchanan, within whose tenure occurred John Brown's attack on the Harper's Ferry Arsenal. Brown was financed by the Eastern cabal, was turned into a hero by William Lloyd Garrison, and then into a martyr after he was tried and hanged. The alleged "sympathy for Brown" and "hatred of the South" in the North was played to the population of the South, to the despair of Southerners still holding pro-Union sympathies.

To emplace the needed Southern political leadership, another highly important figure arose, the historical shroud surrounding whom is ripped away by Chaitkin. His name was Albert Pike, of Newburyport, Massachusetts, a protégé of Caleb Cushing. Pike was brought into the Scottish Rite in 1853, and emerged, shortly after John Quitman's sudden death in 1858, as the Grand Commander of the Southern Scottish Rite Supreme Council, which he extended for the first time over the entire South. In March of 1860, Howell Cobb of Georgia, Buchanan's Secretary of the Treasury, was brought into the Supreme Council as an active member. A few months earlier, John Breckinridge of Kentucky, Buchanan's Vice President, had likewise been brought in. In its 1860 convention, under the chairmanship of Caleb Cushing, the Democrat Party would be split, with Breckinridge emerging as the secessionist candidate for President, running against the "Northern Democrat" Stephen Douglas of Illinois, the "Democrat Unionist" John Bell of Tennessee, and the Republican Abe Lincoln of Illinois. Whether he knew it or not, Breckinridge's chain of command went to Pike, then Cushing, the Essex Junto, and the English oligarchy, which was momentarily under the generalship of Lord Palmerston.

The election of 1860 was won by Lincoln with 1,867,000 popular votes, with 1,379,000 for Douglas, 854,000 for Breckinridge, and 591,000 for Bell. The secessionist Breckinridge thus received only about 22 percent of the total vote, and also only 45 percent of the vote within the slave states, where, with Lincoln excluded from the ballot, the non-secessionist total votes (for Douglas plus Bell) exceeded Breckinridge's vote by a 55 to 45 margin. It was hardly a landslide in favor of secession.

Chaitkin then details the mechanics, state by state, which brought about the creation of the Southern Confederacy. We will summarize the bare bones of Chaitkin's findings. In South Carolina, the home of the Scottish Rite's Southern headquarters, the legislature, says Chaitkin (p. 238), under the urging of Governor William Gist, "called a convention which met on Dec. 20, 1860, and passed an Ordinance of Secession, announcing that the state's ratification of the U.S. Constitution was 'repealed.'" They then urged the other southern states to do the same. Gist was one of the many who had been trained up in revolutionary skills by Dr. Thomas Cooper (p. 297, supra) at South Carolina College. No popular election for President was ever held in South Carolina in 1860, nor was a referendum held to vote on secession.

In Mississippi, the state's Young America leaders called a convention which on December 20, 1860, passed an Ordinance of Secession drawn up by one Lucius Lamar, of the Lamar banking family of Georgia and New York, whose Bank of the Republic in New York, says Chaitkin (p. 355), "...would manage the New York financial affairs of the Southern secessionists." On that same day, the U.S. Secretary of War John Floyd, another pupil of Dr. Thomas Cooper, ordered that cannon from the Pittsburgh military arsenal be sent to certain unfinished and undefended forts in Mississippi and Texas, where they could easily be seized by insurrectionists.

In Florida, an election for convention delegates was held on Dec. 22, yielding a tiny vote with about 60 percent favoring secession. The secessionists were led by Senator David Yulee, a prominent Florida spokesman for the Young America movement.

In Alabama, a convention election on Dec. 24 ran about 35,000 to 28,000 in favor of the secessionists. The Alabama secession leader was William Yancey, who was raised by his stepfather Nathaniel Beman in Troy, New York. Beman was the abolitionist President of Rensselaer Polytechnic Institute, the creation of the family of K.H. Van Rensselaer, the Northern Scottish Rite leader who set up the Knights of the Golden Circle. A couple of other Alabama leaders were Caleb Huse (of Newburyport, Mass.), who excelled in procuring arms from Europe in support of the Southern insurrection, and John Mallet, a British citizen and member of the same family into which Aaron Burr married.

Mallet, a visiting chemist working at the University of Alabama, later was appointed head of the Confederate Ordinance Laboratories, designing weapons of war for the Confederacy.

In Georgia, a questionable convention vote favored secession by 44,000 to 41,000. Leading secessionists there were Howell Cobb (President Buchanan's Secretary of the Treasury), the Lamar family, and Albert Pike's good friend Senator Robert Toombs, later to be appointed to the Rite's Supreme Council.

In Louisiana, a convention election on Jan. 7, 1861 produced 20,000 secessionist votes to 18,000 for their opponents. The most powerful secessionist leader was John Slidell, a New Yorker brought up within Aaron Burr's political machine, and brought into Louisiana politics by Edward Livingston, previously described as a co-conspirator with Burr in the 1807 secession attempt (p. 281, supra).

In Texas, the pro-Union Governor Sam Houston declared that secessionist efforts were illegal, and refused to call a convention. He was forcibly replaced by an armed coup which installed his secessionist enemies. They called for a secession "election" and announced the results to be 40,000 for and 10,000 against. Some believe that we haven't advanced much in electoral credibility in the 140 years following that event.

At any rate, no other state than the seven listed above voted in favor of secession, though elections were held in every Southern state including and to the south of Missouri, Kentucky, Virginia, Maryland, and Delaware. The seven states with announced secessionist majorities met in February of 1861 in Montgomery, Alabama, under chairman Howell Cobb of the Scottish Rite Supreme Council. They proclaimed the establishment of the Southern Confederacy, and designated the Mississippian Jefferson Davis, an acceptable "front man," to be President. Other states later to be counted as within the Confederacy (Virginia, North Carolina, Tennessee, and Arkansas) were only "dragged in" after the war had started. "West Virginia" separated from "Virginia" and remained as a separate state loyal to the Union.

In November of 1860, two weeks before Lincoln's election and four months before his inauguration, Governor Gist of South Carolina began to arm his state for war against the U.S. by arranging with President Buchanan's Secretary of War John Floyd to sell 10,000 government rifles to South Carolina. After Lincoln's election win was announced, Gist began a military buildup in Charleston aimed at seizing the U.S. fortifications in the Charleston harbor. If the forts were to prevail, they would need to be reinforced. Gist told Buchanan that South Carolina was moving toward secession, and that it could be done bloodlessly if the forts were not reinforced. Gist's arguments were backed by Treasury Secretary Howell Cobb, a Scottish Rite Supreme Council member, and by New York Senator William Seward, the leader of the abolitionist wing of the brand new Republican Party. Buchanan caved in, symbolizing to enraged patriots, says Chaitkin (p. 252), "...the manifold treason of the Buchanan administration."

Upon Lincoln's inauguration on March 4, 1861, he determined to resist the secession movement, and to reinforce Fort Sumter. To "balance his cabinet," he had appointed William Seward his Secretary of State. Seward traitorously encouraged the secessionists by assuring them that Lincoln would not reinforce Fort Sumter, and upon learning that Lincoln had ordered gunships and reinforcements to be sent, secretly arranged for orders to be given the fleet commander to divert the force to Florida. The attack on Fort Sumter then started, and was even observed by the reinforcing force, which stood off in accordance with what they believed to be their orders. The fort surrendered after 36 hours of bombardment.

Lincoln was aware, however, that Washington was crawling with traitors, and that the secession was not a popular movement but rather the treasonous activity of a cabal of conspirators. He accordingly turned to leading the nation into a fight to the death to defeat the conspirators and to save the Union. He called for volunteers for a Union Army, and by the time the war had been won, the U.S., having restored in substantial part the policies of Hamilton, J.Q. Adams, and Henry Clay, had created the strongest military force in the world, and had hugely increased the country's financial and productive clout, creating a steel industry from scratch, and starting what would soon become the world's greatest railroad system.

Lincoln was also aware of the international nature of the conflict, and when a pact was made among England, France, Belgium, Spain, and Austria getting up a Mexican invasion force, and enthroning a European Hapsburg as Emperor Maximilian, Lincoln supported the Mexican President Juarez as best he could during the Civil War, and that support was continued by his successor Andrew Johnson. The Europeans, seeing their American Civil War lost, and probably not wishing to engage the strong and unified United States over Mexico, withdrew their invasion army, whereupon Maximilian was tracked down and executed.

Although Lincoln may have been well aware of the nature of his opponents, the great bulk of the population certainly was not, and a great opportunity to enlighten the population was lost when Lincoln was assassinated. Chaitkin points out one of the many consequences of this ongoing ignorance: the appointment of Edward "Colonel" House as President Wilson's personal advisor during the years of World War 1 and the Versailles Treaty. His father, Thomas House, had been a British merchant who had made a fortune carrying arms from England to Texas in opposition to Sam Houston. Edward, educated in England, returned to America to tend his father's plantations, and retained for the rest of his days a fierce loyalty to Britain and hatred for the United States.

Chaitkin covers much more of great interest and value in his incredibly erudite book, with the subject matter extending up through World War 2. [One small item: He wrote (p. 323) that an 1896 biography of a pro-British Columbia College president quoted his declaration in an 1841 speech that Cardinal Wolsey had at one time held the position of Grand Master of the English branch of the Masonic Order, a connection we ourselves had speculated about (p. 246, supra).] However, we have covered the material in Chaitkin which best illuminates our theme, which has to do with the great success that our oligarchical enemies have had with their practiced use of secrecy and dissimulation in gaining objectives which they could never otherwise have attained. We suffer today from their continuing success, exercised, for example, by their control of the history being taught by the American education system (e.g., see HTWRW, pp. 75-80), and by their secret control of the American mass communication media, which prevents the widespread dissemination of historical truth once a skilled researcher, such as Chaitkin, manages to dig out a sizeable chunk of it. Contributing to that continuing success has been their creation and use of more modern secret society incarnations, one of which has only very recently been uncovered and brought into public view. We shall take up that matter next, and follow it finally with our proposed action plan.

Chapter 11

"AMERICA'S SECRET ESTABLISHMENT"

(By Antony Sutton, pub. 1986 by Liberty House Press, PO Box 80650, Billings, MT 59108. Also available from Omni Publications, PO Box 900566, Palmdale, CA 93590, 805-274-2240. Also prominently referenced in this chapter is "The Anglo-American Establishment," by Carroll Quigley, pub. 1981 by Books in Focus, Inc., PO Box 3481, Grand Central Station, New York, N.Y. 10163. Also available from www.amazon.com.)

In 1982, about three years before Chaitkin's book was published, Antony Sutton, one-time professor of economics at California State University, and research Fellow at Stanford University's Hoover Institution, received in the mail an eight-inch stack of documents which listed the historical membership roster of an American secret society, as a result of which he published, in 1983 and 1984, the several sections of the above named book, and then in 1986 the completed book in its entirety. He had previously written some 16 books, which raised lots of questions, but not many answers. The material sent to him provided the answers his inquiring mind had long sought, and he hastened to produce the present book, which he regarded as his *magnum opus.*

Members of the secret society refer to it as The Order, though it is more informally referred to as "Skull and Bones," or just simply "Bones." It's charter, as Chapter 322 of a German secret society, was brought back from Germany in 1832 by a visiting American student, William Huntington Russell (1809-1885), who, with Alphonso Taft as co-founder, established The Order as a Senior year society at Yale University. Fifteen new members were thereafter selected annually from among resident Juniors, the Yale class of 1833 being the first to graduate a group of American "Bonesmen," which included Messrs. Russell and Taft. About 2500 Yale grads have become members up to the time that Sutton wrote his book. The Order was incorporated in 1856 under the name The Russell Trust, the first president of which was William H. Russell.

The nature and aims of The Order's German antecedents are not factually known, but the aims of The Order may be discovered by examining which societal fields The Order's members chose to enter, a study which Sutton has meticulously pursued. Its aims might also be more quickly inferred by examining the main fields of endeavor of The Order's founders, particularly the Russell family of Middletown, Connecticut. (Such a study appears in Chap. 7 of *George Bush: The Unauthorized Biography*, by Tarpley and Chaitkin, which appears on Tarpley's web page at www.tarpley.net, and from which the following is excerpted.) Among Yale's founders (in 1701) was one Rev. Nodiah Russell. His descendants have been involved with running Yale ever since. In 1823, Samuel Russell, second cousin to Wm. H. Russell, established Russell and Co., the main function of which was to smuggle Turkish opium into China, with British cooperation. "By the 1830's," Tarpley-Chaitkin write, "the Russells had bought out the Perkins syndicate and made Connecticut the primary center of the U.S. opium racket. Massachusetts families (Coolidge, Sturgis, Forbes and Delano) joined Connecticut (Alsop) and New York (Low) smuggler-millionaires under the Russell auspices.... The incestuously intermarried Massachusetts and Connecticut families associated themselves with the British East India Company in the criminal opium traffic into China. These families made increased profits as partners and surrogates of the British during the bloody 1839-42 Opium War...."

The Order's real purposes are pursued by its graduates, or *Patriarchs*, who hold annual meetings on Deer Island in the St. Lawrence River, but without, of course, leaving behind any public record of their proceedings. The society is, after all, a *secret* society, with rules, rites, and aliases, whose members are sworn to silence, instructed to deny membership, and required even to avoid conversations concerning The Order. What Sutton instantly recognized was the immense power wielded by The Order, clearly apparent by simply scanning the names of its members over the years. As a first example, its co-founder Alphonso Taft, who became President Grant's Secretary of War in 1876, was the father of William Howard Taft, future President of the U.S. and Chief Justice of the Supreme Court. In all, eight Tafts have been members of The Order, down to Alphonso's great grandson Robert Taft, Jr., a "conservative Republican."

From his examination of the membership roster, Sutton presents three hypotheses concerning what ails America, which we shall briefly repeat. The first reads (p. 17), "There exists in the United States today, and has existed since 1833, a secret society comprising members of old-line American families and representatives of financial power." In support, he lists the following family names appearing in the membership lists: Bundy, Davison, Gilman, Harriman, Lord, Payne, Perkins, Phelps, Pillsbury, Rockefeller, Sloane, Stimson, Taft, Wadsworth, Weyerhaeuser, and Whitney. Current members reside predominantly on the Eastern seaboard, and are nearly all WASPS (White Anglo-Saxon Protestants) descended from 17th century English Puritan immigrants who intermarried with or invited into membership indigenous money moguls whose sons in turn became members.

Sutton details two of these families – the Whitneys and the Harrimans. One of the eight Whitney Bonesmen was the immensely wealthy William Collins Whitney, the power behind the Cleveland administration, who supplemented his wealth by marrying into the Payne family, which shared a good bit of the Standard Oil wealth of the Rockefellers. Among the Harrimans, W. Averell Harriman, the power behind the Democrat Party for much of the 20th century, merged his W.A. Harriman & Co. in 1930 with the Brown Bros. financial house of New York and Philadelphia, founded in 1800, to form the private banking firm of Brown Brothers, Harriman. In the 1970's, no less than nine members of The Order had been taken into this company as partners, including Sheldon Prescott Bush, the father of former President George Herbert Walker Bush (The Order '49), and grandfather of the George W. Bush (The Order '68) who, in mid-November, 2000, is still fighting with Al Gore over which of them won the Presidential election.

Before proceeding further, Sutton pauses to inquire about the connection between The Order and other secret groups overseas, and focuses at this point on the English secret society centered around Cecil Rhodes, a subject which we discussed (in HTWRW, pp. 27-30) in our review of Carroll Quigley's *Tragedy and Hope*. Sutton, writing in 1983, had before him the newly published *The Anglo-American Establishment*, containing a preface by Quigley dated 1949. It remained an unpublished manuscript until 1981, when it was published, says Sutton (p. 30), "by a small anti-establishment publisher," because Quigley, who died in 1977, couldn't find a main-line publisher who would touch it. "This is not surprising," says Sutton. "The book blows the lid off the British equivalent of The Order." While the scope of Quigley's *Tragedy and Hope* encompassed the whole world in the first half of the 20th century, his *Anglo-American Establishment* centered more tightly on the people and events in Britain. In particular, Quigley focuses on who was and who was not a member of the secret society running Britain. He writes in his preface, "The society has been known at various times as Milner's Kindergarten, as the Round Table Group, as the Rhodes crowd, as the *Times* crowd, as the All Souls [of Oxford] group, and as the Cliveden set.... I have chosen to call it the Milner Group." Then, throughout his book, he shortens the name to simply The Group.

Sutton undertakes (p. 30) to describe the importance of Quigley's revelations: "Quigley describes in minute detail the historical operations of the British establishment controlled by a secret society and operating very much as The Order operates in the U.S." We will display just one such example. In his opening paragraphs (p. 3), Quigley relates how The Group was born out of an 1891 conversation in London held by three well known members of the British establishment: "The leader was Cecil Rhodes, fabulously wealthy empire-builder and the most important person in South Africa. The second was William T. Stead, the most famous, and probably also the most sensational, journalist of the day. The third was Reginald Baliol Brett, later known as Lord Esher, friend and confidant of Queen Victoria, and later to be the most influential advisor of King Edward VII and King George V." Rhodes was to be the top leader, and the innermost circle under him was to consist of Stead, Brett, and Alfred Milner, who was added to the society by Stead. The point which we are taking some pains to note is that Brett, who was soon to be "the most influential advisor of King Edward VII," was also operating at the very apex of, in Quigley's words (p. 3), "the secret society that was, for more than fifty years, to be one of the most important forces in the formulation and execution of British imperial and foreign policy." In short, The Group was in a prime position to guide King Edward VII through the foreign policy manipulations described by Tarpley (p. 265, supra) which produced World War 1.

Returning now to The Order, Sutton examines the professional areas chosen by graduate Bonesmen, and then formulates his second hypothesis (p. 25): "The Order has penetrated or been the dominant influence in sufficient policy, research, and opinion making organizations that it determines the basic direction of American society." What societal functions or entities would have to be invaded in order to obtain such control? Sutton rattles off such a list (p. 31): Education, money, law, politics, economy, history, psychology, philanthropy, medicine, religion, media, and continuity of control. He states his intention of detailing each of these areas in subsequent volumes, and actually completed a chapter on education which is included in the present book. (Special attention is given to Yale itself, having been taken over and now being run essentially as an extension of The Order. He lists on p. 70 some 44 Order Patriarchs who have been employed as Yale professors or other staff members.) He may have given up writing separate volumes on the other fields out of exhaustion. However, he incorporates lots of "for instances," which we will sample.

The Order's efforts in the public education arena have produced, says Sutton (p. 32), "the educational morass of the 80's where most kids – not all – can't spell, read, or write, yet can be programmed into mass behavior channels." Concerning the related matter of the philanthropic founda- tions, Sutton continues, "They got all the big ones – Carnegie, Ford, Peabody, Slater, Russell Sage and so on.... The Order has usually maintained a continuing presence [in such Foundations] over decades." (See also our HTWRW, Chap. 4.)

In the field of religion, a key penetration involved the Union Theological Seminary, affiliated with Columbia

315

University. Henry Sloan Coffin (The Order '97) was a professor at the seminary from 1904 to 1926, and then its President up to 1945. Its philosophy was broad enough to include a campus Atheists Club. Coffin's son, Henry Jr. (The Order '49), was, says Sutton (p. 28), "one of the Boston Five indicted on federal conspiracy charges."

Major law firms in New York "are saturated with The Order," says Sutton. Thus, the firm Lord, Day, & Lord, one of whose current clients is the New York Times (p. 9), was founded by George DeForest Lord (The Order 1854) and his father Daniel Lord, also a graduate of Yale. The firm Simpson, Thacher and Bartlett, presently enjoying the largest billing on Wall Street (p. 138), and with former Secretary of State Cyrus Vance as a current partner, was founded in 1884 by Thomas Thacher (The Order '71), whose son Thomas, Jr. (The Order, '04) worked for Henry Stimson (The Order '88). Thacher's firm represented the U.S. interests of the Soviet State Bank while the Soviets were preparing the first of their Five Year industrial plans. Lastly, the law firm of the ubiquitous Rockefeller family rated a brief mention by Sutton as one of The Order-saturated firms.

In the publishing field, Bonesmen include Henry Luce of Time-Life, William Buckley of National Review, and Alfred Cowles of Cowles Communications, among the several others whom he lists. He notes also that Harvard's prestigious Nieman Fellowship award in journalism was administered by the Nieman Fund, the original director of which was Order member Archibald McLeash.

Many major industries are linked to The Order, including such as Standard Oil (via Percy Rockefeller, the Paynes and the Pratts), Shell Oil, Socony Vacuum, Dresser Industries, Weyerhaeuser Lumber, and many others. In the finance arena, the first Chairman of the New York Federal Reserve, the major banking entity within the Federal

Reserve System, was Pierre Jay (The Order '92), who was elevated from an obscure position as a Vice President of the Manhattan Bank, the bank created over one hundred years earlier by Aaron Burr (p. 278, supra). In the political field, major penetrations have been made by Order members named Taft, Bush, Stimson, Chafee, Lovett, Whitney, Bundy, and more. Sutton devotes a chapter to just one of these – the Bundy family – and declares that a separate volume would be required to definitively cover The Order's domination of politics.

The breadth of The Order's societal control is indicated by the breakdown of the occupations undertaken by their membership over the years, which Sutton lists (p. 41) as follows:

Occupation	Percent of Members
Law	18
Education	16
Business	16
Finance	15
Industry	12
Total	77

Thus, over three quarters of the membership has become engaged in these five areas of endeavor, which are the key ones for controlling a society. The "occupation" of politics is undertaken by revolving members into and out of their more formal occupations listed above.

Of great importance is Sutton's third hypothesis. He leads up to it by noting and then asking why it should be that Order members were found on *both* sides of so many societal conflicts. For example, Bonesmen William Howard Taft and Theodore Marburg founded The League to Enforce the Peace, which was active both in promoting peace and in urging the U.S. to enter World War 1. As a second example, W. Averell Harriman, against State Department regulations, helped create Ruskombank, the first Soviet commercial bank, and put Max May, the Vice President of the Harriman-Morgan dominated Guaranty Trust, in charge of its foreign operations; simultaneously, Harriman's brother Roland, plus Order members E.S. James and Knight Wooley, "were prime financial backers of Hitler." Then there was McGeorge Bundy, National Security Assistant to Presidents Kennedy and Johnson, simultaneously supporting the official U.S. pro-NATO policies and also the pro-Marxist policies of anti-NATO organizations such as the Institute for Policy Studies. Another is William S. Coffin, Jr., who served in the CIA while it was (secretly) helping to prosecute the Vietnamese War, but also became a leader of such organizations as Clergy and Laymen Concerned about Vietnam, which vociferously opposed the war.

The answer to these contradictions is that, from The Order's point of view, there *is* no contradiction, because their goal is to *create the conflict*, not just to support one side against the other. Out of the turmoil of conflict, they will then seek to engineer their own outcome, perhaps unrelated to the outcomes desired by either of the two combatants. The methodology has been extensively written about, and has a name that we should all become familiar with: *Hegelianism.* Sutton describes it succinctly (p. 34):

"The dialectical process did not originate with Marx as Marxists claim, but with Fichte and Hegel in late 18th and early 19th century Germany. In the dialectical process a clash of opposites [thesis and antithesis] brings about a synthesis. For example, a clash of political left and political right brings about another political system, a synthesis of the two, neither left nor right. *This conflict of opposites is essential to bring about change....*

"Furthermore, for Hegel and systems based on Hegel, the State is absolute.... An individual does not exist for himself... but only to perform a role in the operation of the State. He finds freedom only in obedience to the State. There was no freedom in Hitler's Germany, there is no freedom for the individual under Marxism, [and] neither will there be in the New World Order. And if it sounds like George Orwell's *1984* – it is."

The examples in our own history begin to emerge from the historical fog. The British gave up their failed frontal attacks on our new republic, such as the Workman Plan involving Aaron Burr and Edward Livingston, and turned to planning the pure Hegelian conflict which was the Civil War, clearly spelled out in the correspondence of George Cabot (p. 285, supra) and in the simultaneous pro-slavery and abolitionist agitation of Caleb Cushing. World War 1 was brought on by escalating a conflict between Germany and Britain, resulting in the destruction of the Hapsburg, Hohenzollern, and Romanov dynasties, the establishment of the Bolshevik regime in Russia, and the first attempt at forming a system of world governance. World War 2 was created by building up both Stalin and Hitler as archenemies, out of which has come a Russian military capable of challenging the U.S., a new potential enemy in Communist China, and a much more potent candidate for managing world governance – the United Nations. Both pro-war and anti-war sides were supported during the Vietnamese war, the main outcomes being greatly increased drug traffic into the U.S., the beginning of the purchase of America by foreigners, and the start of the long downward moral and economic spiral in which we are presently caught.

As Sutton takes pains to point out, the right-left or conservative-liberal or Republican-Democrat conflicts are purely Hegelian, since The Order substantially controls all of these societal categories, and always maneuvers the conflicts toward increasing the power of the State. He now puts his third hypothesis into words (p. 57): "The Order uses the Hegelian dialectic process to bring about a society in which the State is absolute, i.e., all powerful."

Noting that William H. Russell returned with The Order's charter following his immersion as a student in the German intellectual stew, Sutton examines that stew for clues concerning The Order's lineage. At Jena University (near Leipzig) there existed simultaneously in the early 1800's an interesting philosophic quintet consisting of Johann Herder, Johann Fichte, Friedrich Schiller, Johann Goethe, and Georg Hegel. The first four of these, says Sutton (p. 79), "are either known members of the Illuminati or reputed to be close to the Illuminati Order." The "known" Illuminati were Herder (alias *Damascus pontifex*) and Goethe (alias *Abaris*). Fichte, the creator of the formalized dialectic, passed it on to the older Goethe, who was instrumental in promoting Fichte to his position of chair of Philosophy at Jena. Hegel, for some reason, got the historical credit. Fichte, says Sutton (p. 34), "was a Freemason, almost certainly Illuminati, and certainly was promoted by the Illuminati." The notion that the end justifies the means, paramount within the Illuminati, was of course created by evil men many centuries before Weishaupt was even born, but was carried easily into both Illuminism and Hegelianism. This was the stew into which William Russell immersed himself in Germany, while Goethe and perhaps Hegel were still alive, and from which he returned with a charter to form Chapter 322 of the still unidentified German secret society. The circumstantial evidence of course points to the Illuminati.

Sutton covers a great deal more than what we have discussed. In his Part 2, he discusses how The Order captured Yale and then undertook to subvert and control the American education system (e.g., the look-say scam). In his Part 3, he discusses how the Hegelian system of creating wars was operated, first creating the Soviet Union out of

320

World War 1, and then building up both of the two sides that clashed in World War 2, out of which the United Nations was born. Presently, the Third World is being systematically bankrupted, and China is being turned into a modern military giant, preparing for a future conflagration with a yet another synthesis. (One such synthesis is described in lots of detail in Orwell's *1984*, as we discussed in our own HTWRW, pp. 126-128.) In Sutton's Part 4, he discusses the available information concerning the physical presence, property, documents, and practices of The Order on the Yale campus. If you have never yet had your eyes opened to the truth of the "conspiracy theory," this is the book that may do it.

Though our subverted education system and the pernicious strategy of Hegelianism are proper subjects of study, the simple *existence* of The Order in the present day United States is what is of the most importance to our own theme, so we will depart from Sutton at this point. While the internal structure of The Order may be very different from that of Masonry or the Illuminati, it is clear that the important elements of those secret societies have been incorporated, including oaths of secrecy, willingness to follow orders from unknown superiors for unknown purposes, and the giving of economic and professional assistance to other members in preference to the "profane." The importance of this matter to us, of course, is that the millennial-old techniques of utilizing secret societies for accomplishing societal aims which could not be done in the light of day are still with us in today's United States of America. It could never be clearer that we will never recover the health of our nation, or the freedoms which our hard-won constitutional government sought to guarantee, so long as those aiding the conspiracy remain unidentified and unchallenged. Our task is to identify, challenge, and replace such people with truthful persons willing and able to properly serve a free people. Our last chapter will deal with how we propose to do exactly that.

Chapter 12

"LET'S FIX AMERICA!"

(By Alan B. Jones, pub. 1994 by ABJ Press, PO Box 2362, Paradise, CA 95967. Also available from Amazon.com, PO Box 81410, Seattle, WA 98108, or www.amazon.com, or orders@amazon.com.)

The above title, hereinafter abbreviated "LFA," is of course our own book. It was written to answer the question, Given a willing Congress, what could it do to fix up the many foreign and domestic problems facing our country? That was the easiest of the questions we struggled with, and we would not presently change the bulk of the corrective actions we prescribed. Our second book, *How The World Really Works*, sought to answer the question, Where did all our problems come from? The answer that emerged was that a publicly undeclared war was long ago secretly declared against our country, and especially our middle class, leading us to undertake a preliminary identification of the malefactors and their primary strategies. This third book, *Secrecy or Freedom?*, has been aimed at completing the identification task closely enough to enable the successful removal of our attackers from their positions of social and political leadership, and their replacement by honest representatives of the great bulk of the American public.

How is it to be done? We tried in our LFA (Chapter 20) to address the matter of how to elect responsive Congressmen, but we soon saw that acquiring controlling majorities of such people could not be done without media resources on the order of what is available to those we wish to displace. However, in our present volume we have much more clearly identified our enemy, and more importantly, we have learned enough about its modus operandi to perceive what looks very much like an Achilles Heel – a weakness we can clearly exploit, and in the process regain our own freedom and the prospect of freedom for the rest of the world.

Our plan for the remainder of this chapter is to describe a program and its rationale for obtaining a Congress which can set matters right (replacing LFA Chapter 20), and then to present a list of the societal goals to be pursued and the needed actions, mostly legislative, to attain those goals. Not surprisingly, most of these goals and actions have already been treated at some length in our LFA, but where a subject is new, or where we have seen the need for revision of our previous work, we will spell out the new material in some detail. A complete picture of our proposed program will then consist of our LFA modified by the contents of this Chapter 12.

The two prime tools used by the oligarchs in their attempt to gain control of the whole world have been their tremendous wealth and the secrecy of their operations. Their wealth permits, among other things, their purchase or other control of the world's organs of communication. In the United States, that is a necessary but not quite sufficient condition for them to snatch and retain complete control, since the bulk of our people still believe that the people elect and ultimately control their governments. The oligarchs, though they enjoy a large measure of control, nevertheless remain a tiny minority in gross numbers, and probably understand that, given our citizen army and an armed population, they can't yet mount a coup which can successfully replace the Congress and the Constitution with their own dictatorship. Secrecy will therefore remain necessary during what they probably hope are their final preparations.

Secrecy has in past centuries been so necessary that it has been organized and codified, creating what have been called "secret societies." Our book has been devoted to digging out their history, and has uncovered such names as the Manicheans, the Assassins, the Council of Ten, the Knights Templar, the Scottish Rite Masons, the Illuminati, the Jacobins, the Carbonari, The Order, The Group, and including finally the secret core entity, whatever it may be called, which is directing the multiplicity of agencies preparing the way for the New World Order. The need for secrecy has produced, as an inevitable corollary, the need not only to lie, but to lie expertly and convincingly, to obfuscate, to prevaricate, to dissemble, and to dissimulate. As Voltaire put it in a letter to a disciple (p. 129, supra), "Lying is a vice when it does evil. It is a great virtue when it does good. Be therefore more virtuous than ever. It is necessary to lie like a devil, not timidly and for a time, but boldly and always." This need to lie is the weakness we propose to attack.

In days of yore, kings and others dealt with the lies of their captured enemies, when they wished to extract the truth from them, by ways which the more civilized among us tend today to frown upon. Thus, the rack, the threat of burning, and a great variety of other physical tortures are still practiced by many countries, though not very publicly, out of the growing sensitivity of most of the common populations of the world. A prohibition against compelled self-incrimination was even written into our Constitution, and properly so. However, a better and more acceptable tool has been newly created – voluntary, non-invasive, and non-hurtful – which can readily be harnessed into the service of a free people who want to remain so. It is called the polygraph, or lie detector.

Although polygraph results are not today admissible as evidence in court, they are nevertheless widely used in police investigations, in background checks of governmental employees, and even today in the investigation of employees or potential employees by private companies. Polygraph examiners are professionally trained, and are licensed by the various states to permit them to practice their profession for public purposes. However, though the purpose we have in mind is very public, it will be managed by private entities rather than by any entity in the pay of government, since it is the entrenchment of an abusive government that we are doing our best to prevent.

If a government can see fit to administer polygraph examinations to those it hires to develop the country's weapons of war, how much greater should the incentive be to examine those whose job it will be to write the laws defining the policies by which the country will operate, and thus define how we will interact with the rest of the world (e.g., declare war). The Legislatures make the laws, and the Executives are required to faithfully administer the laws. The laws originate, however, in the legislatures, which happen also to be the elements of government whose members are most closely beholden to the voters back in the local districts hungering for change. Our primary targets are going to be those legislators, particularly those running for a state legislature or the U.S. Congress.

What are the questions we would like a candidate for office to answer while hooked up to the polygraph? Five yes/no questions should do the trick. He should be asked whether he seriously intends to uphold and defend the Constitution, and the guaranteed rights of U.S. citizens under that Constitution; whether he intends to reject and to publicize any attempts to bribe him; whether his past contains anything serious enough to enable a blackmailer to influence his official actions; whether he feels any subservience or adherence to any social or political organization, person, country, or other entity having programs or goals not in accord with the words or purposes of the Constitution; and whether he believes that the attainment of his personal, official, or political goals might ever justify his use of illegal or immoral means, such as lying, conspiring, cheating, or breaking any law. These questions should evolve to a standard set, and become well-known both to the general public and to potential legislative candidates.

The agency administering the examination might best be a local organization created for that sole purpose, and which can become well known to the local public and to the "County Committees" or equivalent of the various political parties. We will for the moment refer to that agency as the local "Truth in Politics," or TIP Committee. When a candidate, including an incumbent seeking reelection, first announces his intention to run for a given office, i.e., prior to a party's primary election, an invitation should be issued to him requesting that he submit to a standard TIP polygraph examination, and that he agree to permit the results to be publicized within his electoral district. The candidate can, of course, refuse to take the examination, but the TIP Committee will likewise be free to publicize that refusal, a result which the electorate should find useful. The polygraph results of tests which *are* taken will no doubt turn out to be even more useful.

But how can one trust the integrity of the examiners, or of the TIP Committee itself? Briefly, they should not be permanently trusted, as attempts to control these positions will surely be made by those who have spent whole careers honing their lying skills. Polygraph technology is such that polygraph data can be independently evaluated by multiple examiners. Both examiners and TIP Committee members should themselves be periodically examined and independently evaluated, and the results locally publicized.

How about the issue of erroneously finding a response to be untruthful? Or, to address the issue with

327

greater clarity, how might a truly honest Constitutionalist feel about taking the test when such a possibility exists? First, the statistics generated within the polygraph testing profession show such outcomes to be rare, and measures will be taken to assure that they *remain* negligibly remote, such as submitting test results to multiple independent examiners, and repeating tests at the request of either examiner or candidate. Also, no matter what the outcome of a test, the electorate will have the final word. Experience will rapidly indicate to the public and to candidates whether false results are a minor issue or a sufficiently large problem that the technique can't be brought into general use. We expect that the former will be the case, and that even if a rare honest error is occasionally made, the overall good to the electorate at large should remain so great that even an aggrieved candidate may find it possible to philosophically accept an erroneous result personally affecting him.

As the system develops, it is to be expected that fewer and fewer persons will enter the legislative arena with hidden intentions to subvert it, to the great benefit of the whole public. The earliest effects might be on the state legislatures, closely followed by the House of Representatives in Washington, DC. The higher proportion of honest legislators should then begin to affect the choice of senatorial candidates nominated for election or reelection in each state, and the U.S. Senate should gradually come around to better representing the interests of the bulk of the public. Finally, with better representation throughout the state and federal legislatures, the national parties themselves will undergo an integrity resurgence, and better candidates for President will be nominated. Even the Supreme Court and the inferior federal courts will eventually be brought back into the fold via the appointment and confirmation processes. (Perhaps the *Senate* will choose to employ background polygraph tests!) We will shortly find ourselves able to seriously approach the task of taking our country back, and actually passing legislation aimed at *solving* our many national and international problems.

Observe what it is that we have done. We have rejected the notion that all we can do is mount a rear-guard action, seeking, as we retreat, to occasionally win a skirmish or two (like beating back fast-track). On the contrary, we have decided, like the army general or the football coach, that without an offense, we will surely lose in the long run, no matter how strong our defense might be. We must, therefore, develop and put in the field a vigorous, credible, viable offense aimed at *defeating* our opponents. If we fail to do so, we are headed for a worldwide Dark Age out of which the world's humanity may *never* emerge, so powerful and astute are our opponents. Our efforts go beyond simply trying to educate the public about each of the new outrages which our wannabe masters perpetrate. We seek instead to stop them, emasculate them, and take back the control of our country.

Once we have a Congress and an administration willing to undertake the task of turning matters around, here are some of the goals which we would have that administration set:

1. Protect legislators and the legislative process from the corrupting influence of great oligarchic wealth.

2. Assure the honesty of elections, and that they cannot be dominated by individuals or organizations of great wealth.

3. Expose and eliminate the secret promotion of oligarchic goals in our public schools and universities.

4. Expose and disempower the secret oligarchic monopoly controlling our major news media.

5. Expose the secret facilitators in government and banking of the worldwide narcotics trade, bring the

domestic trade to a halt, and help other countries do the same.

6. Reestablish a constitutional monetary system having a stable, non-depreciating currency.

7. Establish a federal fiscal system which precludes an accumulated national debt, and which caps the tax load on U.S. citizens.

8. Replace the income tax with a tax on consumption.

9. Reinstitute the authority and validity of the Tenth Amendment, dropping federal involvement in pension, medical, and welfare delivery systems.

10. Reestablish the development of the American infrastructure, standard of living, and economic and political independence as a higher priority than promoting international interdependence, i.e., dependence on others.

11. Redefine and strictly enforce laws regarding immigration, citizenship, and the rights and obligations of non-citizens.

12. Disengage the U.S. from international institutions created to further the goals of the oligarchs, their banks, and their multinational companies.

13. Create and lead new international institutions composed of countries seriously seeking to guarantee the rights and freedoms of its individual citizens.

We will consider each of these goals in order, noting where each is treated in LFA, and modifying or adding to that treatment as we deem appropriate.

Goal 1 was addressed in LFA Chapter 19, items 1 to 4 on pages 212-214. We would presently rescind our Item 1, which called for legislative term limits, because that aim can be better accomplished by TIP polygraph testing prior to a legislator's run for reelection. By this means, good legislators can be kept on the job so long as they remain in the honest service of our citizenry. We would not change items 2 and 3, which provide respectively for the financial maintenance of legislators, and their expulsion from office for accepting or failing to report any gift of significant value. We would put more teeth in item 4, providing penalties for attempted extortion, blackmail, or bribery of a legislator severe enough (e.g., jail time plus 10 percent of a culpable corporation's net worth) to expunge these practices from our social fabric.

Goal 2 was not addressed in LFA, and three different aspects will be outlined here: "third" party manipulation, campaign funding, and ballot integrity. With respect to third parties, we propose that state election laws be modified making it much more difficult for a small party to bring about the election of a major party candidate having only a plurality but not a majority of the votes cast. For example, in 1912, Teddy Roosevelt's Bull Moose effort drained Republican votes from William Howard Taft, causing the election by plurality of Woodrow Wilson. In 1992, Ross Perot's Reform Party drained votes from George Bush, causing the similar election of William Clinton. Such distortions of the electoral process by small, wealthy groups can be avoided by the expedient of passing state laws (no Constitutional Amendment is needed) requiring that, in all primary elections, and in all general elections except for President, if no candidate receives a majority of the popular vote, a runoff election will be held between the top two candidates. As a special case, general elections for President shall be held between only two candidates: Candidate A, who individually received the greatest number of final primary election votes throughout the country, and Candidate B, who received the greatest number among all the candidates of parties other than that of Candidate A.

Concerning campaign funding, we have two primary goals: to enable viable candidacies by persons of moderate means, i.e., from among the 90 percent of the population

who can't presently compete, and to limit campaign donations such that those dollars represent the wishes of individuals as opposed to the wishes of accumulated organizational wealth, be it corporate, union, foundation, or other.
Thus, in primary and general elections for federal office,
whether an original or runoff primary election, or an original
or runoff general election, federal taxpayer dollars will be
provided to pay for an "adequate" campaign, defined by
statute, and covering the cost of a basic campaign infrastructure, topped by a specified number of television (or
other mass media) hours which a candidate may utilize as he
wishes. The money provided should be in rough proportion
to the size of the electorate for the particular office.

Candidates (or their supporting organizations, including political parties) contracting for media hours beyond
those limits, but without the agreement of opposing candidates or their supporters to similarly contract for the same
excess hours (because, for example, they don't have the
money), will be required to purchase equal excess hours for
the use of such opposing candidates. Thus, wealthy candidate A can't simply swamp his less-wealthy opponents by
grossly outspending them beyond the "adequate" campaign
limits. Individuals and organizations, excepting only political parties, shall be limited to annual donations of $1000 in
cash or kind, including gifts of television access. No more
than 25 percent of such contributions may come from
persons not residing in the electoral district of the candidate.

With these reform measures in place, campaign
activities will no longer be focused on channeling large
blocs of money from wealthy contributors to candidates,
whether demanded by a candidate or pushed on him by the
contributor. An elected candidate may then remain focused
on how he can best serve the public, without having to be
concerned with the particular interests of large campaign

contributors. Such financing reforms should similarly be applied to candidates running for state offices.

We will now address the issue of ballot integrity. Our two reforms will deal with illegal casting and illegal counting of ballots. We therefore desire first that voting be limited to "non-repetitive votes by validly registered live citizens." Federal statutes should be enacted requiring that a person wishing to vote in federal elections must undergo a thorough local registration process, verifying his U.S. citizenship, his birth date, and his place of residence. Proof of citizenship should be no less stringent than that required when applying for a U.S. passport, including birth certificate, citizenship papers if any, etc. His place of residence should be physically verified. Other identification data shall be requested, including driver's license and social security numbers. These shall be used to help verify the identity and existence of the applicant in these other records. State records identifying felons shall be used to deny the voting privilege to those so affected.

When satisfied, the local registrar shall assign the applicant a "Voter Number" which shall be entered in a National Voting Registry (NVR), to assure future identification and non-duplication. The number shall include the state, county, and precinct in which he is eligible to vote. A voter's Identification Card will be issued to him, containing a photo ID, his name, age, and Voter Number. When voting, he will present the card, and upon satisfying the precinct election workers as to his identity and his existence in the precinct voting list (a public record prepared by the registrar prior to the election), he will sign the voting list and be handed a ballot upon which to register his votes. Equivalent safeguards should be employed when issuing absentee ballots to voters prior to the election.

If a voter moves, he must reapply for a new Voter Number and card, and the NVR will be correspondingly updated. County officers recording deaths shall periodically submit such records to the local registrar, who will be responsible for marking such persons as "deceased" in the local records and the NVR. Lastly, federal law should provide for required periodic verification by independent auditors of the completeness and legality of all changes made in registration records in each registrar's jurisdiction since the previous audit. With all of the above reforms in place, we may begin to feel a little more secure that the votes entering our ballot boxes represent only the single votes of live, legally registered citizens.

But assuring that only honest ballots are cast gets us only halfway to an honest result. We must now assure that the ballots are counted and reported honestly. The basic protection will be provided by requiring that the media on which a voter records his vote must be a media which can be physically saved, such that votes can later be recounted by computer or by hand (without computers) if that becomes necessary. A precinct's ballots will ultimately be received and semi-permanently stored by the County Election Commissioner, or other official having jurisdiction over the precinct, but the essential safeguards will be performed before the ballots leave the precinct. We propose a procedure along the lines described below.

Each political party, the candidates, and the public at large will be informed at least six months prior to an election as to what the ballot media will be, such as cards to be punched, or squares to be blackened, etc., with all the detail necessary to enable an "Interested Party" to non-destructively read the voters' choices appearing on the ballots, and thereafter count the results with computer software which he may create for that purpose. Interested Parties (hereinafter IP's), such as a local Truth in Politics (TIP) Committee, will be invited to do so, provided that they agree to make the source language of their software publicly available, so that others can read, understand, and compile and use it on their own computers. Test ballots, marked up, will be provided by the County Election Commissioner's office. If and when the software of an IP produces the "correct" results, the Commissioner will designate that IP as one of at least two count verifiers that he will appoint in every precinct. He will also assure that his own official equipment for ballot reading and counting is available and manned in each precinct.

When a precinct balloting station closes, the raw ballots, including all the absentee ballots previously mailed in from residents of that precinct, will, under the watchful eyes of *all* of the IP's, be read into the official counting system and into that of each of the IP's. (The absentee ballots should be required to be in the hands of the County Election Commissioner several days before the election, to permit them to be bundled and sent to the precincts for counting on election day.) If the vote totals from these computers all agree, and if they all record the number of ballots cast to be equal to the number of absentee ballots received plus the number cast by voters appearing in the precinct, then the total number of votes for each item appearing on the ballots will be printed, signed as accepted by each IP, and transmitted to the media for public dissemination. The totals will also be transferred, by whatever modern means available, to the next higher summation point, e.g., the county, along with the physical ballots. The county election officials will sum up the inputs they receive from their constituent precincts, and send the precinct inputs and the county totals back to the individual precinct officials and IP's, who will be asked to verify that their precinct inputs are correct. When their verification is recorded, the precinct officials and IP's are done, and may go home and go to bed.

SECRECY OR FREEDOM?

Only after all of the precinct inputs are verified may the county officials send their totals to the local media of record for public printing, and the totals for the state and federal races to their State Election Commissioner. That person will go through the same process of summing over the state, obtaining a recorded verification from every county of its inputs, and then releasing the state totals to the media for public dissemination. Results may then also be sent to the Federal Election Commissioner, so that federal results can be accumulated concerning control of the Congress and what the Electoral College outcome will be if a presidential election is involved.

The public media might also be trusted to add up those federal results correctly, given the announced state totals. However, they should *not* be trusted to declare "winners" based on exit polling, crystal balls, or Ouija boards before at least all the West Coast polls are closed. Our main thrust, after all, is to define reforms which will eliminate electoral distortions by accumulated wealth, which our establishment media clearly represents.

We will lastly take on the issue of resolving disagreements among the results obtained by the official and the IP computers in a given precinct. First, each ballot must have an identifying number on it, readable by the computers, and known only to the voter who cast that ballot. (He should have received a ballot stub containing that number.) Thus, functionally equivalent computer software can be defined to locate and display any differences in the ballot data loaded into the several machines. For example, regardless of the *order* in which the data may be loaded into each machine, each one can sort the data by ascending ballot number, and store those results into new files. Cumulative sums from lowest toward the highest ballot number can then be computed and stored for each item appearing on the ballot. If the total votes for some item fails to agree between two of the computers, the accumulations can be printed, or selectively displayed, until a ballot is found containing a discrepancy.

That physical ballot should then be found and examined. If, in the judgment of *all* of the IP's and precinct officials, the intent of the voter is clear, and matches one or more of the computers, the computer(s) showing the discrepancy should be altered to match that intent, by changing the data in the sorted data file such that the accumulation to that point matches the other computers. The accumulations and totals for the affected computer can then be recalculated and the comparison and search for differences continued. If, however, the IP's and officials are not unanimous in their judgment of voter intent, that ballot vote will be marked as "under review," and not to be presently counted. The totals will then be recomputed, skipping that vote, and the process continued until no more discrepancies exist. The total number and identities of such "under review" votes will be reported to the County Election Commissioner, who will have the responsibility of making final determinations if the number of such "under review" votes could conceivably affect any election outcome.

Goal 3 concerning education is addressed in detail in Chapter 13 of LFA, and summarized on pages 302-303 of HTWRW, especially relating to the matter of utilizing vouchers to establish control by parents, rather than by the oligarchy's education establishment, over the education of their own children, from preschool through high school. The only federal involvement which we would retain is the "GI Bill" for college education, which we regard as an element of payment for military service. An addition which our present work suggests, not dealt with in LFA, is to request local owners and superintendents of private schools, as well as school board candidates and superintendents of local public schools, to voluntarily submit to the same TIP polygraph tests that political candidates are being asked to take. We believe that educators with honest, constitutional beliefs will soon attain ascendancy, to the great benefit of our children.

Bringing similar change to our institutions of higher miseducation will be slower, probably requiring the prior reform of a majority of a state's legislative and executive personnel. These are the people usually needed to effect changes in a public university's board of directors (highly important prospects for TIP polygraph testing), and eventually in its staff and educational offerings. This latter work is very important, however, since the great bulk of the work of ruining public education was undertaken within such hallowed halls (e.g., see HTWRW, pp. 74-81), and the oligarchs will be very loath to lose their control over the methodology of public education, in which they have invested so much for so many years.

Goal 4 is aimed at acquiring for our country the kind of national media system envisioned by Franklin, Jefferson, and others of our founders. It was supposed to keep a sharp eye out for corruption and accumulation of political power in our federal government, in order to protect the citizenry. As history has shown, it has failed to do so, and has instead become the corrupt servant, a prostitute, of those criminal oligarchs who would control us. How can we reacquire an honest, independent media? Our LFA did not address this issue, perhaps its most important omission, nor did HTWRW, though the latter contained numerous references to various media cover-ups and other manipulations.

We suggest a two-pronged campaign, with keywords *attack* and *replace*. The Attack aspect is our reformed federal government's response to the existence of an obvious cartel controlling news delivery in the United States, which should be just as vulnerable to anti-trust indictment and judicial penalty as is a cartel fixing prices on electric generators or hiding the delivery to the public of known poisonous carcinogens in cigarettes. They may hide behind the First Amendment, but that amendment does not give a media cartel the right to conspire to defraud the American public, to deliver poisonous misinformation to it, or to prevent the growth of *any* large-scale competitive media. The issue should be joined, and the public made aware that this long-festering issue of media monopoly is finally going to be addressed.

At the same time, the Replace aspect can be approached by myriad local communities around the country acting in concert with the national anti-trust effort. Local publishers and editors, and radio and TV station managers, can be asked to submit to TIP polygraph testing. If they refuse, the owners of such media can be approached with the same request. Refusals and testing results should be publicly disseminated, the object being to support the honest folk and expose and replace the dishonest. These exposures should be accompanied by explicit offers of support to parties who will take on the challenge of creating replacement media which the public can trust, displacing those who are unable or unwilling to serve the public honestly.

Thus, the grass-roots attack will add credibility to the national legal attack, while simultaneously making a start at replacing the corrupt cartel which the national effort is trying to expose and shut down. The battle should be fought as publicly as possible, with a major effort made to attract consumers and local advertisers to the newly emerging honest media. When the public begins to catch on as to what they have been missing, the battle will be essentially won, a result which many of us have been longing for many years to see.

Goal 5 deals with the worldwide scourge of narcotic drugs. Chapter 11 of LFA only proposed the legal delivery of such drugs to medically certified addicts, and only to such addicts, as a way to take the profit out of the trade, and thus cripple it. This seemed sufficient until Chapters 9 and 11 of HTWRW clearly showed that the growth of drug use was not a naturally-occurring happenstance of nature, but rather a deliberate effort by evil people to enrich themselves while simultaneously weakening the will of target populations to facilitate their takeover. This presented us with a highly important new task, namely, to publicly identify the perpetrators, and make every effort to indict and incarcerate them and destroy their industry. Our HTWRW noted the need for such a larger effort on pages 301-302. Thus, our revised program for exposing and then eliminating the worldwide narcotic trafficking industry includes the following elements:

a. Trace and publicly identify the major domestic and foreign financial institutions through which drug money flows, and into whose accounts it is ultimately deposited.

b. Prosecute, fine, and incarcerate the CEO's and board members of banks caught laundering drug money, and fine such banks severely enough to jolt their stockholders or private owners.

c. Freeze and confiscate the assets of casinos and other large-scale gambling or cash-handling establishments that are caught laundering drug money, and prosecute and jail their managers and owners.

d. Freeze and confiscate the visible assets, material and financial, of companies caught transporting drugs into or within the United States.

e. Terminate the practice of covertly raising funds from illicit drug operations to support any government program or bureaucracy, especially including law enforcement, military, and intelligence agencies, and prosecute and incarcerate agency heads and other individuals, at both higher and lower levels, who are found culpable.

f. Trace and publicly identify the foreign sources of narcotic drugs, and the identity of individuals, organizations, and countries covertly supporting such production. Mount a publicly funded and highly publicized campaign to help rout the criminal drug lords and their private armies out of those countries, and assist in the international prosecution of those financing, arming, or otherwise supporting such criminal entities.

g. Destroy the business of street pushers and the criminal activities of addicts by permitting states to make low-cost addictive drugs or their substitutes available from state agencies exclusively to medically certified drug addicts, and then help such addicts get totally free of drugs.

h. Mount state programs of public education against the use of narcotic drugs with at least as much enthusiasm as the similar campaign against tobacco.

Goal 6 has to do with defining a replacement for the *un*constitutional, *un*stable Federal Reserve System, a private banking cartel whose notes are forever depreciating, constituting a miserable store of value. We have considerably improved the corrective actions described in LFA, however, by making the Treasury, rather than the private banking system, the constitutional issuer of currency and the guardian of the gold stock which will be used to maintain the currency's stability. A little reflection will illuminate the motivation for this change: the interests of the federal government and that of the private banks, in particular the large private banks, simply do not coincide. The banks serve the interests of their stockholders or private owners, while the Treasury serves the interests of the taxpaying public. So we will stick with the Constitution, and make the U.S. Treasury the boss over the nation's currency, with full audits being performed annually and submitted to the Congress. We believe that we can trust the Congress and the Executive to properly handle these responsibilities *after* the TIP polygraph system has brought the requisite honesty to Washington, DC.

To get to our new system, we shall merge the primary assets and liabilities of the Federal Reserve System back into the U.S. Treasury, and abolish the Federal Reserve. (The Fed's assets of Gold Certificates and U.S. bonds will both be extinguished, as will the corresponding Treasury liabilities. The Fed's major liability – the unredeemable Federal Reserve Notes that it has issued – will be assumed as a Treasury liability, as will the reserve deposits of U.S. banks.) Upon public request, circulating Federal Reserve Notes will be replaced by the Treasury, one for one, by Treasury Gold Certificates (TGC's) of the same denominations, which will also be issued upon cash withdrawals from bank or Treasury deposit accounts. The TGC's will be redeemable in revalued gold (see below) at any bank upon demand. Banks will obtain such gold from the Treasury upon presentation of the TGC's, the Treasury being the one and only depository of the metallic gold reserve which will henceforth comprise the backing for our currency. The unredeemable FRN's will in this manner be replaced by our new gold-redeemable TGC's.

Banks will be required, over a period of time, to dispose of their holdings of federal government bonds, and will thereafter be prohibited from acquiring more. The bonds will eventually be paid off, extinguishing the national debt, but without having an effect on the amount of currency in circulation. Federal and state governments shall be required by statute law to conform to the constitutional proviso that only gold, or gold-backed currency, may be used in payment for goods and services either purchased or sold by the federal or state governments. Short of a national calamity requiring immediate huge expenses, the Federal government will have no need or authority to create TGC's to pay its bills or debts, as the accumulation of a modest surplus via the taxing power will automatically suffice for such purposes, as discussed in Goal 7 below. Statute law will be written to enhance banking stability (e.g., permit geographic diversification), and to prevent any future accumulation of a dangerous concentration of financial power (e.g., by capping assets permitted to be held by a single bank, prohibiting interlocking banking directorships or ownership of one bank by another, etc.).

The "price" of gold will be set by law to provide 100 percent redeemability of all the circulating currency and demand deposits in the hands of the public, presently amounting to around $1000 billion dollars. There presently exists about 0.25 billion ounces of Treasury gold. The presently computed gold redemption price would therefore be $1000/0.25 = 4000$ dollars per ounce. This price would obviously attract publicly held gold for sale to the Treasury. Anticipating this, and to determine how much total Treasury gold will later be held, the Treasury should advertise for and accept "commitments" for such sales for six months or so prior to issuing the new currency. The committed gold would be verified by accepting and storing it into "escrow depositories." The Treasury should further keep the public continuously informed as to how much has been committed, and what the resulting redemption price would be (using a recent annual average of publicly held currency and demand deposits). When that computed redemption price has stabilized, new commitments will be closed, and the legal price set. If the total Treasury gold then amounts, say, to 0.40 billion ounces, the gold price will be set to $1000/0.40 = 2500$ $/oz. Those who have committed their gold will thereupon be paid for it at the rate of 2500 dollars per ounce, and Congress shall declare the "dollar" to be defined as $1/2500 = 0.00040$ ounces of gold.

It is to be expected that long-term changes will occur in both treasury gold and average short-term banking liabilities. Consequently, the government should continuously recompute and track the "100 percent reserve gold redemption price," smooth it by, for example, averaging it weekly over the preceding 52 weeks, freely inform the public of those weekly computations, and thereafter announce periodic, perhaps annual, small modifications in the legal redemption price to keep up with such long term changes, thereby retaining continuous 100 percent redeemability of the national currency. (While TGC's issued upon presentation of "new gold" will immediately add to short term liabilities, they will soon thereafter automatically be converted into long term deposits and loans, reflecting the public's transfer of funds not needed in the short term into interest-earning investments.)

The "high" price placed on gold reflects its much higher-value use as backer of the country's currency than any other alternate use to which it may be put, such as jewelry. With access to 100 percent reserves for their short-term liabilities, banks will no longer be subject to bank runs, provided they exercise prudence in managing the timing between receiving repayments of long-term loans, and delivering payments on maturing time deposits. Short-term deposits, i.e., demand deposits, must never be considered by the banks as a part of the basis for making new loans.

This new monetary arrangement is in proper accord with the Constitution, with money being issued only by the government (not by a private cartel), and with the "dollar" defined by Congress. (Art. 1, Section 8: "The Congress shall have the power... to coin money... [and] regulate the value thereof...") Other countries, observing the good results obtained by the U.S., can be expected to follow its lead. As they do so, they will similarly be acting to protect their own currency from the depredations of wealthy currency speculators and central bank owners, and return control of their monetary affairs to their own elected governments.

Goal 7 is dealt with in Chapters 3 and 4 of LFA, and involves eliminating the national debt and capping the federal tax load. Chapter 3 lays out a congressional budgeting process to which we still fully subscribe, in which the federal departments will submit revenue-dependent variable budgets, which Congress and the President will review, modify, and ultimately approve. The departments will then be required to reduce approved expenditures if new budget items are later added, and to adjust expenditures quarterly in proportion to realized Treasury revenues. At the end of each fiscal year, and shortly before the general elections, the realized surplus or deficit will be respectively remitted or billed to the states, in proportion to each state's population. An allowance will be included in each fiscal year's budget to pay down on any still-existing accumulated debt, and ultimately accumulate in its place a substantial reserve for emergencies.

We believe that TIP-tested legislators honestly responding to the interests of their constituents will find this system both workable and politically attractive. Since our new monetary system described in Goal 6 no longer requires the existence of government debt at the foundation of the nation's monetary system, there is no reason why the national debt and its annual expense cannot be rather quickly extinguished, and prevented from ever again arising. The inflation spawned by the Federal Reserve's debt-based currency will be a thing of the past, our new currency will soon be seen as a safe store of value, and the habit of saving for the future will again be seen as proper, prudent, and responsible.

Chapter 4 of LFA describes a formula for defining an upper limit, or cap, which an annual federal budget may not exceed, such as to limit the total federal, state, and local tax load on the citizenry to a specified maximum percentage of the country's "national income," perhaps measured by the total of personal and corporate receipts from the sale of goods and services. We continue to support the Chapter 4 methodology. An unexpected or emergency expense could then be dealt with via the following hierarchy of actions: 1) Budget it in the next fiscal year; 2) Include it in the current budget, but automatically reduce all other budget items as needed to leave the total unchanged; 3) If the other items cannot be sufficiently reduced, increase the budget total to the statutory budget cap.

If money is needed in excess of the budget cap, it may be raised by the "emergency" means listed in items 4, 5, and 6 below. The expenditure of such funds, however, shall not be included in the calculation of the fiscal year deficit to be billed to the states. The emergency means are: 4) Pay for the excess over the cap by withdrawing funds from the carefully accumulated "substantial reserve" referred to above; 5) If still more is needed, borrow by selling bonds (to American citizens and corporations only), creating or increasing the federal debt; 6) If national survival requires it, inflate the currency by issuing the additionally needed TGC's, as noted in Goal 6 above, but with the intention of withdrawing them via taxation as quickly as possible. Issuing such currency without adding any corresponding gold backing constitutes, of course, the classical act of inflation, and if the currency is not withdrawn, will cause rising prices, including an increase in the long-term gold redeemability price. Devalued TGC's will be redeemable in a little less gold, and the stored value of all TGC-denominated savings diminished. The governmental issue of unbacked currency will be shown once more to amount to nothing more than a hidden tax forced on those holding fixed dollar-denominated assets.

Goal 8 involves the replacement of the income tax, and is discussed at length in LFA Chapter 5. However, we have presently defined that proposal much more tightly, as follows. The federal income tax should be replaced with a uniform tax on all previously untaxed goods and services (excepting only food) sold by state-licensed foreign or domestic businesses for consumption by domestic not-for-profit entities (i.e., by non-business consumers). The tax will be collected by the several states and transmitted to the federal treasury, one check per quarter per state. The 16th Amendment will be repealed and the IRS abolished. Our LFA Chapter 5 discussion was much the same, but quite erroneously treated wages to individuals as the sale of a service, whereas in reality they represent the addition of value to a product or a service later to be sold to a consumer.

Goal 9 asks that we revalidate the Tenth Amendment, and reinforce its enforcement. This issue was precisely the theme of Chapter 19 of LFA, and we would change hardly a word of the methods discussed there for accomplishing that goal, though one additional method might be to make adherence to the Tenth Amendment a "litmus test" for Supreme Court nominees. Three of the most egregious violations involve the federal intervention in pension, medical, and welfare delivery systems to individual American citizens, all in violation of the Tenth Amendment. These three areas are dealt with in LFA Chapters 6, 7, and 9 respectively, about which we would likewise change hardly a word.

Social Security, presently nothing but an intergenerational pyramid scheme, can readily be replaced with an actuarially sound non-federal system of grossly greater value to retirees, and blessed with a huge pool of real savings of great value to our private sector economy. Medicare can similarly be replaced by a non-federal system involving annuity provisions to account for the higher medical expenses to be expected at advanced ages. (Both Social Security and Medicare reforms obviously require as a prerequisite a non-depreciating currency, and hence the monetary reforms of Goal 6.) Other needed medical reforms discussed in LFA Chapter 7 concern malpractice insurance, the FDA (the unconstitutional birthplace of high prescription costs), and the AMA (where acceptable qualifications, procedures, treatments, drugs, and other medical matters are defined and enforced via its monopolistic licensing power). The federal welfare system has cost the public over $5 trillion since LBJ's War on Poverty was declared about 35 years ago. It hasn't reduced the incidence of government-defined "poverty," but it has functioned brilliantly as a source of waste, and contributed mightily to our current national debt. We continue to insist that the only place that it can be gotten under control is at the local county level, to which any really needed programs should ultimately be transferred.

Another category of Tenth Amendment violations is treated in LFA Chapter 10, entitled "Bailout Surprises." Several examples in this area are treated in some detail, but the general principle, to which we still adhere, is to abolish essentially *all* federal insurance, price guarantee, loan, and loan guarantee programs, none of which are among the enumerated powers of Congress. The federal liability for such programs is estimated to have grown to around $5 trillion, representing the rightful obligations of private individuals, groups, or companies which the government has been conned, bribed, or otherwise persuaded to gratuitously assume in the name of U.S. taxpayers.

Goal 10 resets the national priority to improving the American standard of living, and building the economic and political *independence* of the American society as opposed to its *interdependence* with (i.e., dependence upon) other countries. Some proposals responding to this goal were laid out in LFA, and some in HTWRW. Two from LFA (Chapter 18) and then several more from HTWRW are:

a. Terminate U.S. government loans and grants for the economic or military development of foreign countries. No more foreign aid!

b. Prohibit future U.S. government bailouts of foreign or domestic economic losses realized by U.S. or foreign citizens or companies, or by foreign governments.

c. Knowing that our new gold-backed dollar will come under attack by the oligarchs, careful attention should be paid to its protection (cf. HTWRW, p. 309). Thus, the gold conversion rate must be set to avoid disastrous gold loss upon the presentation of foreign-held dollars. This first protection has been dealt with in Goal 6 by defining the conversion rate such that sufficient gold will always be available to cover all outstanding short-term claims, i.e., currency and demand deposits.

d. A second protection will be sought by avoiding, as a minimum, the legal accumulation of foreign-held dollars via a long-term negative balance of trade (cf. HTWRW, p. 309). Impose a uniform U.S. tariff on imports of foreign-produced goods, automatically adjusted annually such as to target and maintain the accumulated long-term net balance of payments at close to zero. (Illegal outflow of dollars via the drug trade won't be affected by this measure, however. Suppression of the trade itself is needed to stanch this outflow of dollars.)

e. Tax American investments in foreign enterprise (cf. HTWRW, p. 309). President Kennedy had tried to impose an Interest Equalization Tax on American funds invested abroad, as he saw American investment banks and multinational companies chasing the higher interest rates available abroad rather than investing their funds at home in modernized factories and the maintenance of the physical infrastructure of the U.S., especially the roads, rivers, bridges, and ports used in interstate commerce. However, Kennedy was assassinated and the tax was gutted (cf. HTWRW, p. 13). To support the fully adequate growth and maintenance of the American physical infrastructure, the tax should be reimposed, without loopholes, taxing any loan to, or investment in, any foreign entity by any U.S. person, bank, or company, including their foreign branches if any.

    f. Terminate the obstructionist policies (detailed in HTWRW, Chapter 8) which use fraudulent "environmental" or "occupational safety" arguments to prevent the full utilization of American resources, technology, and ingenuity to further the growth of American production and resulting standard of living. Abolish OSHA, EPA, and any other federal agencies created by the Congress and given a *general mandate* to define what was needed to be done and then to enforce their findings. Such agencies were charged with goals which were in violation of the Tenth Amendment, and were unconstitutionally granted legislative, executive, and judicial powers. Unsurprisingly, the agencies became despotic, and came to be feared almost as much as the IRS, the mother of such agencies.

    g. Create law aimed at preventing the use of foreign dollars for buying up American companies or the control of such companies, and instead encouraging the use of such dollars for purchasing the natural or manufactured products created by American industries. (Thus, Goal 8 imposes no sales tax on foreign purchases of American products.) The wholesale use of dollars accumulated abroad from the drug trade and our own historical profligacy, and used by the oligarchs for buying into our major American financial institutions, is described in HTWRW, pp. 288-290.

    Goal 11 aims to put some backbone into a meaningful U.S. policy with respect to illegal immigration. The issue is addressed much more fully in LFA Chapter 17, to which we still adhere. The most important of the changes in federal law which we propose are the following:

a. Pass federal law denying the granting of any federally-funded public services to illegal immigrants, and permitting states to deny similar state-funded services.

b. Pass federal law permitting states to assist the Immigration and Naturalization Service (INS) in border monitoring measures to prevent illegal immigration, by identifying and holding suspect illegal immigrants within the state for investigation by the INS, by assisting in their deportation if such is ordered, and by helping detect and prosecute domestic individuals and organizations financing or otherwise aiding illegal immigrants or illegal immigration efforts.

c. Pass a constitutional amendment denying citizenship to babies born in the United States to illegal immigrants.

d. Pass federal law requiring the immediate deportation of any illegal immigrant found guilty of a felony, and the expeditious deportation of any immigrant unable to prove lawful entry within 30 days of detainment.

e. Expose and publicize the criminal movement by Mexican legal and illegal immigrants to return the southwest portion of the United States to Mexican ownership and/or control. Seek the support and assistance of the legitimate Mexican government in this effort. Identify and prosecute, where possible, American and foreign individuals or organizations giving financial support or other aid and comfort to this movement. Penalties shall include the confiscation of assets of organizations found culpable.

Goal 12 seeks to terminate U.S. support of oligarchical institutions seeking to establish a world government, and to free the U.S. of the pernicious influence of those institutions. LFA Chapter 18 proposed most of the items below, HTWRW Chapter 12 added a few more along with a much higher level of urgency, and the last two are appended from our current vantage point. We thus propose the following actions:

a. Terminate membership in the United Nations and its several agencies, including NATO, and eject the UN, its agencies, and its activities from the United States.

b. Terminate membership in the IMF and the World Bank, and recover US investments or deposits therein.

c. Terminate membership in NAFTA, GATT, and the WTO.

d. Terminate the use of US military forces to implement UN directives or other imperatives requiring a world police presence.

e. Revive and pass the "Bricker Amendment" to the Constitution, to provide that no treaty or other governmental agreement shall be deemed effective as internal law unless it could have been passed by valid, constitutional, congressional legislation. This will prevent international or foreign entities to which we may become connected by treaty or agreement from imposing upon us law which our own system would find unconstitutional.

f. Terminate governmental funding of Non-Governmental Organizations (NGO's) that are doing organizational work for the oligarchs around the world.

g. Strengthen and enforce the Logan Act, penalizing US private citizens or organizations for negotiating with or lobbying foreign entities, including foreign members of NGO's, such as to bring about changes in provisions of US laws, treaties, or policies.

Goal 13 seeks to have the U.S. take the lead in creating a new international organization composed of member nations: 1) whose citizens are already living under governmental charters which seek to guarantee the maintenance of their citizens' freedom; 2) who desire to join with other countries of that kind for the purpose of giving and gaining mutual help in strengthening those guarantees; and

3) who are admitted into the new organization by the sufferance of the existing members. Thus, we propose that a new International Freedom Organization (IFO) be created in which:

a. Membership is limited to countries having a constitution, and a conforming government, whose core purpose is to guarantee the rights of its individual citizens to life, liberty, and the pursuit of happiness, with lesser priorities assigned to the rights of any other political, social, or business entity in the nation.

b. Membership is granted, and may be rescinded, by vote of the existing membership, but only after whatever detailed examination of the applicant or member government and its governing officials may be deemed necessary by the IFO, including possible polygraph examinations.

c. The IFO charter is continually examined by the IFO membership for possible improvements, with agreed-upon changes submitted to member countries for ratification or other action, including abdication of membership.

d. Knowledge is shared of mechanisms and policies (such as protective tariffs) which promote national security, independence, economic growth, and citizen well-being (as opposed to Malthusianism).

e. Mechanisms are developed for negotiating proposed solutions to any significant disagreements among members, such solutions to be returned to member countries for ratification and/or other action.

f. A standard is raised demonstrating to non-member governments and populations how well the fundamental interests of a country's citizens can be served by patterning their governmental organization after those of IFO members.

g. Advice and help is offered to non-member nations concerning changes which would have to be made in a country's governing institutions in order for that country to become eligible for membership.

* * *

Having finally arrived at the end, we are led to congratulate ourselves for finishing the job we set out to do. We can see now who it is (roughly) that is waging a secret war against the citizenry of the world (the Venetian-spawned oligarchy), and what its two crucial weapons are (money and secrecy). Having identified its weapons, we perceive that one of them (the secrecy) may be directly attacked via modern technology, making the ultimate over-throw of the oligarchy a foregone conclusion if the attack is mounted quickly enough.

A time of troubles is clearly before us, however, as we cannot expect the oligarchs to graciously submit. Many hands will be needed to break the chains which presently bind our society, and I plead with those members of the American society who must fight this fight – whether you are black or white, male or female, conservative or liberal, Protestant, Catholic, Jew or Muslim, old or young, rich or poor – to keep your eyes on the goal of freeing our society and our posterity from the criminal oligarchs. Do not let yourselves be led off into tangential fights among your-selves. The oligarchs are experts at creating these conflicts, so let us all try to become expert in recognizing such con-flicts for what they are, and in husbanding our resources for attacking and overcoming our real enemies.

I will close with a personal note. I fear that my age precludes me from witnessing the completion of this strug-gle. However, I hope that my efforts will be found useful to those unknown future heroes who will be found in the front lines of the struggle. One former writer foresaw and printed a description of the world desired by the oligarchs (*1984*, by

George Orwell). I foresee something much different, as may be visualized by a world accepting the existence of an IFO having the functions and purposes that I have described immediately above. I pray for the success of those of you who share this latter vision, and who may find yourselves in the 21st century fighting to realize that vision. If you are successful, the world may yet be turned into a proper habitat for human beings desirous of nothing more than to contribute to the ongoing growth and well being of each individual member of the whole human race, each one having been created in the image of God.

INDEX

Bundy, McGeorge & fam. 312, 317-18
Buonarotti 161
Burr, Aaron 272-85, 294, 297, 299, 305-6, 317, 319
Bush, Prescott, George, & George W. 311, 313, 317, 331
Byzantine Empire 237, 240-41, 243-44
Cabala (Yetzirah + Zohar) 181-91
Cabalistic Masonry 26, 33-34, 77, 85, 181-91, 249
Cabot, George & fam. 285-90, 319
Cairo, Grand Lodge of 195, 197
Calvin, John 250
Calvinists 131, 204, 227, 228, 248, 250, 252, 273
Cambrai, League of 237, 245-49
Cambridge 225, 234
Canada 255-56, 274, 283-84, 294
Carbonari 138-42, 143, 145, 154, 165, 197, 200, 258, 261, 325
Carey, Mathew & Henry (father & son), 272, 284, 286
Cathari 28, 30, 191, 198, 199, 204
Catherine de' Medici 227
Catherine of Aragon 204-9, 220, 225
Caussidière 161
Cecil, Robert 251, 292
Cecil, William 220-21, 224-34, 246, 251
Central Intelligence Agency (CIA) 318
Charles I of Spain, 204-5, 209-10, 212, 216, 218-24, 226, 249
Charles I of England 86, 252, 253
Charles II of England 253-54
Charles V, Holy Roman Emperor, see Charles I of Spain
Charles VIII 244, 246
Charles X of France, 118, 137
Chigi, Agostino 246-47, 249
China 92, 170, 181, 213, 214, 238, 241, 257-58, 277-78, 284, 288-89, 298-99, 311, 319, 321
Christ, see Jesus Christ
Christian, anti- 8-12, 15, 17-20, 25-32, 39-41, 50, 53, 57, 84, 95, 114, 119, 121-26, 127-30, 138-41, 150-58, 186-89, 210-11, 233, 244, 293
Churchill, Lord John 255
Churchill, Winston 171, 255

General of Illuminism 62-64
Geneva 18, 165, 227, 250, 273, 276, 277, 295
Genoa 208, 212, 214, 246, 292, 293
George I 86, 255
George V 264, 269, 270, 314
Germanic Union 73-75, 78
Germany 13, 81, 96-97, 108, 118, 144-46, 154, 163, 166-67,
    171-73, 210, 211, 212, 218, 219, 221, 228-29, 242, 245-47,
    251, 259-71, 310-11, 318-20
Ghengis Khan, see Mongols
Giovani 250, 251
Girondins 96, 98, 109, 114
Gist, Gov. William 304-5, 307
Glorious Revolution 221, 254, 257, 292, 293
Gnostics 50, 188-90, 192, 198, 199
Goethe 106, 107, 320
Gourgas, John James Joseph & fam. 293, 295, 302
Grand Orient 35, 36, 76, 78, 85, 87, 128, 132, 137
Grant, Ulysses S. 312
Gresham, Sir Thomas, 221, 225, 229, 231, 232
Grey, Sir Edward 268-70
guilds (of workmen), 125, 131, 150, 212, 213
Hakim, Caliph 195-96
Hamilton, Alexander 272, 278-80, 288, 296, 308
Hanover 67, 86, 203
Hapsburg 173, 250, 261, 270, 308, 319
Harriman, W. Averell & fam. 312-13, 317-18
Harrison, William Henry 297
Harvard 277, 290, 316
Hasan Saba 196, 197
Hébert 114, 164
Hegel, Georg 318, 320
Hegelianism 318-21
Henry VIII of England, 204-10, 217, 220-21, 225, 246-47, 249,
    252, 280, 292
Herder, Johann 320
Hermetic Masonry 26-28, 191, 249
Higginson, Stephen & fam. 272, 285-86, 287-88

Hitler 270, 318-19
Hobbes, Thomas 8
Hohenzollern 173, 270, 319
Holbach's Club 15-17, 20, 34, 61, 87
Holland 13, 34, 65, 69, 82, 108, 121, 131, 132, 137, 156, 210,
    212, 218, 221, 226, 231, 248, 250, 276, 277, 302
Hope family 276, 282
House, Edward Mandell 233, 308-9
Houston, Sam 298-99, 306, 309
Huguenots 211, 227-29, 234, 252
Hundred Years' War 242
Hungary 144-45, 210, 241, 245
Illuminati 7, 38-79, 80, 84, 85, 89, 95, 96, 98, 112, 114, 118,
    132-38, 148, 150, 151, 159-61, 165-67, 169, 172, 175-77,
    190, 193, 200-202, 233, 292, 320, 325
Illuminati/Masonry Interrelations 39, 43, 46, 49-50, 51, 60, 62,
    64, 66-71, 73, 75-79, 80-81, 118, 132, 134-38, 150, 167
Independents, see Cromwell, Oliver
India 181, 213, 216, 217, 248, 256, 288, 289
Ingolstadt 40, 64, 71, 72, 169
International, First 147-48, 164-66, 168, 177, 200
Ireland 27, 132, 148, 165, 197, 253, 258
Islam 181, 182, 190, 192, 193, 196, 210, 218
Ismailis 192, 197, 199-200
Italy 27, 29, 69, 82, 122, 132, 134, 136, 138-39, 141, 144-47,
    150, 152-56, 162, 166, 168, 211, 214, 217, 218, 223, 237,
    240, 242, 243-47, 250, 258-61, 263, 266, 267-68
Ivy League colleges 151, 273, 277, 290, 309, 311, 315, 316,
    320-21
Jack the Ripper 264
Jackson, Andrew 281-82, 284, 296-97
Jacobin 23, 30, 79-82, 86-88, 90-117, 135, 153, 166, 197, 229,
    282, 286-87
James I 251-52, 292
James II 132, 233, 253-54, 255
Japan 266
Jefferson, Thomas 278-79, 281-83, 286-87, 338
Jerusalem 182, 198, 212, 240

Jesuits 8, 40-41, 70, 73, 128, 129, 132, 177, 248-49, 291, 292, 293
Jesus Christ 7, 9, 25, 27-28, 40, 50, 53, 130, 139, 151, 183-89, 192, 208
Jews or Judaism, 132, 149, 172, 176-77, 181-89, 191, 203, 210-18, 223, 233, 247-48, 259, 293, 354
Johnson, Andrew 308
Johnson, Lyndon B. 318
Juarez, Pres. Benito 308
Kadosch 24, 25, 37, 76, 85, 197
Karmathites 194, 200
Kennedy, John F. 318, 349-50
Kerensky 171, 197
Kidd, Captain William 280
Knigge, Baron 53, 67-70, 73, 75-76, 82, 176
Knight(s) Templar, see Templars
Knights of the Golden Circle 303, 305
Koran 182, 192
Korean War 262
Kropotkin, Prince 148, 167, 168, 171
Lafayette, Marquis de 35, 99, 101, 286, 291
Lamar, Lucius & fam. 305-6
Le Roy, Mr. 15, 16, 19
Ledru-Rollin 161, 260
Lenin 170-76, 197
Liberty and Equality 18, 22, 23, 31, 35, 39, 52, 54, 57, 58, 69, 78, 85, 112, 138, 191
Lincoln, Abraham 144, 260, 272, 299, 304, 307-8
Livingston, Robert & Edward 280-84, 306, 319
Lord, George DeForest & fam. 312, 316
Louis Napoleon 118, 143, 145, 162, 167
Louis Philippe 118, 137, 145, 162, 260
Louis XI 243, 244
Louis XII 205, 245
Louis XIV 151, 254
Louis XVI 22, 75, 79, 89, 92-102, 107-9, 118, 276
Louis XVIII 118, 137
Louise de Montmorency 226, 232

365

murder 24, 46, 55, 90, 95, 100-105, 110-11, 112-15, 194, 197-98, 228, 280, 296

Naples 155, 244-46, 267

Napoleon Bonaparte 37, 82, 97, 101, 117, 118, 135-39, 151-52, 167, 215, 216, 229, 281, 294

Napoleon III 118, 145-46, 154, 156, 162, 164, 260, 261

Necker, Jacques & fam. 276, 282

New World Order 21, 319, 325

Nicholas II 171, 267, 269

Norfolk, Duke of 205, 208, 209

Nova Scotia 253, 282

Nubius 134, 139-44, 147, 154, 158, 179

Nullification movement 295, 297, 301

oligarchy 236-71, 272-309, 324, 329-30, 337-38, 349-52, 354

Opium War 257-58, 298, 312

Orwell, George 319, 321, 355

Ottoman Turks 82, 145, 204, 210, 211, 216, 218, 237, 238, 243-44, 246, 250, 259-62, 270, 289, 311

Oxford 33, 85, 86, 130, 131, 246, 314

Paganis, Hugo de 24, 26

Palmerston 134, 143-49, 153-54, 156, 163, 166, 167, 237, 257-62, 298, 304

papacy 26, 27, 28, 29, 34, 121-26, 127-29, 135-36, 138-41, 144-46, 150-58, 166-67, 179, 204-9, 220-24, 243-52, 261

Papal States 136, 138, 146, 151, 153-56, 158, 246

Parvus, nee Israel Helphand 172

Paulicians 191, 199

Payne, Oliver & fam. 312-13, 316

Peabody, George 260, 290, 297, 315

Perkins, Thomas, James, George & fam., 272, 288-89, 311, 312

Permanent Instruction 140, 144, 158, 179

Persia 31-32, 180, 184, 190-92, 196, 201

Petty, Sir William 293

Philip II of Spain 203-35, 242

Philip le Bel 25, 27, 28, 32, 199, 293

Philip of Orleans 76, 78, 87, 89-90, 94-95, 97, 105, 109, 114, 132, 137

Philosophers, (French assn.) 7, 8-21, 26, 29, 33, 34, 61, 64, 199

Pickering, Timothy 285-86
Piedmont 146, 147, 153, 154
Pierce, Franklin 259-60, 302-3
Pike, Albert 303-4, 306
Pitt, William 108, 113, 278
Poland 69, 76, 131, 144-45, 165, 241, 259, 260
Polk, James 298-99, 301
polygraph 325-28, 330, 338-39, 342, 353
Pope Julius II 245-47, 249
Pope Julius III 220
Pope Leo XIII 121-26, 127, 128, 158
Pope Pius IX 121, 150-58
Pope Pius VI 136
Pope Pius VII 136, 151-52
Portugal 169, 212, 217, 245, 248, 253, 266
Prevost, James, Theodosia, Augustine & fam., 272-76, 282, 293-95
Priestley, Dr. Joseph 90, 104
Princeton 273
propaganda 11-12, 37, 61, 81-82, 96, 137, 142, 166, 228, 299
Propagandists Club 37-38, 81
property 7, 40, 50, 52, 58, 80, 89, 102, 113, 123, 129, 147, 150, 164, 175, 194
Protestant Reformation 130, 202, 203-35, 236, 248-52, 292
Protocols of the Learned Elders of Zion 175-77
Prudhomme 100, 105, 111
Prussia 9, 89, 103, 105-6, 118, 145, 146, 154, 163, 166, 167
Puritans 86, 252, 312
Quebec 256, 274, 281
Queen Anne (Stuart) 128, 255, 256
Queen Elizabeth 205-6, 208, 221, 224, 225, 227, 229, 231, 234-35, 246, 251
Queen Mary of Hungary, 210, 218, 221, 226
Queen Victoria 143, 258, 263, 314
Quigley, Carroll 21, 233, 310, 313-14
Quitman, John 300-302, 303-4
Reeve, Judge Tapping 285
Regent 54-56, 60-62, 68-69

Regulating Committee 35-37, 78
Renaissance 203, 242-43, 245, 293
Revolution of 1848 118, 143, 145, 152-53, 156, 161-63, 260,
    261
Rhodes, Cecil 279, 313-14
Robespierre 96, 97, 100, 102, 104, 109, 111-16, 118, 159, 171,
    173, 194, 287
Robison, John 114, 135, 176
Rockefeller, Percy & fam. 312-13, 316
Romanov 173, 262, 270, 319
Roosevelt, Theodore & fam. 302, 331
Rosicrucian 24-26, 32, 39, 73, 77, 83, 249, 292-93
Rothschild family 218, 260, 302
Rousseau 18, 19, 58, 256, 299
Ruge, Arnold 259-60
Ruskin, John 279
Russell, John and Francis, 220, 225, 231, 232
Russell, Wm. H. & fam. 272, 310-11, 320
Russia 76, 117, 118, 137, 144, 145, 148, 150, 162, 165, 168,
    170-76, 213, 241, 259-63, 265-71, 316-20
Sackville, Thomas 225, 230-32
Sanders, George 260
Sardinia 154, 155
Sarpi, Paolo 237, 251-52
Savalette de Lange 76, 78, 85
Schiller, Friedrich 320
schools 15, 20, 61-62, 125, 145, 151, 152, 156, 178, 228, 292,
    329, 337-38
science, perversion of 12, 31, 33, 55, 58, 61, 236, 243
Scotch Architect Lodge, see Edinburgh
Scotch degrees 24, 26, 49, 68, 83, 85
Scotch Knight 49-51, 52, 68, 69, 190
Scotch Master 24, 49, 68, 83
Scotland 24, 27, 33, 85, 130, 132, 224, 227, 248, 251, 252, 253,
    256, 276, 278, 280, 292, 293
Scott, General Winfield 302
secession 297, 299, 302, 304-8
secrecy 7, 10, 17, 28, 30, 31, 34-38, 41, 62, 126, 138, 309, 325

Secret Academy, see Holbach's Club

secret societies 42, 46, 49, 51, 52, 60, 62, 71, 74, 83, 87, 88, 118, 119, 127-31, 134, 139, 140, 149, 151, 154, 161, 165, 172, 178, 180-202, 216, 225-26, 230, 231, 233, 258, 261, 292, 309, 310-14, 320-22, 325

Serbia 268-70

Seven Years' War 256, 257, 273

Seward, William 307

Sforza, Francesco 243-44

shadow government 48, 55, 59, 87, 234

Shelburne, Lord 258, 276-77, 280, 288-89, 291, 293

Shiite Muslims 192-93, 196

Shippen, Peggy 273-75

Skull and Bones (see The Order) 310

slavery 30, 35, 53, 175, 238, 240, 253, 255-56, 259, 267, 271, 286, 288-91, 296, 299-304, 319

Slidell, John 299, 306

Smith, Adam 276, 288

Society of Jesus, see Jesuits

Socinians 128, 129, 130-31

Spain 29, 59, 122, 132, 134, 162, 203-35, 245, 247, 250-51, 253, 254, 255, 266, 279, 281, 294, 308

Spinosa 57, 128

Spiridovitch, Gen. A.E. 171-72

spying 45, 63, 65, 112, 218, 233, 239, 276

St. Just 109, 112, 115

St. Mark Basilica 239, 251

Stalin, Joseph 319

Stanhope, Lord 90, 105, 117

State Absolutism 111-12, 160, 164, 168, 171, 174-75, 215, 239-40, 244, 318-20

Stead, William T. 314

Stimson, Henry & fam. 312, 316-17

Stuart 86, 132, 251-54, 292-93

Stuart, Mary 224, 227

Sturgis, Russell & fam. 288-89, 311

Sunni Muslims 192, 196

Versailles 79, 93-95, 96, 270, 308
Vicenza 129, 130, 131
Victor Emmanuel II 146, 154, 156-57, 166, 167
Victor Emmanuel III 267
Vienna 65, 137, 138, 152, 153
Vietnamese War 262, 318-19
Voltaire 8-21, 34, 41, 61, 64, 84, 128-29, 132, 133, 140, 151, 199, 256-57, 275-77, 292, 325
War of 1812 280, 283-84, 286, 287, 294, 296
War of the Spanish Succession 255
Washington, DC 282, 284, 303, 308, 328, 342
Washington, George 272, 274, 281, 296
Wealth of Nations, see Smith, Adam
wealth of secret societies 26, 31, 38, 43, 66, 80, 102, 148, 172, 178, 198, 199
wealth of Ven-Brit-Amer oligarchy 208, 211, 214, 230, 233, 239, 240, 256, 287, 289, 293, 313, 314, 324, 329, 331, 332, 336, 344
Webster, Daniel 298, 302
Weishaupt 38-77, 82, 85, 87, 110, 114, 118-19, 129, 133-44, 147, 149, 158, 164-66, 169, 172, 175-78, 190, 193, 195, 197, 201-2, 292, 293, 320
Weyerhaeuser, Frederick & fam. 312, 316
Whitney, William Collins & fam. 312-13, 317
Wilhemsbaden conference 67-69, 75, 134, 137, 150
Wilkinson, James 280-82, 284
William I of Orange 221-22, 226, 232
William I of Prussia and Germany 163, 167, 168, 261, 263, 265
William II of Germany 172, 263, 265-66, 269-70
William III of Orange 86, 221, 232, 254-55
Williamson, Charles 277-78, 280
Wilson, Woodrow 308, 331
Wolsey, Cardinal Thomas 208, 246-47, 309
Workman, James 279-82, 319
World War 1 118, 173, 237, 261-71, 308, 315, 317, 319, 321
World War 2 170, 179, 262, 270, 271, 309, 319, 321
Yale 151, 273, 311, 315, 316, 320-21
Young ... 145, 154, 155, 162, 258-60, 299-302, 305

Order from ABJ Press (prices include shipping costs):

Let's Fix America! $15
How the World REALLY Works $15
Secrecy or Freedom? $15

Total for one each of the above $30

Two or more books in any
combination of the above 3 books $10 per book

Send check, made out to ABJ Press, to:
ABJ Press, PO Box 2362, Paradise, CA 95967

Low-cost case lots are also available for those wishing to undertake re-selling or other bulk distribution. Note that carte blanche permission has been granted, and is here restated, to reproduce these books in whole or part in order to further their distribution. Each of the three books is available on floppy disk, and republishing from these disks is invited. Several such disks have already been distributed.

Alan B. Jones
February, 2001